W9-CMJ-242

Postmodern Proust

Postmodern Proust

Margaret E. Gray

UNIVERSITY OF PENNSYLVANIA PRESS   Philadelphia

Library of Congress Cataloging-in-Publication Data

Gray, Margaret E.
  Postmodern Proust / Margaret E. Gray.
     p.   cm.
  Includes bibliographical references and index.
  ISBN 0-8122-3149-X
  1. Proust, Marcel, 1871–1922. A la recherche du temps perdu.
  2. Postmodernism (Literature)—France.   I. Title.
PQ2631.R63A795   1992
843′.912—dc20   92-16747
                                                                          CIP

Contents

Acknowledgments

"Only three more weeks," wrote my mother in her journal as I neared completion of my undergraduate thesis, "and Margot will be through with Proust forever." Since then, I have contrived, with the help of many along the way, to stave off such an unhappy fate. After David Ball's insistence at Smith College that I acquaint myself with Proust's critics, Peter Brooks of Yale warned how artfully I would need to dodge among their numbers. When I realized that the Proust I had struggled to domesticate in my dissertation was so endlessly interesting precisely for all that eluded domestication, the project of a "postmodern" Proust was born (between two inspired sips of a cappuccino in Durham's Ninth Street Bakery, Marcel, after all, having largely sewn up the tea possibilities).

Opportunities to rehearse my arguments in public have been valuable. Material from my introduction was presented at the Twentieth-Century French Studies Colloquium in Austin, 1991. A primitive version of my first chapter was given at the 1987 MLA in San Francisco; of my third, at the Twentieth-Century Literature Conference in Louisville, 1988. Evolving phases of Chapter 4 were presented at the Modern Literature Conference in East Lansing, 1986, and at the Romance Languages Conference in Cincinnati, 1987, before appearing in penultimate form in *Modern Fiction Studies* 34.3 (1988). I first threshed out the work of Chapter 5 at Smith College in 1986, at the kind invitation of Mary Ellen Birkett, and, in a more "postmodern" cast, at the Twentieth-Century French Studies Colloquium in Iowa City, 1990. My sixth chapter was initially presented at the Twentieth-Century French Studies Colloquium in Durham, NC, in 1987 (my thanks to Jean-Jacques Thomas for giving me a forum), and appeared in *MLN* 104.5 (1989). An early form of my final chapter was given at the Narrative Literature Conference in Madison, 1989. Permission to reprint copyrighted material is gratefully acknowledged. Particular thanks go to Ed Arno, Phyllis Herfield, and Sempé for permission to reproduce their work.

I was fortunate to have thorough and perspicacious readings from Mary Lydon and Richard Macksey. I am also grateful to my Bloomington colleagues Matei Calinescu and Gil Chaitin, whose names will recur in the pages ahead, and Emanuel Mickel, whose support of this project was timely and crucial. J. Theodore Johnson, Jr., was unwaveringly responsive to my queries; without material compiled in the "paraproustology" sections of his *Proust Research Association Newsletter*, I could not have written my final chapter. The students of my 1988 Proust seminar here at Indiana University/Bloomington were as rigorous an audience as I've ever faced. I owe much to the interest, steadfast encouragement, and expert guidance of editors Jerry Singerman and Mindy Brown. Sustenance of another sort in the latter phases of this project has been provided by Oz Kenshur's patience, humor, and stir-fried dinners.

The devotion and support of many family members, in countless small ways and big, is to be read between every line of these pages. This book is for them.

Introduction

*Post*modern Proust? Few writers are so confidently cited as high modernist. And along with the modernist label comes its invariable implication: "dead, stifling, canonical" (Jameson)—in other words, obsolete. Such assertions, perhaps not surprisingly, are particularly plentiful in discussions of postmodernism—as if the obsolescence of Proust's modernism were a final indisputable piece of bedrock before the thicket of postmodernism's competing definitions and indefinitions. Thus, runs the postmodernist litany, Proust is among the "giants of modern fiction" (Holland), the "modernist masters" (Fiedler); his *A la recherche du temps perdu* "the modernist text par excellence" (Spanos), among the "major documents of modernist literary production" (Silverman). His great novel subscribes to the modernist program in that it "recreates reality" (Hassan); his enthusiasm for hypothesis and conjecture is an example of the writing from possibility that characterizes the modernist work, as opposed to postmodernist writing from impossibility (Fokkema). And modernist works, runs the argument, have nothing more to offer us. "The masterpieces of modern literature once seemed formless," asserts one variation, "but we have now discovered their form: they once appeared enigmatic, but now we know their meaning" (Martin). "What is clear," pronounces Jameson, summing up the postmodernist's stance, "is that the older models . . . Picasso, Proust, T. S. Eliot—do not work any more."[1]

The confidence alone of these assertions suffices to warrant a second look. Take Lyotard's treatment of the *Recherche*, paradigmatic of this pervasive tendency among theorists of postmodernity to use Proust as a springboard to illustrate the difference between modern and postmodern esthetics. Lyotard argues that the modern aesthetic is essentially a nostalgic one, informed by a yearning for the "unpresentable" sublime. This sublime, absent "unpresentable" (in Proust, according to Lyotard, the identity of awareness, however deferred throughout its extension in time) is sensed, but safely from within the consoling, compensating pleasures of an established narrative and syntactic tradition. Thus, although he admits that the tradition of Balzac and Flaubert is nevertheless subverted in Proust (in that the hero, no longer a character, is now the inner awareness of time), Lyotard claims that the writing's identity with itself is not questioned in the *Recherche*. With Joyce, now, runs Lyotard's argument, the "unpresentable" is rendered apparent, rather than repressed; Joyce's writing embodies the "unpresentable" within its very signifiers. Proust's recourse to formal unity, however, or "bonnes formes" in Lyotard's claim, disqualifies him as a postmodern (1986, 32–33).

It isn't only so lately, however, that Proust has been thus dismissed. Sartre complained that Proust's esthetic should have had him writing like Faulkner, who had the courage of his convictions and "decapitated" time. Proust, wrote Sartre scornfully,

> est un classique et un Français; les Français se perdent à la petite semaine et ils finissent toujours par se retrouver. L'éloquence, le goût des idées claires, l'intellectualisme ont imposé à Proust de garder au moins les apparences de la chronologie. (77)

> is a classical writer and a Frenchman; the French lose themselves carefully, and always manage to recover themselves again. Eloquence, a taste for clarity, and intellectualism obliged Proust to retain at least the semblance of chronology.[2]

Proust's "temps retrouvé," however, is a far more fraught solution, more difficult and improbable, than Sartre realized.[3] In similar dismissive vein, Sarraute objected to Proust's relentless analysis, as she saw it, of elusive, instantaneous movements of the psyche: what she called "tropismes" and claimed to evoke rather than dissect (1956, 98), not recognizing that Proust's analysis dissects nothing so much as the futile efforts of analysis itself. Further resistance to the daring of Proust's text is apparent in Ricardou's work on metaphor; noticing Proust's and the New Novelists' similar use of figuration, he hastens to preserve the differences and distance that separate them rather than recognize how far more coercive, because more surreptitious, the same strategies are in the *Recherche*. The misreading of Proust's audacity continues in Genette's renowned "Discours du récit," which attempts to analyze the *Recherche*'s "formidable," as its narrator puts it, "jeu avec le Temps" [game with Time] (IV, 490); but the very terms of Genette's apparatus falsify this time-game, imposing upon it a notion of temporality too conventional, too chronological. Genette's examination of the difference between events ("histoire") and narrative ("récit") assumes that both can be represented in terms of "ordre," "durée," and "fréquence." Such terms, however, postulate a temporality of succession; time is broken into discrete units, which are then aligned ("ordre"), an alignment then measured ("durée"), and the recurrence of temporal units then identified ("fréquence"). Such a conviction of temporality as, essentially, reducible to linear chronology (the confusion, as Sartre puts it, of temporality with chronology [71]) is peculiarly *modern*, as Lyotard suggests (1986, 120), and Bergson before him. Collapsing temporality to chronology leads Genette to assert flatly that the narrating present is a single instant without duration (1972, 234): a claim I am at some pains to dispute in Chapter 3, for temporal activity in the *Recherche* is far more subtle than Genette's apparatus is able to convey.

One might also trace in Genette, however, as well as in other recent critics, moments of tacit recognition that the *Recherche* is more daring a text than its accounts would have, beginning in particular with its account of itself in its own theorizing. Genette admits that the Proustian vision is more "modern" than its theorizing (1972, 53). A similar claim for the daring of Proust's novel launches Descombes's extended displacement of its stuffy theorizing in favor of its self-reflexive, far more intriguing narrative practice. Descombes goes so far as to venture, conditionally, that Proust's disregard for any moral positivism attached to historical evolution would qualify him as a postmodern (153). Adopting a promisingly proto-postmodern approach in emphasizing the importance of competing *perspectives*, Descombes asks whether Proust's theoretical discussion of perspectivism adequately accounts for the perspectivism actually at work within his narrative discourse (225).

But Descombes ultimately reads the *Recherche* as, implicitly, a Balzac novel recounted from an "interiorized" perspective, which leads him to emphasize the distance between what he calls "facts" and "experience." Relating the facts, he asserts, does not account for the way in which they have been lived, experience (264).

Enfin, et c'est là le pas que fait Proust au-delà du roman psychologique conventionnel, il faut dramatiser le conflit de la version 'du dedans', celle du héros, et de la version 'à vol d'oiseau', celle de l'observateur indifférent. La véritable aventure racontée dans le récit n'est plus sociale ou mondaine, mais intellectuelle. (171)

Finally, and this is the step Proust takes beyond the conventional psychological novel, what must be dramatized is the conflict between the "inner" version, that of the hero, and the "bird's eye" version, that of an indifferent observer.

The true adventure recounted in the narrative is no longer social or worldly, but intellectual.

Descombes's promising emphasis on multiple perspectives is thus reduced to the familiar distinction between the outer, social, Balzacian mode and that inner rewriting of social "fact," subjectivity. Descombes thus rediscovers, somewhat post hoc, a modern *Recherche* departing, with its "invention de la vie intérieure," from the worldly, public tradition of Balzacian realism.

Just how great, how decisive, is the departure from Balzac actually accomplished by the *Recherche* is more successfully demonstrated by Deleuze, whose early "apprenticeship in signs" model argued for a Balzacian *Bildungsroman* movement toward understanding via penetration of the signifying systems of "mondanité" or "worldliness," love, impressions, and, finally, art. Originally published in 1964, however, *Proust et les signes*, through successive revisions and additions, presents an increasingly "postmodern" Proustian text. The "Avant-propos" to the second edition in 1970 shifts Deleuze's original emphasis from the narrator's efforts to interpret the "logos" of signs to the resistance of the text's many pieces—in the machinery of its "anti-logos"—to recuperation by organizational and interpretive efforts (158). The fourth edition (1976) contains yet another additional chapter, now returning to the hero's interpretive efforts to argue that the narrator-hero does not function as a subject. The narrator is presented by Proust, Deleuze writes, as incapable of seeing, remembering, or understanding (217); the inquisitive, desiring *Bildungsroman* hero of the 1964 edition has, by 1976, become an absent postmodern character, himself a baffling and baffled effect of the text's "anti-logos."[4]

Such growing recognition of the elusiveness of Proust's text most lately finds expression in cautious yet increasingly explicit references to a "postmodern Proust." Compagnon, for example, suggests that the meandering Proustian sentence with its "cascading" conditionals was itself already postmodern (1990, 160). Arguing that "postmodernism has reinterpreted the past," Szegedy-Maszak proposes that "one could go even further back than to Gertrude Stein, Raymond Roussel, and Borges, and point out circularity and repetitious structures in Proust" (47). And for Lang, the "transition from modern to postmodern mentality" (11) is exemplified in Proust in that his novel scrambles the categories of fiction and autobiography (136).

This critical aporia between postmodern theorists, with their insistence on an obsolete Proust, and Proustian critics' halting but increasing recognition of his "postmodern" text demands further attention. Such contradictory accounts of Proust's position in the postmodern climate would themselves justify scrutinizing the question more thoroughly. But there are other reasons to return to the *Recherche* in the context of postmodernity. For one thing, a "postmodern Proust" may not be so daring a claim after all. Arguments for any radical rupture are vitiated by the very inscription within the word "postmodern" of the "modern" from which it might attempt to extricate itself.[5] Honoring the "modern" within the postmodern is thus to situate postmodernity as a widespread cultural climate or "episteme" *within* the modern—thereby implicitly espousing a "de-periodized" conception of postmodernity, as in the "inclusive" positions of Hassan, Calinescu, Lyotard, and, most particularly, Compagnon. Opening the way for such deperiodization of literary history was De Man's suggestion that all literature is "modern" or "in crisis" (1983). Spanos goes further to "de-historicize" postmodernism with his conception of a postmodern occasion as "not fundamentally a chronological event in a developing plot but rather an inherent mode of human understanding" (194). Speaking of the temporal permeability of culture, its openness to "time past, time present and time future," Hassan claims, "we have reinvented our ancestors, and always shall" (89).

Such an inclusive understanding of postmodernity as part of—indeed, inhabiting—modernity itself would suggest that we have at last extricated ourselves from the fetters of chronological before/after ordering: that is, the notion of historical evolution upon which modernity erected itself. This overturning of chronological ordering is most apparent in Lyotard. Understanding the prefix *post-* in postmodernism as a mark of chronological succession is itself typical and symptomatic of modernist thinking, he claims; for modernity is defined by the very imperative to break with the past and tradition in order to inaugurate an entirely new order (1986, 121). Lyotard argues instead for a postmodernism understood as a recurring moment within modernism, a postmodernism not only non-periodized, but in an audacious reversal, actually *preceding* modernism in its allusion to an "unpresentable" that is then silenced and repressed by modernism. According to Lyotard, the ambivalence of modernism's fear and desire for an absent sublime follows upon the postmodernist embodiment of the "unpresentable": an idea repeated by Hassan's suggestion that "postmodernism may be a response, direct or oblique, to the Unimaginable which Modernism glimpsed only in its most prophetic moment" (1975, 53). Postmodernism recognizes and names that "unpresentable" silenced by modernism with the notion of the "futur antérieur," the future-perfect naming of what will have been: the configuration that retrospectively points to what we have since learned to recognize.

While Lyotard's recurring postmodern moment *within* modernism ostensibly undoes chronology, it surreptitiously, as Compagnon points out, reinscribes one of the great dogmas of modernism. In suggesting that the postmodern advances to an "unpresentable" from which modernism retreats, Lyotard subscribes to the belief in historical evolution or overcoming, and thus embraces what Compagnon calls the "modèle historico-génétique" (1990, 170). Lyotard thus rejects the great determinisms only to have the "evolutionary" model creep back into his argument. As the embodiment of the "unpresentable" within presentation itself, "le postmoderne," claims Compagnon,

se conçoit comme la vérité du moderne, comme l'accomplissement des possibilités non encore réalisées dans le moderne, et donc comme un dépassement de plus vers l'essence de l'art. (1990, 171)

understands itself as the truth of the modern, as the completion of possibilities not yet realized within the modern, and thus as yet another "overcoming" toward the essence of art.

Compagnon develops this formulation of the postmodern as the *truth* of the modern, daringly proclaiming Baudelaire as having inaugurated a postmodernism situated entirely within modernism. While he recognizes an implicitly "bad" postmodernity—"le kitsch éternel" of commodification—Compagnon unhesitatingly identifies "good" postmodernity with Baudelairian modernity (1990, 174). If postmodernity is essentially no different, however, from Baudelairian modernity, we are back to the old question of what point there may be in establishing a "postmodern" within the modern.

Other critics, however, see postmodernism's relationship within and negotiation with modernity as more aggressive. Hassan points to the fertility of postmodernism's negotiation of continuity and discontinuity (1987, 88), "sameness and difference, unity and rupture, filiation and revolt": polarities that argue for Huyssen's claim that "what is at stake is a constant, even obsessive negotiation with the terms of the modern itself" (217). Foster repeats the "negotiation" of modernism by postmodernism, whose strategy is "to deconstruct modernism not in order to seal it in its own image but in order to open it, to rewrite it; to open its closed systems" (1983, xi). Calinescu sees it similarly as a "quizzical" stance, a point from which to ask questions about modernism from within the modern itself: "insofar as modernism always aspires toward its own dissolution, postmodernism should be seen as one of the most typical products of the modernist imagination" (Calinescu and Fokkema 1987, 168). LaCapra also implies the inherent self-doubt of the modern, its "inbuilt negation of itself," when he asks "whether any 'great' text—and certainly any modern 'great'—both tries to establish something—a genre, a pattern of coherence, a unified order—and calls it into doubt" (55).

But this understanding of postmodernity as the self-doubt and quizzical self-deconstruction already inhabiting modernity, even defining it, would seem to obviate the need for postmodernity as a concept. We are back to the recurrent question dogging the postmodern; what's the point of a new notion of transgression when it was the very ethic of transgression that fueled modernity? There seems to be no alternative but to resort to flat distinctions in an effort to find a way out of the impasse. One answer is to assert that postmodernism reverses the hierarchy of modernism in privileging those features that were peripheral in modernism and marginalizing those that were preeminent (Jameson 123). Understanding this reversal in what he calls the "dominant" more specifically, McHale argues that the epistemological preoccupations of modernism, concerned with such questions as how we know the world, have now been usurped by postmodernism's more ontological outlook—what worlds are there? The difficulty with such distinctions, however, grounded as they are in putatively autonomous and objective textual features, is that they presume too static, too fixed, a text. They are unable to account for the different texts solicited by different readings; they thus deny, or foreclose, the activity of interpretation itself. Such a stance then produces crude evaluations of an "in" or "out" status—as in the occasional pronouncement that Joyce's *Ulysses* is a modern text, while *Finnegans Wake* is postmodern—and threatens to deteriorate into what Barth calls "a favorite activity of postmodernists," haggling over who "is to be admitted to the club" or "clubbed into admission" (65).

More useful than belligerent typologies might be a shift of perspective, locating the postmodern not in the text itself, but in its *reading*; we might think of the postmodern as a sort of lens: in Proust's own image, the eyeglasses that transform our world as the oculist polishes them and places them on our nose, saying "Maintenant regardez" [Now look]. "Et voici que le monde nous apparaît entièrement différent de l'ancien, mais parfaitement clair" [And now the world appears to us entirely different from the old one, but perfectly clear] (II, 623). A postmodern reading would be a way of perceiving the text retrospectively, through techniques that have since become more visible, acquiring shape and definition; [6] again in Proust's image, the text, perceived through such lenses, suddenly acquires a new form of organization, in the way that an admission from Albertine transforms "un passé rétrospectif que tout d'un coup on apprend à lire" [a retrospective past one learns, all of a sudden, to read].

Arguing for such a retrospective reading of the past *through* the thickness of all that separates it from the present is Lyotard's understanding of the postmodern as the future perfect, "le paradoxe du futur (post) et antérieur (modo)," the round trip implied by "what will have been." The postmodern writer, argues Lyotard, writes "sans règles, et pour établir les règles de ce qui *aura été fait*" [without rules, and to establish the rules of what *will have been done*]. There ensues, continues Lyotard, a belatedness that is also an anticipation: text and "oeuvre" "arrivent trop tard pour leur auteur, ou ce qui revient au même, que leur mise en oeuvre commence toujours trop tôt" [arrive too late for their author, or, and this amounts to the same thing, their execution always begins too soon] (1986, 33).

Such a "futur antérieur" approach is mapped in the Borges tale of Pierre Menard, who sets out to write, word for word, in exact replication, Cervantes's *Don Quixote*: not "another *Quixote*—which is easy— but *the Quixote itself*" (39). But this is not to be accomplished as if Menard himself were Cervantes. "To be, in some way, Cervantes and reach the *Quixote* seems less arduous to him—and, consequently, less interesting—than to go on being Pierre Menard and reach the *Quixote* through the experiences of Pierre Menard" (40). A comparison of Menard's *Quixote* with Cervantes's suggests the differences produced by the same sentence: "Truth, whose mother is history, rival of time, depository of deeds, witness of the past, exemplar and adviser to the present, and the future's counselor." As written by Cervantes in the seventeenth century, "this enumeration is a mere rhetorical praise of history." But, continues the narrator, "Menard, a contemporary of William James, does not define history as an inquiry into reality but as its origin. Historical truth, for him, is not what has happened; it is what we judge to have happened" (43). The same sentence as written by Cervantes and Menard thus acquires dramatically different meanings.[7]

A "postmodern Proust," then, would be our writing or production of Proust's text as by Menard, from the vantage point of our contemporary understanding. Thus, such claims as the assertion that style is a question of vision (IV, 474) might now be read differently, thanks to our new "Menardian" approach; style, rather than a "question" of the writer's vision, might be read according to the *reader's* vision. Proust even asserts this explicitly: "Je m'étais rendu compte que seule la perception grossière et erronée place tout dans l'objet, quand tout est dans l'esprit" [I had realized that only a clumsy and erroneous form of perception places everything in the object, when in fact everything is in the mind] (IV, 491).

Le lecteur a besoin de lire d'une certaine façon pour bien lire; l'auteur n'a pas à s'en offenser mais au contraire à laisser la plus grande liberté au lecteur en lui disant: "Regardez vous-même si vous voyez mieux avec ce verre-ci, avec celui-là, avec cet autre." (IV, 490)

The reader needs to read in a certain fashion in order to read properly; the author must not be indignant at this, but, on the contrary, must leave the reader all possible liberty, saying to him: "Look for yourself to discover whether you see best with this lens or that one or this other one."

The first imperative, then, is to maintain this thickness—our own postmodern perspective—in our return to Proust. Any authentically postmodern inquiry must then be Janus-faced in Hassan's claim, its self-scrutiny, or confession of its own "intricacies of will and desire," as urgently its intention as its interrogation of another text. It must both see its object and see its own gaze seeing, each gaze destabilized by the threat of becoming itself the object of another gaze; for in the widened cultural context of postmodernism, criticism becomes creative activity—criticism's claim to objectivity now debunked, and the myth of theory's separateness collapsed. A postmodern perspective restores the tangled participation of each within the other, abolishing the imposed boundaries that have segregated the two.

An initial chapter accordingly loosens these traditional borders by opening our inquiry with the ambiguous genre of Proust's own literary criticism and its complex connection to his fiction. Any critical act, theorists of postmodernism (Said, Arac) argue, must scrutinize itself, accounting for its "embeddedness" in a context that enables, produces, and empowers it. Such self-scrutiny will begin here by tracing the tangle of "violence and desire" (Hassan) informing Proust's own two critical essays on Baudelaire. Both are staged as dialogues that, in fact, displace and rewrite Baudelaire's voice to Proust's purposes, producing instead a model of the dialogic as understood by Serres: the dialogue as exclusion rather than exchange. The appropriation and reproduction, or "pastiching" of Baudelaire's voice in ways that evoke Proust's own discourse in the *Recherche* point to the generic scrambling of confession, autobiography, and fiction that inhabits any critical act, entangling it within the critic's own agenda. But the critic's agenda is itself entwined within cultural circumstance, as suggested in the eventual adoption of Proust's daring "écriture" (in accordance with Gallimard's explicit policy of risk) by the emerging intellectual elite of the publishing house. Such institutional "affiliation" (Said) in turn provided backing for Proust's second critical essay on Baudelaire, indicated by Rivière's eagerness to have any critical piece at all from a "commentateur" of such importance. Baudelaire's own voice in this critical saga, however, is increasingly obscured as it is appropriated and rewritten.

Providing a point of entry into the *Recherche* itself is another voice, the "monstrous" (Genette) narrating voice of the "monsieur qui dit 'je.'" While the *Recherche* is indeed usually read as the rich, interiorized, almost obsessively analyzed experience (Sarraute) of a powerful subjectivity, that subjectivity is as contested as it is developed, for the very ubiquity of the narrating voice ultimately produces a different experience of selfhood. Interiority, my second chapter argues, becomes the immanence of a fragmented, dispersed postmodern self, passive and voyeuristic, lacking in depth and motivation. Theorizing voyeurism as the fascination with one's own absence (Baudrillard), we might trace in the *Recherche*'s "voyeur" scenes an "absent" narrating self. This faintly paranoid self produces hypotheses in increasing quantity; but contrary to Sarraute's subscription to such analysis, and to Bowie's more developed claim for its scientific "muscle," this hypothesizing is an ever more anxious and futile effort to control what resists interpretation. Such hypothesizing eventually deteriorates in the "Albertine" volumes to the flatness of formulaic maxims—as if, his attempts at interpretation manifestly unsuccessful, the narrator resorts to shrill legislative efforts to impose coherence: a move from epistemological inquiry to frustrated ontological fiat.

This anxiety and ineptness of the narrating voice invites further scrutiny of the "gnarus," or narrator as "one who knows." Narration as the knowledgeable display of memory's contents—however panoramically ordered and reordered, in Genette's demonstration—might more properly be read in the *Recherche*, my third chapter argues, as the incessant invention and revision of those "contents." Such a shift from the notion of memory as fixed record to memory as ongoing invention finds interdisciplinary support. At the "micro" level, new developments in neurology imply that the mechanics of memory—the ceaseless reorganization of material ("recategorization" in the work of the neuroscientist Edelman) through new relationships among mental maps—are tantamount to the ongoing elaboration of fictions. At the "macro" level of organization, one might cite historiographic arguments for the tropological structuring of a historic past. The past, whether personal or historic, is increasingly formulated as a retrospective creation cast from the present. Such emphasis on the present points to the narrating act's duration and its importance; for it is over that duration that changes, shifts, in the presentation of material become perceptible. An anecdote given twice in the *Recherche*, intriguingly modified the second time—Morel's unfathomable interest in algebra—provides a particularly visible example of memory (narration) as incessant invention and revision.

From the act of narration, the discussion turns to narration's object, the "world" represented in the *Recherche*. Recent elaborations of the "feminine" use it as that "space" in the text that subverts narrative mastery. The "feminine" is used similarly here to question representations of sexual difference, "dissolving" (in the idiom of Proust's passage on Albertine's desire for molded ices) the possibility of representation itself—and throwing into question those differences the narrative claims to master. Marcel's failure to derive a coherent narrative of Albertine's past and sexual inclinations—a failure critics have resisted in order to repeat Marcel's claims of mastery—implicitly overturns the narrative's mimetic assertions, scrambling gender polarities and the power relations based upon them.

Representation now questioned from within its own mimetic forms, my fifth chapter disputes the usual handy answer to such problems, namely that the text refers to itself rather than to some putative outside "world." In Ricardou's argument, Proust's use of figure may challenge representation and narrative coherence, but the narrative, to rephrase Sartre, always manages to find itself again; figuration, maintains Ricardou, is always subordinated to mimetic purposes. Further scrutiny, however, uncovers in Proustian figuration a sophisticated device that fractures the textual web and immobilizes differential narrative movement—and this from within the very representational forms of a mimetic fiction. A rereading of signal figural moments through cultural theorizations of the simulacrum (Baudrillard) encourages us to recognize the subversiveness of metaphor's implicit claims to represent. In the figural behavior of passages on the magic lantern, the "clochers de Martinville," Swann's "faire cattleya," the initial vision of the "petite bande" on the boardwalk of Balbec, the Opéra as marine cave, and the homosexual encounter of Charlus and Jupien as the fertilization of an orchid by a bee, Proust's extremes of mimetic representation displace the outside world they evoke. Narrative progression is arrested by obsessive, simulacral images. Notions of the postmodern as perpetual present, a suspended schizophrenic landscape cut off from past and future (Jameson), help identify the peculiarly anti-interpretive behavior of figuration in the *Recherche*.

While the end of the *Recherche*'s narration is generally read as the beginning of writing and the replication of Marcel's story as literature—the "solution" Sartre so scorned—postmodern suspicion of such totalization uncovers the neglected tensions that undermine such closure. In particular, a psychoanalytic apparatus suggesting a textual unconscious might be used, as my sixth chapter demonstrates, to trace tensions that call into question the text's explicit claims—and to point to a singularly postmodern refusal to conclude, to the open-endedness of hesitation, delay, deferral. The passage from narrating to writing is more problematic, more unlikely, more respectful of the difficulty of literature than the traditional interpretation of closure suggests.

Concluding by returning to my opening inquiry into Proust's own critical writing and the "violence and desire" (Hassan) of its personal and cultural appropriations, my final chapter addresses conditions of criticism in the postmodern era. Critical attention to a canonical text can no longer ignore, it would seem, other attentions and energies that now inhabit that text. This chapter investigates the current cultural phenomenon of the popularization of Proust, tracing a "vernacular" simulacrum through iconography, jokes, anecdotes, and the columns of Russell Baker. How does such commodification and consumption of Proust affect what Benjamin called the "aura" of the work of art? What transactions are operated between the "official" culture of the high canon and its subcultural appropriation? Such "kitschification" or reduction of Proust's canonical work, however, may itself be inscribed in the idolatrous behaviors of Swann and the narrator Marcel. The *Recherche* may thus implicitly provide the map for its own kitschification, programming its own appropriation by mass culture. Yet a more anxious energy may be at work here than kitschification suggests, and notions of the part-object or fetish help investigate the unease behind these various reductions of Proust, as in the tendency to conceive the madeleine scene synecdochically for all of the *Recherche*. The anxious cultural ambivalence through which we now read Proust cannot but inform and reshape his text. Citing Duchamp's mustachioed and goateed Mona Lisa entitled *LHOOQ*, Foster points to the impossibility of returning to the canonical work once its "aura" has been "defaced": an assertion substantiated by Duchamp's subsequent invitation to a gallery opening depicting the original Mona Lisa—that is, minus mustache and goatee—significantly retitled *Rasé LHOOQ* [Shaved LHOOQ].

Within the frame provided by these opening and closing chapters on the cultural conditions that attend criticism is an exercise in what shapes the obsession with which postmodernism negotiates modernity—the plural, indigenous to the postmodern climate: "the irritable condition," Hassan calls it, of "postmodern discourse" (1987, 167). For pluralism is the critical imperative of postmodernity. As an antidote to totalitarianism, it eschews any "dominant discourse." "Philosophical, ideological, psychoanalytic, and rhetorical analyses," writes Schor, "share an ecumenical critical forum, free of polemical posturing and terrorist intimidation" (xii), free, moreover, of "insidious attempts to homogenize meaning" (Hartman 105). Not content merely to endorse pluralism, the postmodern calls for suspicion of the nonplural; for "totality as a political scheme—totalitarianism—has made us suspicious of all systematic thought as it rationalizes what is and what is not . . . as it aspires to the total intelligibility of history or envisions an ultimate order" (Hartman 98). Hassan puts this more sweepingly: "to think well, to feel well, to read well . . . is to refuse the tyranny of wholes; totalization in any human endeavour is potentially totalitarian" (1980, 17), while Lyotard gloriously and polemically proclaims, "guerre au tout" [Let us wage a war on totality] (1986, 34).

Enlisting the "toolkit" (Foster, Deleuze) of contemporary critical idioms, we will thus "engage different objects with different tools" (Foster 1985, 3), our purpose being to tease out the enigmatic fringes of the *Recherche*'s behavior: from those that complicate the critical enterprise itself to those that render the *Recherche* distinctly postmodern as they unravel conventions of narratorial mastery, subjectivity, representation, closure, and reception. As even the most scrupulous critics have tended to organize the *Recherche*—through imposition of a particular critical language—as a powerful totality, thereby confining and domesticating any behavior that would threaten its coherence, it is time to solicit the *Recherche* rendered possible by a postmodern attention, an attention receptive to a multiplicity of critical strategies and to the different textual energies they make available. For we have learned to read not only Cervantes's *Quixote*, but Menard's. If "our eyes," as Hassan asserts, "have learned to recognize postmodern features" (1987, xvi), it is with the aid of a multiplicity of critical lenses figured, perhaps, in the collection of eyeglasses Proust once sent Céleste to fetch for his perusal. When Céleste came back with ten or twelve pairs, Proust kept those he preferred on his table and never, apparently, returned the others.[8] Let us consider them part of his heritage.

Notes

1. These assertions for a canonical, high-modernist Proust are taken, in order, from Jameson 1983, 112; Holland 1983, 293; Fiedler 1983, 233; Spanos 75; Silverman 1990, 2; Hassan 1987, 108; Fokkema 1984, 14; Martin 147; Jameson 1983, 112.

2. Unless otherwise indicated, translations from the French are my own. Where I provide page citations to both French and English editions, the latter reference is to the English edition indicated under "Works Cited." I have,

however, freely modified all translations in the interest of accuracy and faithfulness to the original.

3. It might be cruelly observed that Sartre's own *Nausée* can be read as resorting to the ready solution he so deplored in Proust. "Sartre's *La nausée*," writes Christopher Butler, for example, "moves to a typically modernist (indeed Proustian) conclusion, in which the protagonist's ephiphany leads to his decision to redeem his experiences in art" (4).

4. This assertion of Deleuze's evolving depiction of the *Recherche* as an increasingly postmodern text was part of an argument presented at the Eighth International Colloquium in Twentieth-Century French Studies in Austin, Texas, in March, 1991; a parallel discussion emphasizing Deleuze's evolution as a critic was presented at the same conference by Jean-Jacques Thomas.

5. This ritual point—the lexical contradiction of construing a "postmodern" utterly other, different from the modern—is rehearsed in many opening paragraphs on postmodernism, such as those by, among others, Huyssen 183, and Compagnon 1990, 143–44.

6. I am indebted here in part to Gene Moore's argument for the postmodern as a reading strategy in "Postmodernism and 'le petit tortillard,'" MLA Convention, Washington, DC, 28 December 1989.

7. Floyd Merrill offers a valuable discussion of the important implication of Borges's story, the idea that "texts . . . are invariably naturalized from within variant and even incompatible contexts" (5).

8. This multiple-eyeglass anecdote is cited by Céleste Albaret (322), and by Philip Kolb in his "Avant-propos" to *Correspondance de Marcel Proust: 1916*.

Chapter 1
Criticism, Violence, and Desire

"No critical gesture," writes Hassan, "that fails to confess even as it questions the intricacies of violence and desire—desire for love or death, for being or power—can come near to wisdom" (1987, 151). Confession of its own "intricacies of violence and desire" even as it continues to scrutinize those of another text would seem, increasingly, to be the requisite gesture of every responsible critical act. Such a critical gaze constantly refigures itself as object, occupying not only the position of minister in Poe's story, perceiving the letter of the queen's anxiety and the king's blindness, but in turn the position of the detective Dupin—himself perceiving the gaze that perceives. For the critic, as Foster puts it, "also writes to an other who supervises his meaning." Criticism has entered "with its object in an investigation of its own place and function as a cultural practice" (1983, 2), and Dupin's agenda is as "supervised" by intention as the minister's and the queen's. Understanding the implication of critic within work "criticized" is consonant with the collapse of such myths as scientific objectivity; the observer is a part of the experiment observed, just as the psychoanalyst's implication in the analysis, the transference that is always mutually transactional, reshapes the very exercise of psychoanalysis.

The implication of critic within production of criticism—criticism as closet "confession," in Hassan's suggestion—would then scramble generic distinctions separating criticism and autobiography, the critic's own "story" becoming as inscribed in the critical act as that act's object-text. The loosening of such boundaries continues in further generic scrambling, as in Hartman's interrogation of the difference between critical and creative writing, the collapse of T. S. Eliot's flat claim—"You cannot fuse creation with criticism" (74)—in the face of assertions that criticism can only be creative, can only be "paracriticism" (Hassan). In suggesting that "the line between original text and critical commentary may always have been precarious," Hartman quotes Sainte-Beuve, who remarked "the commentary has invaded the text" (90–91). Sainte-Beuve, himself an object of Proust's "invasions," may well have been anticipating the part of confession, ideology and invention inscribed within Proust's critical writings.[1]

For violence and desire are expressed with particular gusto in the early "critical" sketches, the pastiches of Balzac, Flaubert, Sainte-Beuve, Regnier, the Goncourts, Michelet, Faguet, Renan, and Saint-Simon: pastiches Proust called "de la critique littéraire en action," explaining,

c'était, par paresse de faire de la critique littéraire, amusement de faire de la critique littéraire en action. Mais cela va peut-être, au contraire, m'y forcer, pour les expliquer à ceux qui ne les comprennent pas.[2]

they were, because I was too lazy to write literary criticism, an amusement—literary criticism in action. But this will perhaps, on the contrary, force me to write criticism in order to explain my pastiches to those who don't understand them.

This is generally understood to name the transition from the pastiches to the essays posthumously collected in competing editions of *Contre Sainte-Beuve.*[3] In his introduction to *Le carnet de 1908*, Philip Kolb suggests an even more explicit link between the pastiches and the critical essays, however, in pointing out that it was while writing his pastiche of Flaubert that Proust had the idea of accompanying it with a second pastiche, a pretended critique of the Flaubert pastiche "by" Sainte-Beuve (18). But if Proust's literary criticism begins with pastiche, its beginning is also unusually marked by a peculiarly literal enactment of both violence and desire. While pastiche has been argued as innocent play, the empty trying-on of masks in a cultural void where innovation is no longer possible (Jameson 1983, 114), another look suggests pastiche as the wrenching or decentering of style from its cultural, historical context: its "reification" (Foster) in an appropriation or wresting of form from history. Literary pastiche enacts this peculiar violence as an appropriation of voice, a swallowing-up or absorption, as Said notes in distinguishing between the essay and the pastiche. The essay is essentially, eternally unfinished, without an "organic" end (1983, 52), whereas the pastiche is an introjection, a swallowing-whole of voice. Citing Proust's pastiches of Flaubert, Balzac, Renan, and the Goncourts, Said argues that "in making over the authors he imitated, Proust set himself the aim of producing them from the opening to the conclusion of a passage" (1983, 157). The critical act is thus marked in Proust by an aggressive absorption or arrogation, both violent and desiring, of voice.

From this appropriation of voice, this swallowing-up, emerge two "essays" on Baudelaire. The 1909 piece, "Sainte-Beuve et Baudelaire," is part of Proust's *Contre Sainte-Beuve* project, and contains Proust's attack on Sainte-Beuve's policy of evaluating the genius according to the man—as Proust put it,

A ne pas séparer l'homme et l'oeuvre, à considérer qu'il n'est pas indifférent pour juger l'auteur d'un livre . . . d'avoir d'abord répondu aux questions qui paraissent les plus étrangères à son oeuvre (comment se comportait-il, etc.), à s'entourer de tous les renseignements possibles sur un écrivain. ([1954] 1971, 221)

Of not separating the man from the work, of considering that it is not irrelevant, in order to judge the author of a book . . . to have first answered those questions seeming quite foreign to his work (how did he behave, etc.), to surround oneself with all the possible facts about a writer.

In this early essay, Sainte-Beuve's hesitations, qualifications, ambiguous praise, and general waffling whenever in a position to help Baudelaire are detailed in stinging lines, before Proust, having aroused the reader's indignation, goes on to discuss the greatness of the poet Sainte-Beuve refused to appreciate. The later essay, "A propos de Baudelaire," published in 1921 by Jacques Rivière in the *Nouvelle Revue Française*, drops much of the Sainte-Beuve material to concentrate on Baudelaire the poet, occasionally mentioning similarities with Proust's own work. Could Baudelaire have hoped for a more eloquent admirer and defender than Proust? Curiously enough, Proust's defense is not quite what Baudelaire might have wished, for it replicates more subtly the very gesture of censure it deplores in Sainte-Beuve.

In both essays, Proust's praise of Baudelaire is extravagant. Baudelaire is categorically "le plus grand poète du XIX siècle" [the greatest poet of the nineteenth century] ([1954] 1971, 243). In his shorter poems, Baudelaire is "incomparable" (624). No poet has treated the subjects of death or the populace more powerfully. Baudelaire's universe is exhaustive—"Est-il rien qu'il n'ait peint?" [Is there anything that he did not depict?] (256) asks Proust. His technique, the materiality of his symbolism (a quality Benjamin also was to admire) draws lavish praise from Proust. No other poet is such a master of renewal—as in an abrupt change of tone—in the middle of a poem (624). Proust defends the cruelty of "Les petites vieilles," comparing it to Beethoven's late quartets, their dissonance also their peculiar beauty. Baudelaire's own sympathy for these broken old women, according to Proust, is silenced for the sake of his artistry, and thus "une marque du génie, de la force, de l'art supérieur à la pitié individuelle" [a sign of genius, of strength, of an art superior to individual compassion] (252). Each image is unique to Baudelaire's genius, "formes d'une planète où lui seul a habité et qui ne ressemblent à rien de ce que nous connaissons" [forms from a planet where he alone has dwelt and which resemble nothing of the world we know] (253).

This "defense" becomes increasingly suspect, however, in spite of Proust's clear mission to defend Baudelaire from Sainte-Beuve's stinginess—or perhaps because of it, for the act of defense carries a tricky ideology. Less apparently so, perhaps, than in the pastiche, it is nonetheless an implicit appropriation of voice, the arrogation of a right to speak on behalf of, somehow in place of, for—as Derrida notably suggests of Foucault's claim to restore to madness its proper voice, silenced by incarceration since the seventeenth century. Feminist criticism grapples with the similar problem of who is to speak the feminine, as Shoshana Felman, among others, points out in her discussion of Irigaray's *Spéculum de l'autre femme*. "Is Irigaray," asks Felman, "speaking the language of men or the silence of women?" (1975, 3).[4] And Barbara E. Johnson adduces a powerful example of the ideological manipulation of voice when she points to the use of apostrophe by the anti-abortion lobby: the animation and ventriloquizing of a subject in, for instance, the film "Silent Scream" (191). To what extent is a "defense" only a more powerful, more coercive because more surreptitious, swallowing-whole or absorption of voice than that of the pastiche?

These questions become pertinent in Proust's essays as the very act of defense, suspect to begin with, becomes an insidious attack: a paradigm anticipated in Sainte-Beuve who, as Proust himself observes, exploits the act of defending Baudelaire as a way of avoiding praising him. When Sainte-Beuve publishes his letter to Baudelaire on *Les Fleurs du mal*,[5] it is, says Proust, "en faisant valoir, pour diminuer sans doute la portée de l'éloge, que cette lettre avait été écrite dans la pensée de venir en aide à la défense" [emphasizing, no doubt so as to lessen the weight of his praise, that this letter had been written with the idea of coming to the aid of the defense] (244). Proust's indignation notwithstanding, his own essay will repeat Sainte-Beuve's gesture of substituting defense for praise, for Proust's extreme praise is repeatedly qualified and undermined in his "defense" of Baudelaire. His statement in the 1909 essay that Baudelaire was the greatest poet of the nineteenth century recurs in the 1921 piece, when the same claim is now followed by the interjection "avec Alfred de Vigny."

Baudelaire is thus in the same line given the honor and made to share it. Again in the later essay, Proust immediately adds yet another qualifying remark, that he doesn't mean Baudelaire wrote the greatest *poem* of the nineteenth century. That honor goes to Hugo for "Booz endormi"; Proust then devotes two pages to "Booz" in a digression that obscures his claim for the greatness of Baudelaire. Proust's claim that Baudelaire is "incomparable" in the shorter poems is followed by a much lengthier discussion of how his longer poems "se soutiennent par de la rhétorique" [are sustained by rhetoric] and "tombent à plat" [fall flat] at the end. Proust announces, "Je ne peux pas dire que Baudelaire surpasse Hugo dans la peinture de l'amour" [I cannot say that Baudelaire surpasses Hugo in the portrayal of love] (628). Baudelaire's repeated lines, says Proust, are tiring and pointless. "Quand on a dit au premier vers 'Pour savoir si la mer est indulgente et bonne', à quoi bon redire au cinquieme 'Pour savoir si la mer est indulgente et bonne?'" [When one has said in the first line, "To find out whether the sea is indulgent and good," what's the point of repeating in the fifth, "To find out whether the sea is indulgent and good"?] (631).

The implicit arrogating of voice entailed by any defense recurs in more specific form when Proust lists a series of lines by Baudelaire with the claim that each sounds as though it had been written by someone else. One might think, says Proust, that Baudelaire's line "Et les grands ciels qui font rêver d'éternité" [And the great skies that make one dream of eternity] (258) were Hugo's; that another line belonged to Gautier; that further Baudelaire lines were by Sully Prudhomme, Racine, Mallarmé, Sainte-Beuve, and Nerval. Once Baudelaire's voice has been thus divided up and ascribed to other poetic voices, Proust concludes by suggesting that the white-haired Baudelaire toward his death even *looked* like other poets in "une ressemblance fantastique avec Hugo, Vigny et Leconte de Lisle"—and Proust goes on, "comme si tous les quatre n'étaient que des épreuves un peu différentes d'un même visage" [as if all four were but slightly different proofs of a single face]. Proust has now allocated to others Baudelaire's face as well as his voice. This alienation from himself in a purloining of Baudelaire's voice and face reaches a pathetic extreme when Proust, toward the end of the 1921 essay, describes the episode of a friend bringing a mirror to Baudelaire's deathbed for him to comb his hair. Baudelaire doesn't recognize the face in the mirror, and greets it.

A further example of Baudelaire's appropriated voice is to be found in the very structure of Proust's essays. Both are written as addresses, apostrophes—but to a third presence rather than to Baudelaire himself. The first is structured as a "conversation avec maman," whose dialogic presence as "addressee" is constantly invoked. The essay's opening line begins "Un poète que tu n'aimes qu'à demi . . . " [a poet whom you only half-like . . .], introducing a maternal presence that is thereafter not allowed to disappear: "Et tu as vu quelles phrases . . . " [And you have seen what sentences . . .], "Tout cela vient à l'appui de ce que je te disais" [all this bears out what I was telling you], "Je comprends que tu n'aimes qu'à demi Baudelaire" [I understand your only half-liking Baudelaire] (248–50).[6] The 1921 essay, written as a letter to Jacques Rivière, incorporates the same dialogic structure—this time, with Rivière as "vous" in place of the earlier maternal "tu." The conversational tone is maintained; Proust apologizes that illness prevents him from writing an article about Baudelaire, and says "Tenons-nous en faute de mieux à quelques petites remarques" [Let's confine ourselves, for want of anything better, to a few brief remarks] (618), chattily throwing in such colloquialisms as "ces sentiments que nous venons de dire" [these feelings we have just been speaking of] (628), "nous disions que" [we were saying that] (629), "Est-ce que ce n'est pas bien joli, mon cher Rivière?" [Is that not very pretty, my dear Rivière?] (637).

Proust's earliest references to this critical project suggest the significance of this dialogized essay form for him. From the "contre Sainte-Beuve" essay's earliest inception, notes on a "conversation avec maman" as one form the essay might take bespeak Proust's preoccupation with a dialogized presentation. Proust writes of his hesitation between an "article de forme classique" and a dialogized "récit d'une matinée" [account of a morning]: "Maman viendrait près de mon lit et je lui raconterais l'article que je veux faire sur Sainte-Beuve. Et je le lui développerais" [Mother would come to my bedside and I would describe to her the article I want to write on Sainte-Beuve. And I would develop it for her].[7] This early preoccupation with a dialogized form continues in the two Baudelaire essays, where a closed-circuit exchange is established in which another dialogue, that of Proust with Baudelaire himself, is neatly and assiduously avoided. The persistence with which Proust dialogizes his addressee, whether his mother or Rivière, eclipses Baudelaire's voice. Not only does such insistent and obsessive direct address to someone else effectively shut out engagement with Baudelaire's voice itself, but the message's "phatic" (Jakobson) function—the verification that the channel of communication is open through use of the maternal "tu" or Rivière's "vous"—overwhelms and obscures the poetic function: the message of Baudelaire's greatness as a poet.

As other communications with his mother and Rivière suggest, however, Proust's dialogues are anything but dialogic; instead, dialogue screens a powerful monologue deaf to any other voice. This is particularly apparent when one remembers Proust's mother is dead by the time Proust first sketches his idea of a "conversation avec maman." The maternal voice, ventriloquized by Proust without any risk of interference, is conveniently acquiescent and manipulable. The theatrics of dialogue thus become, in effect, a way of silencing or avoiding engagement with another voice. As Alain Buisine has pointed out, Proust's letters are also elaborate strategies of evasion, the more powerful in that they appear to solicit rather than refuse the other's presence. Buisine cites Proust's habit of exchanging letters with his mother while the two shared the same apartment, leaving their notes in the vestibule (Proust tending to go to bed in the morning just before his mother arose) in an exchange that establishes and maintains distance within intimacy (30). This distancing maneuver is inscribed in other letters as well, according to what Buisine calls the "pratique typique de la lettre proustienne à ses ami(e)s: insister sur son désir de voir l'autre tout en multipliant les empêchements et les obstacles" [typical practice of the Proustian letter to his friends: emphasize his desire to see the other person, all the while multiplying the interferences and obstacles] (27). When Rivière asks to come see him, Proust replies with an ambiguous invitation:

Gide qui a eu la bonté de vouloir venir me voir et que j'en ai dissuadé, vous dira qu'en effet je ne reçois personne (pas même mon frère). Mais il peut m'arriver à certaines heures (surtout le soir) d'être assez bien. Si c'était un de ces soirs-là que vous me telephoniez je serais trop heureux de causer avec vous. Seulement il faudrait que vous me permettiez de rester couché. Comme je ne peux guère me lever (et pendant quelques heures seulement) qu'une fois par quinzaine, ou au plus par semaine, je profite de ce que ce jour-là pour sortir un peu au lieu de rester levé dans ma chambre, de sorte que tous les autres jours je ne quitte pas un instant mon lit. L'ennui est que souvent l'atmosphère de ma chambre est rendue bien désagréable par les fumigations que je suis obligé de faire. Mais je tâcherais de m'en abstenir pendant les heures qui précederaient votre visite. Ne prenez en tous cas pas la peine de me répondre. Vous déciderez ce que vous voudrez, ne m'écrivez pas.

Gide who has been kind enough to want to come see me and whom I have dissuaded will tell you that, in effect, I receive no one (not even my brother). But it can happen that at certain times (especially at night) I feel well enough. If it were to happen that you should call me one of those evenings, I would only be too happy to chat with you. But you would have to allow me to remain in bed. Since I can scarcely get up (and that only for a few hours) but once a fortnight, or at most once a week, I take advantage of that opportunity to go out a bit instead of staying in my room, so that all the other days I don't leave my bed for an instant. The problem is that often the atmosphere of my room has been made quite disagreeable by the fumigations I am obliged to have.

But I would try to avoid them during the hours preceding your visit. Don't in any case go to the effort of answering. Decide what you would like, don't write to me.[8]

Thus a dialogic exchange with another becomes a means of manipulating and confining a discursive other, a powerful silencing. Proust had an "acute understanding," in Said's claim, of the "asymmetry" of the dialogic situation, "more usually like the unequal relation between the colonizer and colonized, oppressor and oppressed." Said suggests that Proust's "representations . . . of the discursive situation always show it in this power-political light" (1983, 48). Another model of the dialogic situation, however, might even more precisely render the case of Proust and Baudelaire. Such asymmetry is construed by Michel Serres not as that between oppressor and oppressed, or between two speakers, but as that asymmetry with which dialogue becomes the exclusion of a third. "Dialoguer" [To dialogue], he claims, "c'est poser un tiers et chercher à l'exclure" [is to posit a third and seek to exclude this third]; "une communication réussie, c'est ce tiers exclu. Le problème dialectique le plus profond n'est pas le problème de l'autre. . . . C'est le problème du troisième homme" [successful communication is this third excluded. The most profound dialectical problem is not the problem of the other. . . . It's the problem of the third man] (41). All dialogue, claims Serres, emerges "contre les phénomènes de brouillage et de confusion" [against phenomena of interference and confusion], against what Serres calls "noise"—"voire contre des individus ayant quelque interêt à rompre la communication" [that's to say, against individuals having some interest in interrupting the communication] (41). Dialogue then becomes, it would seem, not so much communication as a constant, aggressive defense against interference. Proust's dialogic defense *of* Baudelaire, we begin to see, is really a defense *against* him, an effective screen shutting out his poetic voice. Thus the dialogic or phatic function, the effort to establish a channel of communication through direct address, perversely for Proust becomes a means of foreclosing communication (Jakobson): the theatrics of soliciting a dialogue about Baudelaire become a screen for refusing a dialogue with him.

Such a structure, an apparent invitation masking a deft refusal, recurs in the very gesture of address itself in Proust, where the rhetoric of intimacy and informality masks a highly meditated, elaborated discourse. In the 1921 essay addressed to Rivière ("Mon cher Rivière"), Proust excuses the informality of what follows, suggesting that this substitution of a letter for the planned article is due to a "grave maladie" [serious illness]—thus, "Tenons-nous en faute de mieux à quelques petites remarques" [Let's confine ourselves, for lack of anything better, to a few brief remarks]. This spontaneity is entirely fictive, however, as Proust's correspondence with Rivière and Gallimard demonstrates. Proust himself first proposes an article on Baudelaire to Gallimard in April 1921. The formal term "article" recurs in Rivière's responses to Proust expressing his enthusiasm at the prospect of "un article de vous sur un si beau sujet" [an article from you on such a fine subject] (13 April 1921) and, upon lending Proust *Les Fleurs du mal*, "Comme je serais heureux que vous y trouviez l'inspiration pour un article!" [How delighted I would be if you should find therein inspiration for an article!] (mid-April 1921). That the article has in fact taken shape as a letter to Rivière is mentioned by Proust to Gallimard: "Si vous voyez Rivière dites-lui que j'ai fait les trois-quarts de l'article qui est très long, très mauvais et qui est une longue lettre adressée à lui" [If you see Rivière, tell him I've completed three-quarters of the article, which is very long, very bad, and a long letter addressed to him] (19 or 20 April 1921). This factitious essay-as-epistle is again explicit when Proust writes: "Gaston [Gallimard] a-t-il pensé à vous dire que j'avais fait un énorme et assommant article sur Baudelaire (forme: mon cher Rivière)" [Has Gaston [Gallimard] thought to tell you that I've written an enormous and tedious article on Baudelaire (form: my dear Rivière)] (21 April 1921). The very form of direct address is discussed and analyzed by Proust to Rivière himself:

Comme vous m'aviez dit quand j'avais voulu inscrire mon cher Rivière en tête du hâtif Flaubert, si cela vous déplaît encore je mettrai mon cher Gide, comme il a écrit une préface (que je regrette tant de ne pas connaître) mais cela me semble mieux adressé à vous. (22 April 1921)

As you'd told me when I'd wanted to inscribe my dear Rivière at the beginning of the hasty Flaubert, if you still don't like this I'll put my dear Gide, since he's written a preface (which I so regret not knowing) but I feel it seems preferable to address this to you.

The easy informality of "mon cher Rivière," this article in letter form, is thus entirely stylized, assumed, contrived: the direct address to Rivière in fact meditated and discussed with Rivière himself, suggesting the evasion of the formality of an article, in spite of the effort Proust devotes to the project: "J'ai mis les heures de travail doubles pour Baudelaire" [I've put double-time into Baudelaire] (22 April 1921). In the end, it is the myth of "epistolarity" that prevails. Rivière announces, "Je crois pouvoir donner pour titre à votre Baudelaire: 'Lettre sur Baudelaire'" [I think I can give as title to your Baudelaire: 'Letter on Baudelaire'] (May 1921).

What is Proust avoiding? His exploitation of dialogue and epistle effectively refuses to engage Baudelaire's text directly. Such a silencing takes the form of appropriation, as in Proust's defense of Baudelaire, in a peculiarly vivid gesture configuring both the violence and desire of the critical act. But the abusive power of such appropriation becomes increasingly clear as appropriation turns to disfiguration—Baudelaire's lines are frequently misquoted. The misquotations include changes of subject, as when Proust rewrites Baudelaire's "le plaisir vaporeux fuira vers l'horizon" [vaporous pleasure will flee towards the horizon] as "le printemps vaporeux fuira vers l'horizon" [the vaporous spring will flee towards the horizon]. These misquotations include changes of verb tense; Baudelaire's present tenses are often rewritten by Proust in the imperfect, a tense Proust himself, as critics have shown, was to exploit in new ways.[9] Proust operates an occasional chiasmus of terms, writing Baudelaire's "pauvre et triste miroir" [poor and sad mirror] as "triste et pauvre miroir." There are omissions; when Proust quotes the line, "Dans ces soirs solennels de célestes vendanges" [In these solemn evenings of celestial harvests], he leaves out Baudelaire's adjective "solennel," producing an extremely disfigured alexandrine, one missing three syllables. Baudelaire's "Des trônes, des Vertus, des Dominations" are rewritten by Proust with definite articles: "Les trônes, les vertus, les Dominations." On one occasion, a faithful quotation—"L'autre, que son époux surchargea de douleurs" [Another, whose spouse overburdened her with miseries] (1971, 253)—is taken up again in the next line only to be misquoted there as the adjective "surchargé" of the verb "surchargea," attributing the miseries to the husband, rather than to the wife upon whom he heaped them.

These two means of "purloining" Baudelaire's own voice, the obsessive address to someone else and the relentless rewritings, converge in the most interesting misquotation of all, a mistake that betrays the silenced real dialogue. Baudelaire's line on the pipe, "Je fume comme la chaumine" [I smoke like the thatched cottage] (1971, 257), is revealingly misquoted by Proust with "tu" [you] as its subject instead of "je" [I]. It is as if the real "tu," the real addressee, Baudelaire himself, erupts in Proust's inadvertent, misquoted pronoun. Baudelaire's poetic "je" is both disfigured, misquoted as "tu," and suddenly addressed directly by Proust through that very mistake. This sudden and different "tu" ruptures the surface of the screen dialogue with the other "tu," "maman."

The decisiveness of Proust's appropriation of Baudelaire's voice is demonstrated in the Pléiade text of "Sainte-Beuve et Baudelaire." Throughout most of Proust's essay, Pierre Clarac's editorial practice is to cite Baudelaire faithfully, giving Proust's misquotations only in endnotes as a list of "Proust a écrit . . . ," "Proust a substitué . . . " [Proust wrote . . . , Proust substituted . . .]. In the text of Proust's essay proper, the Pléiade editor thus revises Proust's revisions and restores Baudelaire's voice to accuracy. But Proust's insistent revisions eventually prevail in the Pléiade text, for Clarac's policy has inexplicably reversed itself by the end of the essay. Proust's piece now gives the misquotations, "naturalizing" a disfigured Baudelaire within the body of the essay, while Baudelaire's original lines are marginalized in endnotes. From the earlier endnote litany of "Proust a écrit . . . ," "Proust a mis . . . " [Proust wrote . . . , Proust put . . .], Clarac's endnotes now read "le texte de Baudelaire est . . . ," "le vers de Baudelaire est . . . " [Baudelaire's text is . . . , Baudelaire's line is . . .] in yet another usurpation of Baudelaire's voice by Proust.

At the end of his 1921 essay, Proust exploits anew the informality of the letter form to excuse these misquotations: "quand j'écrivis cette lettre à Jacques Rivière, je n'avais pas auprès de mon lit de malade un seul livre" [when I wrote this letter to Jacques Rivière, I did not have a single book by my sickbed] (638). In fact, however, Proust had gone to some lengths to obtain a critical edition of *Les Fleurs du mal*, as his correspondence with Rivière and Gallimard indicates. Upon learning of Proust's intention to write an article on Baudelaire, Rivière writes "Je suis prêt à vous faire envoyer . . . le Baudelaire le plus scientifique que je pourrai trouver (je m'informe des éditions)" [I'm ready to have you sent the . . . most scientific Baudelaire I can find (I'm looking into the different editions)] (13 April 1921). Proust refuses the offer, saying he himself is having the best critical edition purchased (mid-April 1921). But Rivière persists: "Dès demain matin je vous ferai chercher et envoyer (dans l'après-midi) l'édition Crépet" [Tomorrow morning I'll have the Crépet edition picked up for you and sent (in the afternoon)] (mid-April 1921).

Contrary to his sickbed disclaimers, Proust thus had access to not less than three editions of *Les Fleurs du mal*. He wrote to Gallimard, "Je vous ai renvoyé le Baudelaire que vous aviez la gentillesse de me prêter, mais je venais de l'acheter le matin même" [I've sent back to you the Baudelaire you were kind enough to lend me, but I had just bought it that same morning] (19–20 April 1921), and to Rivière a day or so later, "Pardonnez-moi de ne pas vous avoir renvoyé votre Baudelaire qui ne me sert pas" [Forgive me for not having sent back your Baudelaire, which I'm not using] (21 April 1921). This borrowed collection notwithstanding, however, Proust ignores Baudelaire's voice itself: "Et d'ailleurs j'ai fait les citations de mémoire" [And besides I've quoted from memory], echoed in his "article" as "je ne prétendais que feuilleter ma mémoire" [I claimed but to be leafing through my memory] (638).

This use of "feuilleter," suggesting Proust's memory as a book to be leafed through, announces yet another appropriation: the usurpation of Baudelaire's own text by Proust's memory of *Les Fleurs du mal*. Ignoring his several editions of *Les Fleurs du mal*, Proust "leafs through" his memory instead, in a memory-as-text image that suggests his literal "memory-as-text," the *Recherche* itself. Under the guise of criticism—Proust's discussion of *Les Fleurs du mal*—is a slippage toward the fiction that is the *Recherche*: a slippage that seems to figure the move from *Contre Sainte-Beuve* fragments to the emergence of the *Recherche*. This slippage toward fiction—the precise relationship of *Contre Sainte-Beuve* and the *Recherche*—is the enduring enigma of Brun's question, "Le *Contre Sainte-Beuve* a-t-il donné naissance au roman ou bien l'a-t-il simplement précédé?" [Did *Against Sainte-Beuve* give birth to the novel or did it simply precede it?] (153). The editors of two editions of *Contre Sainte-Beuve* offer opposing arguments, Fallois suggesting a taut, linear progression from critical to fictive text, Clarac maintaining that essay and novel were always separate projects. Brun offers a more subtle view by stressing the simultaneity of Proust's critical and fictive gropings in sketchy drafts, and argues persuasively for a more subtle sort of evolution, "une écriture en progrès" [an evolving writing], whereby the hesitation between "l'essai de Taine en moins bien" [a mediocre version of the Taine essay] and the "conversation avec Maman" ends up producing a wild "prolifération": "la matinée de conversation se gonflant par l'évocation de la nuit qui l'a précédée, nuit d'insomnies, de rêves, et de réminiscences, et par la multiplication des personnages secondaires, à côté du héros et de sa mère" [the morning conversation swelled by the evocation of the preceding night, night of insomnia, dreams, reminiscences, and by the multiplication of secondary characters in addition to the hero and his mother] (Brun, 173–74). The "récit," originally intended simply to introduce the "essai," eclipses it and proliferates, but is far from being as yet the novel.

This simultaneity would offer an explanation for the ideology of Proust's appropriative move: Proust was indeed "practicing" in the pastiches and the Sainte-Beuve fragments not only literary criticism, but fiction, in a "trying-on" of voice. Such a distancing move—the trying-on of other voices before assuming one's own fictive voice—is argued in Germaine Brée's claim that the movement from the third-person narration of *Jean Santeuil* to the first-person narration of the *Recherche* is not a "return" to an autobiographical "je," but the highly conscious assumption of an autobiographical voice, exercised and trained in the pre-texts of *Jean Santeuil*, the pastiches, and *Contre Sainte-Beuve*. The dialogue maneuver becomes not only a means of avoiding Baudelaire's text, but of absorbing and rewriting another poetic voice. The high degree of fiction that informs Proust's essays—the dialogue with a mother now deceased, the "quelques petites remarques" [few brief remarks] screening a careful article, the meditated informality of "mon cher Rivière," and the dismissive "je n'avais auprès de mon lit de malade un seul livre" [I did not have a single book by my sickbed]—suggests the imbrication of criticism and fiction for Proust.

Proust is thus, even as he writes his first fragments on Baudelaire, at work appropriating and rewriting Baudelaire's voice in his own text. The first essay's plaintive "est-il rien qu'il n'ait peint?" [isn't there anything he did not depict?] anticipates the universe that Proust will himself arrogate and depict in his own work. For Baudelaire's work on sensuality and memory, reminiscence provoked by sensation, renders him a powerful precursor for Proust. The narrator of *Le temps retrouvé* might well be speaking for Proust himself when he says

J'allais chercher à me rappeler les pièces de Baudelaire à la base desquelles se trouve ainsi une sensation transposée, pour achever de me replacer dans une filiation aussi noble, et me donner par là l'assurance que l'oeuvre que je n'avais plus aucune hésitation à entreprendre méritait l'effort que j'allais lui consacrer. (IV, 498–99)

I was about to try to remember the Baudelaire poems based thus upon a transposed sensation, in order once and for all to establish my place in so noble a line of descent and thus to give myself the assurance that the work which I no longer had any hesitation in undertaking was worthy of the pains which I should have to bestow upon it.

Such a "filiation noble," however, from its gentlemanly rendition of influence, has come to be read instead as Bloom's agonistic arena of dismemberment and wrestled appropriation. This absorption is complete in the 1921 essay, where the features of Baudelaire's poetics Proust chooses to discuss have now become Proust's. Proust thus describes his own poetics as well as Baudelaire's when he cites Baudelaire's long days: "le monde de Baudelaire est un étrange sectionnement du temps où seuls de rares jours notables apparaissent; ce qui explique les fréquentes expressions telles que 'si quelque soir,' etc." [Baudelaire's world is a strange dividing-up of time in which only a few notable days appear; which explains the frequent expressions such as "If some evening", etc.] (297).[10] Proust discusses Baudelaire's rich interiors ("le mobilier de Baudelaire"); his use of reminiscence (628); Baudelaire's poetics of the city, of crowds, which in Proust become Swann's anguished nocturnal search for Odette on the "grands boulevards," the narrator's fearful visions of Albertine in the midst of sensuous crowds and scenes of illicit homosexual encounters in the furtive, darkened Paris of the war. Baudelaire's lesbian "vierges en fleurs" [blossoming virgins] recur in Proust as the sensuous "petite bande" of Balbec. The appropriation of Baudelaire's poetic voice thus continues beyond Proust's critical essays through the *Recherche* itself, in an extension that realizes the etymological meaning of "purloin": "to prolong." In a sense, we are back where we began in pastiche, for as Jameson remarks, "the allusive and elusive plagiarism of older plots is, of course, also a feature of pastiche" (1983, 117).

Proust mentions that a day comes in which that most powerful of poetic voices could only pronounce "nom, crénom" (260).[11] Baudelaire's words of impatience and frustration at his pain were taken as blasphemies by the mother superior of the convent that was caring for him—and who then forced him to leave. This misreading of Baudelaire's final words of pain stands as a last ironic figure for Baudelaire's purloined poetic voice.

Proust as defender of Baudelaire and the backfired ideology it lays bare has disquieting implications for any critical enterprise. Particularly dramatic here is that a critical intention to defend carries out precisely its reverse, as Proust's extravagant praise of Baudelaire becomes the violence of disfiguration. Is such disfiguration necessarily the implicit gesture of all criticism? Compagnon seems to suggest as much in pointing out that even the most deferential act of quoting has a dismembering violence to it, the cutting and pasting of quotation too akin to the bloody surgery of extracting and grafting. The verb "citer" [to quote], notes Compagnon, is from "cis en deçà" [this side], for it seems as though one is having the quoted writer or passage brought to oneself (1979, 283). This bringing-to-oneself, this absorption or arrogation of another voice, is particularly apparent in Proust's "defense" of Baudelaire.

But we need to go further, and engage the dimension of what Arac calls "wordliness" (281). We have been scrutinizing the "violence and desire" implicit in the critical act, observing the wrestled appropriation enacted in the "filiation" linking Proust to his Bloomian precursor, Baudelaire: the embattled transmission and (violent) transformation and appropriation of a poetics. But critical consciousness, as Said argues, must be read not only as a matter of "filiation," but of "affiliation." Suggesting that what has been read as high modernism teems with the difficulties of biological filiation, Said traces a "transition from a failed idea or possibility of filiation to a kind of compensatory

order that, whether it is a party, an institution, a culture, a set of beliefs, or even a world vision, provides men and women with a new
form of relationship" (1983, 19). In this institutional or "compensatory" order, the former "natural" filial bonds take on new cultural
"transpersonal forms—such as guild consciousness, consensus, colle-
giality, professional respect, class, and the hegemony of a dominant
culture" (20). Foster renders this as a veritable critical "'imperative' to
go beyond formal affiliations (of text to text) to trace social affiliations
(the institutional 'density' of the text) in the world" (1983, xv). A wid-
ening of the "interpretive circle" would thus inscribe Proust's own
critical or "filial" relationship with Baudelaire upon the contextual,
empowering "affiliations" of social and institutional circumstances.

We might undertake such a move from "filiation" to "affiliation" by
returning to the origins themselves of Proust's criticism, his pastiches.
These variations on "l'Affaire Lemoine" were inspired by a news item
that intrigued Proust for its "côté balzacien." Claiming that he had
discovered how to manufacture diamonds, Lemoine extorted 64,000
pounds sterling from Sir Julius Werner, president of De Beers. Lemoine's intention was to provoke a drop in the value of De Beers
stock, which he would then buy up at a favorable rate. Werner having
discovered the truth, Lemoine was questioned in January 1908 and
eventually sentenced to six years in jail. Proust himself, intriguingly
enough, owned stock in De Beers, and initially was quite concerned
at the news of Lemoine's "discovery." [12]

Proust's own implication in the very circumstances that initiated his
critical work is rendered explicitly in the Goncourt pastiche, where he
has the news arrive that "Marcel Proust se serait tué, à la suite de la
baisse des valeurs diamantifères, baisse anéantissant une partie de sa
fortune" [Marcel Proust is rumored to have killed himself following
the drop in diamond shares, a drop wiping out part of his fortune]
(1971, 24): a "false rumor" corrected several paragraphs later. Within
the originary act itself of Proust's criticism—the pastiches inspired by
"L'Affaire Lemoine"—is embedded in parody form the circumstances
providing for Proust's production of criticism: his position as a well-
to-do "rentier" of independent means. Within criticism "en action" is
inscribed the invested independent wealth that empowers not only
the critic, but eventually the novelist as well, as Grasset's publication
of *Du côté de chez Swann* "à compte d'auteur" [at the author's expense]
demonstrates. It is thus within the "affiliative" context of class that
Proust's critical intentions take shape as the pastiches take him to
the essays of *Contre Sainte-Beuve* and an increasingly explicit critical
ideology.

Il me semble . . . qu'en montrant en quoi il a péché, à mon avis, comme
écrivain et comme critique, j'arriverais peut-être à dire, sur ce que doit être la
critique et sur ce qu'est l'art, quelques choses auxquelles j'ai souvent pensé.
(1971, 219)

Thus it seems to me that . . . by showing where he sinned, in my view, both as
writer and as critic, I should perhaps manage to say, as to what criticism
should be and what art is, some things I've often thought about.

Sainte-Beuve's method and its erroneousness will thus serve Proust's
own polemical ends, providing a position from which to legislate what
criticism should be. The critical essays of *Contre Sainte-Beuve* thus
originate with an explicitly ideological, or "performative" (as that
which "achieves something" [Eagleton 115]) intention. Proust's own
performative claim—to show "what criticism should be and what art
is"—again seems to state the implicit ideology of critical and artistic
action: action empowered, in Proust's case, by the performative of
wealth, as Rivière indicates in his notes: "ce qu'était l'argent pour
Proust: seul moyen de se procurer quelque chose dans la vie" [what
money was for Proust: the only means of obtaining something in life]
(1985, 99).

How did Proust manage to enact these performatives? If class
wealth originally provided for the novelist's publication "à compte
d'auteur," it was the novelist's fame that empowered the later critic.
While Proust's 1909 essay wasn't published until 1954, his later essay
appeared within a month of completion on 1 June 1921. The circumstances that delayed publication of the first essay, consigning it to obscurity for many years, and that produced immediate publication of
the second suggest that Proust's emergence as a critic was rendered
possible by his reputation as a novelist. In 1909, three publishing
houses refused his pastiches; in 1921, two-thirds of the *Recherche* had
appeared in print, put out now by the prestigious publishing arm of
the *Nouvelle Revue Française* group, and *A l'ombre des jeunes filles en
fleurs* had won the Prix Goncourt for 1919, establishing, as Rivière
puts it, "l'importance du commentateur." The same confusion and
exchange between critical and creative writings is thus repeated on
the "worldly" level of Proust's reputation as both novelist and critic—a
relationship implied by Benjamin's observation that this "most significant document" of Proust's criticism "came into being on the high
level of his fame" as a novelist (214).

   Just how imbricated were Proust's fame as a novelist and the "coming into being" of his critical text? Jacques Rivière's role was to be
decisive. Rivière first read *Du côté de Swann* soon after its publication
and wrote excitedly to his wife Isabelle, "Je trouve ça *passionnément*

intéressant, et par moments d'une profondeur admirable" [I find it *passionately interesting*, and at times of admirable profundity].[13] Though his letter of admiration to Proust has never been found, Proust's gratified and famous answer begins "Enfin je trouve un lecteur qui devine que mon livre est un ouvrage dogmatique et une construction!" [At last I find a reader who guesses that my book is a dogmatic and constructed work!] (7 February 1914). It was Rivière who persuaded Gide to read the work he had cursorily perused and rejected, leading to Gide's recognition of his error, the withdrawal of the *Recherche* from Grasset, and the publication of its remaining volumes by the *N.R.F.* Rivière's enthusiasm, however, may be anticipated from his three-part article, "Le roman d'aventure" [The novel of adventure] published in the May, June, and July 1913 issues of the *N.R.F.* and thus some months before the appearance of *Du côté de chez Swann* in November. "Le roman d'aventure" is an esthetic manifesto proclaiming the end of Symbolism, for "la littérature a pris une orientation nouvelle" (1913, 748) in which the novel will be the preferred form; not the novel of Cartesian lucidity and analysis, but what Rivière calls the "roman d'aventure," precisely opposed to the clear progression of what has hitherto been "le roman français," in which the intelligence dominates and "le personnage est toujours l'incarnation d'un certain caractère intelligible" [characters are always the incarnation of a certain intelligible temperament] (1913, 64).

Instead, Rivière declares, "l'oeuvre, au lieu de s'éclaircir et de se raréfier, s'augmente et se développe; disons même, s'encombre et se surcharge" [the work, instead of becoming clearer and more rarefied, grows and develops; let's even say, encumbers and overburdens itself] (1913, 58–59). "On perd de vue sa direction, son fil" [One loses track of its direction, its thread], proclaims Rivière, "l'action . . . éclate à la fois en vingt endroits différents, et ne peut [être] racontée tout entière qu'au prix de mille embarras et de mille recommencements" [the action . . . explodes at once in twenty different spots, and can only be recounted in entirety at the cost of a thousand complications and renewals] (1913, 60). Rivière was later to realize the strange prescience of his wishful sketch for a "roman d'aventure."

Cet article est de 1913, et bien que je l'aie écrit sans avoir en vue aucun livre déterminé, il m'apparaît comme l'annonce et presque la prophétie d'une oeuvre qui devait voir le jour vers la fin de cette même année: l'oeuvre de Proust, justement. (1985, 195)

This is an article from 1913, and although I wrote it without having a single specific book in mind, it seems an announcement and almost the prophecy of a work that was to emerge towards the end of that same year: precisely the work of Proust.

Proust's conclusion in his letter to Rivière half a year later corresponds to Rivière's programmatic manifesto for the work of the future. "Cette évolution d'une pensée, je n'ai pas voulu l'analyser abstraitement mais la recréer, la faire vivre" [This evolution of a thought, I didn't want to analyze it abstractly, but to recreate it, to make it live] (28). And Rivière will confirm the conjunction in his postwar writings on the *Recherche*.

[L'oeuvre] est d'autant plus profonde que l'auteur n'a eu ni l'intention, ni la conscience de la produire. . . . Il bouleverse cent fois plus profondément nos habitudes et nos conceptions littéraires que le plus téméraire des "cubistes." (1985, 42)

[The work] is all the more profound in that its author had neither the intention nor the awareness of producing it. . . . He overturns our habits and literary conceptions a hundred times more thoroughly than the most audacious of "cubists."

Echoing Proust's own programmatic declaration of "ce que doit être la critique" [what criticism must be], Rivière's tone in "Le roman d'aventure" is programmatic, legislative—"la littérature a pris une orientation nouvelle" [literature has taken on a new orientation] (1913, 748), in which, says Rivière, "il nous faut enfin un roman où rien ne puisse arriver à être inutile" [we need a novel in which nothing can manage to be without use] (1913, 960)—punctuated with such exhortations as "le livre que nous souhaitons de pouvoir bientôt ouvrir" [the book we hope to be able to open soon] (1913, 64). The imposition of Rivière's ideology is most overt years later in the first *N.R.F.* issue to appear after the war.

Nous essaierons de faire sentir au lecteur que l'âge esthétique qui a commencé avec le Romantisme est aujourd'hui en fait et malgré certaines survivances complètement révolu. (*N.R.F.*, juin 1919)

We will try to make the reader feel that the esthetic age beginning with Romanticism is effectively, in spite of certain vestiges, nowadays completely bygone.

We might wonder here what empowers Rivière's position, not only "authorizing" his programmatic legislation of "le livre que nous attendons de voir" [the book we are waiting to see], but provoking Proust's gratified recognition of Rivière's importance. Proust's original reply to Rivière, following the famous "Enfin je trouve un lecteur . . . " quoted above, continues "Et quel bonheur pour moi que ce lecteur, ce soit vous" [And what a joy for me that this reader should be yourself]. As Alain Rivière was to observe many years later, "Si surprenant que cela puisse nous paraître de nos jours, tant est grande la distance qui sépare leur célébrité, c'était alors Rivière qui faisait figure de personnage connu et Proust qui ne l'était pas, du moins dans le monde des Lettres" [As surprising as this might seem to us today, so great is the distance separating their renown, at that time Rivière was the public personage and Proust wasn't, at least in the world of Letters] (514). In 1913 upon *Swann*'s publication, Proust, author of *Les Plaisirs et les jours* and hence considered an obscure dilettante and darling of society ladies, had reason to be gratified by the approbation of the prestigious *Nouvelle Revue Française*'s editorial secretary. For at the time, the publishing house was emerging as a new center of intellectual power and authority, even as the university—renovated, liberalized, and secularized by the Third Republic—was losing its own elitism through rapid expansion. "Quand le professeur décline" [When the professor declines], as Debray puts it, "l'auteur remonte" [the author rises] (63). Fostered by the institutionalization of the publishing house, the emergence of an independent "milieu littéraire" offered a new select intellectual arena.[14] While the publishing house as commercial enterprise existed well before the turn of the century, Hachette being founded in 1826 and Plon in 1854, the editor as intellectual, "maître à penser" [arbiter of thought], emerged largely in the person of Gallimard at the *N.R.F.* Said's "affiliations" are again apparent in the institutional formations, contextualized as wealth and class, that brought Gallimard to the head of the *N.R.F.* Thirty issues of the review had appeared when Gide, Schlumberger, Drouin, Copeau and Rivière set about to find a benefactor. The decision to open a publishing branch of the *N.R.F.*, with the financial drain and risk it was sure to entail, made a benefactor's fortune imperative. This is clear in the rare combination of qualities sought by the *N.R.F.*:

assez fortuné pour contribuer à l'apport de capital et assez désintéressé pour n'escompter de profit qu'à long terme, assez avisé pour conduire une affaire, assez épris de littérature pour placer la qualité avant la rentabilité, assez compétent pour s'imposer et assez docile pour exécuter les directives du groupe, c'est-à-dire, Gide. (Anglès, quoted without reference in Assouline 44)

wealthy enough to contribute to the acquisition of capital and disinterested enough to forego all profit but long-term, sufficiently informed as to conduct a business, sufficiently committed to literature to put quality before commercial concerns, competent enough to make his word heard and docile enough to carry out the directives of the group, which is to say, Gide.

At twenty, Gaston Gallimard, son of the wealthy owner of the Théâtre des Variétés and himself a "rentier" thanks to the fortune made by his grandfather, "n'apprécie que les loisirs, l'oisiveté, le luxe, les femmes et les amis" [enjoys but leisure, idleness, luxury, women and friends] (Assouline 35). At twenty-five, he is chosen as editor: "A défaut de culture spécialisée, il avait ce flair qui permet de ne pas se tromper sur la qualité d'une oeuvre et d'aller droit au meilleur, non pour des motifs raisonnés mais par une sorte de gourmandise" [Lacking in any specialized culture, he had the sort of flair that allows one not to mistake the quality of a work and to go straight to the best, not for motivated reasons but out of a sort of delectation] (Schlumberger, quoted without reference in Assouline 44–45). The imperative of wealth in the *N.R.F.*'s editorial policy is no less clear some seventy years later in Gaston Gallimard's farewell lines asking the *N.R.F.* to pursue this policy that was his own in its "recherche de nouveaux talents qui entraîne la publication de nombreux manuscrits au succès incertain" [search for new talent entailing the publication of many manuscripts of uncertain success]:

La vocation de l'entreprise, dans ces conditions, consiste à constituer et accroître un fonds littéraire de qualité et non pas à tirer des profits immédiats de succès commerciaux sans lendemain. Cela réclame aussi plus de patience de la part des actionnaires. (quoted in Assouline 14)

The vocation of the enterprise, in these conditions, consists of acquiring and building upon a literary heritage of quality, and not of reaping immediate profits from fleeting commercial successes. This also demands more patience from the stockholders.

The elitist cult of the *N.R.F.* is proclaimed in its second issue (1909): "lutter contre le journalisme, l'américanisme, le mercantilisme et la complaisance de l'époque envers soi-même" [to fight journalism, "Americanism," mercantilism and the complacency of the times] (75). The aristocratic intelligentsia that the *N.R.F.* was destined to become, thanks to its freedom from commercial imperatives, is suggested by Martin du Gard's reaction upon being refused by Grasset.

La phalange de la *N.R.F.* m'offrait tout à coup autre chose: une accueillante famille spirituelle dont les aspirations, les recherches, étaient semblables aux miennes et où je pouvais prendre place sans rien aliéner de mon indépendance d'esprit. (quoted in Morino 79)

The phalanx of the *N.R.F.* suddenly offered me something else: a welcoming spritual family whose aspirations and explorations were similar to mine and where I could take my place without losing any of my intellectual independence.

Proust and Rivière thus each find in the other the embodiment of an ideal, backed by empowering institutional circumstances; having legislated in *Contre Sainte-Beuve* what criticism should be, Proust discovers a perspicacious critic, and Rivière finds a writer who produces what he sees to be the literature of the future, as described in his 1913 article, "Le Roman d'aventure." The intellectual arena of the publishing house will give voice to each, to Proust first as novelist and consequently as critic backed by Rivière's enthusiastic encouragement: "Mon Dieu, quelle joie ce serait pour moi si vous pouviez le finir à temps pour le numéro de juin!" [My goodness, what a joy it would be for me if you could finish it in time for the June issue!] (21 April 1921).

What is Baudelaire's place in this ideologically reciprocal relationship? His powerful presence for Proust is repeated for Rivière, for whom, as a young man, Baudelaire as the precursor of Symbolism provoked enthusiastic response.[15] Now, however, Baudelaire and Symbolism represent a literary moment to be overcome, and Rivière's impatience is already perceptible in a 1910 essay on Baudelaire in which he proclaims, "Il est *poète*, c'est-à-dire qu'il *façonne* des vers comme un ouvrage audacieux, utile et bien calculé" [He's a *poet*, which is to say that he *crafts* lines as in a daring, useful and well-calculated work] (1924, 16). Rebelling ultimately against the "calculations" and artifices of Symbolism, Rivière declares in the opening of "Le Roman d'aventure,"

[le symbolisme] est mort et il n'y a plus rien à faire dans la voie qu'il avait ouverte. Rien ne sert d'obstiner; il y a un mur de ce côté-là; on ne passe plus. (1913, 748)

[Symbolism] is dead and there's nothing remaining to do in the direction it had opened up. It serves no purpose to be obstinate; there's a wall in that direction; it's impassable.

While Rivière cites Mallarmé as the exemplary Symbolist artist, Baudelaire seems to remain for him an oppressive unspoken presence. When the publishing arm of the *N.R.F.*, headed by Gide, Gallimard, and Schlumberger, undertakes during the war to publish Baudelaire's complete works in fourteen volumes, the literary journal, headed by Rivière, ignores this ambitious project. In a letter to Proust, Rivière is aware both of his own silence and of the excitement the Baudelaire publication has generated in other journals. "Et combien," writes Rivière, "le retard de la *N.R.F.* à parler de Baudelaire (sur lequel toutes les revues se sont jetés) serait heureusement compensé par l'importance du commentateur qu'elle produirait!" [And how greatly and happily the delay of the *N.R.F.* in talking about Baudelaire (to whom all the journals have flocked) would be compensated by the importance of our commentator!] (21 April 1921). This delay is echoed by Proust in his response, "J'ai mis les heures de travail doubles pour Baudelaire parce que j'ai trouvé trop fort que seule la *N.R.F.* se soit tue à son sujet" [I've put double-time into Baudelaire because I found it distressing that only the *N.R.F.* should have remained silent on the subject] (22 April 1921).

Thus the same critical itinerary of violence and desire, backed by institutionally and socially empowering circumstances, led Rivière as well as Proust to the same agonistic arena, "Contre Baudelaire." If, initially, Proust's earliest efforts of criticism and fiction were imbricated in his pastiches, yielding to a criticism that then produced fiction, fiction in turn re-produced the critic in the wider circle of institutional affiliation.

Notes

1. Walter Benjamin recognized the part of confession in Proust's criticism, particularly, he implies, in the later of Proust's two essays on Baudelaire examined in this chapter. In Benjamin's claim, "This most significant document is an essay that came into being on the high level of his fame and the low level of his deathbed: 'A propos de Baudelaire.' The essay is Jesuitic in its acquiescence in his own maladies, immoderate in the garrulousness of a man who is resting, frightening in the indifference of a man marked by death who wants to speak out once more, no matter on what subject. What inspired Proust here in the face of death also shaped him in his intercourse with his contemporaries; so spasmodic and harsh an alternation of sarcasm and tenderness that its recipients threatened to break down in exhaustion" (214).

2. Marcel Proust, Letter to Robert Dreyfus, 18 March 1908, quoted in Pierre Clarac, ed. (1971, 821).

3. Pierre Clarac argues for just such an intimate link between the pastiches and critical essays (1971, 190). The "Sainte-Beuve" project itself has been the object of much debate, and exists now in dramatically different versions, one edited by Bernard de Fallois in 1954, the other by Clarac in 1971 according to opposing editorial "visions" of Proust's ambiguous text. The significance and enigma of such different editions will be rehearsed in more detail later in this chapter.

4. The problem of speaking "for" the feminine will be explored at greater length in Chapter 4, where Marcel's efforts to speak "for" Albertine construe her imaged and literary discourse on molded ices as *his* "oeuvre."

5. Sainte-Beuve, *Les Causeries du lundi* (20 juillet 1857).

6. Further apostrophes to the maternal "tu" include "ces belles formes d'art dont je te parlais" [these beautiful art forms I was describing for you] (253); "tous les autres éléments du génie de Baudelaire, que j'aimerais tant t'énumerer, si j'avais le temps" [all the other elements of Baudelaire's genius, which I would so like to enumerate for you, had I the time] (254); "j'ai eu tant de mal à t'habituer à 'La chevelure'" [I had such difficulty in accustoming you to "La chevelure"] (256); "l'automne dont tu sais comme moi par coeur tous les vers" [autumn, all of whose lines you know by heart the way I do] (257); "Rappelle-toi que toutes les couleurs vraies, modernes, poétiques, c'est lui qui

les a trouvées" [Remember that he's the one who discovered all the true, modern, poetic colors] (258); "ses grandes pièces sublimes que tu aimes comme moi, 'Le balcon', 'Le voyage' " [his great sublime pieces that you like the way I do, "Le balcon," "Le voyage"] (259).

7. Marcel Proust, Letter to Georges de Lauris, 1908, in Kolb, ed., *Correspondance de Marcel Proust: 1908* (VIII: 320).

8. Marcel Proust, Letter to Jacques Rivière, 12–13 May 1914, letter 34 of *Correspondance 1914–1922*, ed. Kolb, 1976. All further letters between Proust and Rivière are cited from this edition.

9. John Porter Houston analyzes Proust's use of the imperfect, or what Genette subsequently calls the "pseudo-itératif," which, as Genette sees it, becomes in Proust a veritable "ivresse de l'itération" [rapture of iteration] (1972).

10. Proust's own "long-day" organizational pattern—as in the depiction of a *Combray* Sunday as iterative, habitual—is analyzed by Houston as a feature of Proust's particular use of the imperfect tense.

11. The colloquialism "crénom" derives from "sacré nom de Dieu" [sacred name of God], and might indeed be understood as blasphemous; but this structure ("nom, crénom") also evokes the banal "nom, prénom" [family name, forename]. What Baudelaire's crippled voice might have meant is not clear.

12. An entertaining account (entitled "Remembrance of Dividends Past") of Proust's adventures and misadventures as a stockholder is given by Lillian Friedman.

13. Jacques Rivière, letter to Isabelle Rivière, 5 January 1914, Archives Rivière, quoted in Thierry Laget, 12.

14. In his "Opponents, Audiences, Constituencies," Edward Said reviews Debray's argument for dividing modern French intellectual history into three "hegemonic conquests": the secular universities, ending with World War I; the publishing houses that replaced the overexpanded university system between the wars; and finally, in the sixties, a mass media structure in which, as Said puts it, intellectual legitimacy "slipped from the pages of books to be estimated by frequency of appearance on the television screen" (1982, 154). Said goes on to compare Debray's France to Reagan's America.

15. Baudelaire provoked, in Morino's claim, Rivière's "premières émotions littéraires vraiment profondes" [first truly profound literary emotions] (69), an assertion repeated by Rivière's biographer, who also asserts the "enormous influence of the Symbolists on the young, psychologically vulnerable Rivière" (Levy 8).

Chapter 2
Postmodern Selfhood and the "Monsieur qui dit 'je'"

Providing entry into Proust's *Recherche* itself is the ubiquitous narrating voice of the "monsieur qui dit 'je'" (Proust). It is thanks to the interminability of this voice that the *Recherche* has been read as the rich, interiorized experience of individual subjectivity—and perhaps never so anxiously as in the postmodern era, when such deeply developed selfhood, or its myth, is newly fascinating now as entirely "other" (Jameson). Yet such deeply interiorized subjectivity is as contested in the *Recherche* as it is developed, for the very ubiquity, the "monstrosity" (Genette) of the narrating voice ultimately produces a different experience of selfhood. Critics have become more bold in their discussions of an "absent" narrator (Moore), one whose very act of narrating separates his "I" from itself (Ellison and Doubrovsky): an absence, furthermore, understood as liberating, exhilarating, by Bersani, and as sublime, allusive by Lyotard.[1] Such postmodern evacuations of character, however, now allow us to read Proustian interiority as the immanence of a fragmented, dispersed postmodern self, passive and voyeuristic, lacking in depth and motivation. We recall Deleuze's ultimate claim that the narrator "ne fonctionne pas comme sujet" [doesn't function as a subject]; he is "incapable de voir, de percevoir, de se souvenir, de comprendre" [incapable of seeing, of perceiving, of remembering, of understanding] (1976, 217). Such inner absence is registered in a voyeuristic behavior marked by failure to respond to the illicit scenes he chances upon. The narrator's dispassionate observations continue even into the account of his suffering in the Albertine volumes, somehow curiously flat and devoid of pathos, where any sense of self is fractured by relentless analyses in which the subject increasingly becomes its own object. This analysis produces multitudinous hypotheses in vague efforts to control what resists interpretation. Such hypothesizing increasingly turns to the flatness of formulaic maxims—as if, his attempts to interpret the world manifestly unsuccessful, the narrator resorts to shrill legislative efforts, imposing coherence by decree where there is none.

The need to reconsider the question of selfhood in the *Recherche* has long been apparent in the repeated failure of critical efforts to parse out and label the narrating self. Indeed, the very anxiety and persistence of these efforts to organize and account for an elusive narrating subject imply that self's resistance to such compartmentalizing analysis. This myth of subjecthood begins with Proust himself, who describes the narrator as "un monsieur qui raconte, qui dit 'je' " [a man who narrates, who says "I"]. Ambiguity, however, is immediately afforded by what Benveniste notes as a certain "disponibilité" [availability] inherent in the pronoun, for "je" and "tu" are empty signs susceptible to appropriation by any voice (233). The "signe vide" (Jakobson's "shifter") of the pronoun "je" thus makes it significantly more ambiguous than the objective, noun-like status of the flat, designative pronoun "il."[2] Such ambiguity would provide the *Recherche* a means to maintain a certain undecidability of reference within the narrating voice.

Criticism has persistently resisted this ambiguity, however, dividing this "je" into the narrator Marcel who *says* "I" and the hero Marcel who *is* "I" (Martin-Chauffier 228). Symptomatic of critical unease is the very energy with which criticism has labored to account for the ambiguities of this "I." Its incoherences are not allowed to become problematic; the hero/narrator stratification within the first person pronoun is carefully parsed out and controlled by criticism, producing unwieldy typologies. When the hero is advanced from Martin-Chauffier's reduced role as a sort of puppet manipulated by the narrator—in the way "Golo" pantomimes the script read by Tante Léonie—and given some measure of the "je's" voice, critics impose temporal difference as a means of preserving narratorial integrity. The narration itself is thus usually seen as the definitive difference separating hero from narrator. The hero "acts" until he becomes the narrator, who then proceeds to recount these acts. The incontrovertible difference between hero and narrator is ultimately a function of time; the hero cannot overlap with the narrator, for he temporally precedes him.[3] This distinction between hero and narrator becomes absolute in Ellison's use of the Freudian structure of ambivalence to divide the pronoun "je," concluding that it "designates both protagonist and narrator, but splits them into opposing, noncommunicating functions"; for naive, erring hero and controlling, masterly narrator, in Freud's phrase, "cannot come up against each other" (Ellison 153).

Such extreme polarization of hero and narrator, however, supposes perhaps too traditional and positivist a *Bildingsroman* evolution of mystified hero into masterful narrator. Reading the *Recherche* as the hero's blind and repeated attempt to master an elusive sign, an effort overwritten by the narrator's ulterior knowledge, mastery and control, relies too readily upon temporal development and the premise that the opposition of ignorant and knowing selves is a mere function of "before" and "after," which time, as agent of change and transformation, will reconcile. Implicit in this theory of temporally segregated hero and narrator is the conviction that the events alone of the narrative suffice for the passive, mystified hero to achieve the degree of control, mastery, and knowledge critics have claimed for the narrator. Yet events in the *Recherche* do not align in a causal, *Bildungsroman*esque sequence that would carry the hero through progressive changes toward becoming the narrator. The single "miracle" of involuntary memories at the Guermantes' "matinée," by the very theatricality of its "deus ex machina" intervention, invites suspicion; it is too convenient, too timely. The question left unanswered by the *Bildungsroman* argument is how this original polarization is to be overcome for the hero to become, convincingly, the narrator.

Other indications suggest the speciousness of too firm a distinction between hero and narrator. The moment of transition is elusive, producing anxious attempts by critics to define the transformation. In response to Rousset's claim that at the end of the novel "le héros va devenir le narrateur" [the hero is going to become the narrator], Genette observes that instead, the hero "commence de devenir le narrateur, puisqu'il entre effectivement dans son travail d'écriture" [begins to become the narrator, since he effectively undertakes the work of his writing] (Rousset 144, quoted in Genette 1972, 237). Genette may be referring to a moment when the narrative presents the hero already at work as a writer. Françoise, rummaging in his papers, finds a "récit relatif à Swann et à l'impossibilité où il était de se passer d'Odette" [a story about Swann and the impossibility of his doing without Odette] (IV, 868). Genette goes on to claim that since the *Recherche*'s purpose is to show how Marcel becomes a writer and not Marcel *as* writer, "il est donc nécessaire que le récit s'interrompe avant que le héros n'ait rejoint le narrateur" [it is thus necessary that the narrative be interrupted before the hero joins the narrator] (1972, 237). But the undecidability with which hero and narrator are collapsed within the pronoun "je" suggests the novel's restlessness with such temporal conventions as mystified hero and enlightened narrator. The *Recherche* closes just short of the transformation, the still-to-come moment at which the hero would take up his pen to write. However, the novel's refusal to stage that transformation, as well as its suggestive flirtation with it in the hero's "récit relatif à Swann," implies the collapsing of such temporal and psychological distinctions. Instead, scenarios both preceding and following the supposed "transformation" are given: a "je" not yet at work asking in the face of death, "Ai-je encore le temps?" [Have I still time?] and a "je" having already written the account of Swann's anguish over Odette.

A further problem posed by such segregation of hero and narrator is that it seduces critical efforts into crippling attempts to index local, ambiguous instances and identify the part of hero and narrator in each. Lines such as "je n'ai plus le temps, avant mon départ pour Balbec . . . " [I no longer have time, before my departure for Balbec . . .] would seem to be pronounced by the hero on the point of leaving for the seaside town. But the sentence continues in a voice that seems to be the narrator's: "(où, pour mon malheur, je vais faire un second séjour qui sera aussi le dernier) de commencer des peintures du monde qui trouveront leur place bien plus tard" [(where to my sorrow I am going to make a second stay which will also be my last), to begin depictions of society which will find their place much later on] (III, 139). It is the narrator, not the hero, who knows that his second stay at Balbec will be his last, and that his "peintures du monde" will find their proper place later on in his narrative. A similar example is the *Sodome et Gomorrhe* train journey to visit the Verdurins at la Raspelière, where what would seem to be the narrator's voice details the memories "evoked" by the seaside resort or garrison:[4] "Je me contente ici, au fur et à mesure que le tortillard s'arrête et que l'employé crie Doncières, Grattevast, Maineville, etc., de noter ce que la petite plage ou la garnisson m'évoquent" [I will content myself here, as the little train halts and the porter calls out Doncières, Grattevast, Maineville, etc., to note down what the watering-place or garrison town evoke for me] (III, 463). The movement of the train and the conductor's cries occur in the "histoire," the hero's time; but the much-later act of noting what is *evoked* by the place-names occurs in the time of the narration. Further such examples include "Disons simplement, pour l'instant, tandis qu'Albertine m'attend à St. Jean de la Haise" [Let us simply say, for the time being, while Albertine is waiting for me at St. Jean de la Haise], where "disons" is pronounced by the editorializing voice of the narrator. However, Albertine can only be waiting for the "moi" who is the hero, for she dies before the narrator begins his account. Yet another example is the suggestion "Mais il est temps de rattraper le baron qui s'avance, avec Brichot et moi, vers la porte des Verdurin" [But it is time to catch up with the Baron as he advances with Brichot and myself toward the Verdurins' door]

(III, 722). In this instance, the "moi" is manifestly walking with the baron, while the narrator is recounting his past years and years after it is too late to catch up with the baron at this particular moment on their way to the Verdurins.

Through the indiscriminate agent of the pronoun "je," two remote temporal moments are thus impossibly flattened, pasted smoothly to the same discursive surface. Some critical effort to account for the poetics of such aberrations is made in Steel's observation that they allude to narrative's "linear dimension," to "the exigencies of the narrative felt by the narrator" (7)—and in Genette's claim that such "transgressions" between two worlds ("celui où l'on raconte, celui que l'on raconte" [the one in which one narrates, the one that one narrates]) flirt with a sort of double temporality, "comme si la narration était contemporaine de l'histoire et devait meubler ses temps morts" [as if the narration were contemporaneous with the story and obliged to fill in its dull moments] (1972, 244). Such claims, however, like attempts to parse out the personae inhabiting these incoherences, tend to domesticate rather than demonstrate the audacity of such impossible simultaneity.

No less vexed than the effort to segregate hero and narrator is that of parsing out authorial and narratorial voices. Proust himself endorsed such confusion; in the renowned 1915 account of the planned Albertine volumes, written on the fly-leaf of Madame Sheikévitch's copy of *Du côté de chez Swann*, he constantly uses "je" in referring to the *Recherche*'s Marcel as well as to himself as creator of that Marcel.[5] Elsewhere Proust avails himself of the narrator's "je" in recounting his book ("Ainsi une partie du livre est une partie de ma vie que j'avais oubliée et que tout d'un coup je retrouve en mangeant un peu de madeleine que j'ai fait tremper dans du thé" [Thus a part of the book is a part of my life which I had forgotten and which all of a sudden I rediscover while eating a bit of madeleine I've dipped in some tea]). But here his letter goes unsigned (with the disclaimer "Mais naturellement cela n'a nul besoin d'être signé" [But naturally this has no need to be signed]), in a curious scrambling of identities, fictive and real.[6] A further example of such cohabitation within the pronoun "je" occurs in Proust's 1921 article on Flaubert, where Proust writes,

des pages où quelques miettes de "madeleine," trempées dans une infusion, me rappellent (ou du moins rappellent au narrateur qui dit "je" et qui n'est pas toujours moi) tout un temps de ma vie (1971, 599; quoted in Genette 1982, 293)

passages in which a few crumbs of "madeleine," dipped in an infusion, recall to me (or at least recall to the narrator who says "I" but who is not always myself) a whole period of my life. (1988, 273)

Such self-correction argues for Proust's spontaneous tendency to identify with Marcel, "quitte à se reprendre d'une manière elle-même ambiguë ou partielle" [subject to revise himself in a way that is itself ambiguous or partial], notes Genette (1982, 293). Such ambiguity occurs in the *Recherche* text in warnings such as "Prévenons le lecteur que ce Cartier, frère de Mme Villefranche, n'avait pas l'ombre de rapport avec le bijoutier du même nom!" [Let us warn the reader that this Cartier, Mme de Villefranche's brother, had not the slightest connection with the jeweller of the same name!] (III, 550). The "bijoutier du même nom" exists in the world of the author, whereas "Cartier, frère de Madame Villefranche" exists in the world of the narrator: worlds flattened by such a warning into an expansive, coterminous surface. A final example presents a Charles Swann simultaneously both real and fictive, in an apostrophe pronounced by an undecidable narrator/author.

Et pourtant, cher Charles Swann, que j'ai si peu connu quand j'étais encore si jeune et vous près du tombeau, c'est déjà parce que celui que vous deviez considérer comme un petit imbécile a fait de vous le héros d'un de ses romans, qu'on recommence à parler de vous et que peut-être vous vivrez. (III, 705)

And yet, dear Charles Swann, whom I knew so little when I was still so young and you were nearing your grave, it is because he whom you must have regarded as a little imbecile has made you the hero of one of his novels that people are beginning to speak of you again and that you will perhaps live on.

Here the narrator's account is not, it would seem, the record of his past, the history of his becoming a writer, but a fiction, a "roman," in which the people he knew figure only in "quelques traits" of fictive characters. Yet this voice cannot be ascribed either to the author or to the narrator. Marcel Proust the author did not know a Charles Swann he could apostrophize (he did, of course, know the Charles Haas said to have inspired the character of Swann) and Marcel the narrator is not writing a book as yet, particularly not a novel ("roman").

Critics have also been puzzled by the passage in which Albertine names Marcel, arguing that this naming only underlines the author's absence from his work and loses all "necessary ties" with the outside world (Humphries 44, and Ellison 1984, 184) or, as Lejeune suggests, creates a new textual space—"un espace ambigu"—occupied by such a part autobiographical, part-fictive work.[7] Barthes, however, refers to such authorial intrusion as, rather, appropriation of the author by the fiction; the author becomes a "paper-I," reduced to the flattened carpet-pattern dimension of one of his characters. "No longer privileged, paternal, aletheological, his inscription is ludic" (Barthes 161; quoted in McHale 205). Such contingency destroys any possibility of a totalized self voicing "je," producing instead a "textual differential movement by which the 'I' is separated from itself" (Ellison 184–85).

The most extreme claim for the identity of the *Recherche*'s "je" is Bersani's argument for a "nonattributable autobiographical novel" (404). He points out that the life recounted in the *Recherche* may belong to no one at all—neither Proust, nor a fictional character named Marcel, nor a fictional character *not* named Marcel. For, concludes Bersani, "it is as if the narrator—or Proust—had first of all abstracted his experience to general laws and then deduced another version of the particular from those laws—a kind of second-degree particularity of experience disengaged from existence" (405). This would explain the curious intrusion of the Larivière couple as the only authentic reference in a work in which, claims the narrator, "il n'y a pas un seul fait que je n'ai inventé" [there isn't a single fact I have not invented]. For the voice speaking here is the "already fictive narrator," writes Bersani, "whose invented past would ultimately derive from that narrator's 'real' life—which of course means from an equally fictive life." The fictive narrator Marcel (or not-Marcel) would then be recounting a past not directly his own, but deduced from general laws, "de-particularized," in Bersani's term. This astonishing suggestion—that the life recounted could belong to no one at all, being a sort of double fiction, a fictive life invented by a fictive narrator, and therefore, that the "je" engaged in becoming a writer could be the fiction of a fiction— marks an extreme point of arrival: a moment at which speculation as to *who* this "je" might be culminates at last in the curious possibility that this narration may be a metafiction, a fiction about a fiction, the fictive life of a fictive narrator, belonging to *no one*.

One way to approach these transgressions would be to parse the "worlds" or levels they both create and slip among. We had been reading on one level, supposing the narration to be the true account of the narrator's life; suddenly, an authorial voice claims that this "true" account is fictive, in a peculiarly postmodern overturning or violation of narrative levels: metalepsis (Genette), "tangled hierarchies" (Hofstadter), or "levels of reality" (Calvino). The instability and fragility of any ontological claim is apparent, argues Calvino, in that "Ulysses listens to the song of the sirens" can always too easily be adjusted as "I write that Ulysses listens to the song of the sirens" (104).

The question of which level is "real" and which "fictional" is staged early on in a peculiarly postmodern imbrication. The garden scene of the young hero reading in *Combray* must also, the *Recherche* implicitly argues, be read in hierarchical reverse: fact, reality, is not only the physical sensation of fresh air, of one's seclusion in a sequestered garden amidst the tolling of steeple bells, but the imaged "péripéties" of a running, simultaneous fiction, whether it be a novel by Bergotte or the images of fantasy, memory, or expectation. The garden reading scene is offered by the narrator as a bedrock, grounding "reality" permitting fiction to arise; the child reading seems to anchor the fiction he follows, and the beautiful Sunday afternoons in the Combray garden, he says, progressively surround and contain the strange adventures of his fiction (I, 87). Reality would seem to enclose and contain fiction. However, the subsequent claim that every fact in his own narration is invented (III, 846) implies, as Bersani would argue, that the reading child may himself be an invention, a fiction. Calvino's "first level of reality," the "simultaneous states" the narrator has offered as "real"—the fresh air, the expectation of Françoise's dinner, the pleasures of seclusion, the steeple bells—slips toward fiction, and the novel being read by the young hero toward "reality," in a hierarchical upset.

The idea of hierarchical levels, however, assumes the *Recherche* flirts with, but ultimately endorses the differences among them. The "ontological destabilization" (Bersani 404) produced by the violation of these "levels of reality" notwithstanding, the very idea of "levels" nonetheless implies consistent local, internal worlds in themselves, with identifiable characters and event. Internal coherence thus comes to displace and substitute for overarching unity. The same vexed question returns in a more local form, and critical energies are again tempted into fastidious, debilitating typological efforts to rank the "reality" quotient of each level.

Bersani's argument for the *Recherche* as the account of *no one*'s life, however, now allows us to bracket the notion of subject—with its unwieldy baggage of distinctions among hero, narrator, and author, entailing equally fussy distinctions among fictive and "factual" worlds—and turn to another way of approaching the *Recherche* narration. Rather than concentrating on the identity of the "monsieur qui dit 'je,'"—that is, on the "monsieur" as character—we might think about the act of *saying*, the "dire." We need to think about a Lacanian subject "spoken" rather than a subject speaking (1966, 163), producing as its object the appearance or reflection of a "monsieur."

Considerations of voice itself have invariably been understood as expressions of identity, and thus subordinate to it. Voice has thus always led to claims of formal unity for the immense *Recherche* through recourse to identity, as Picon suggests in identifying the narrator's voice as the "essential element" of the narrative (228). Radicalizing this voice as a sort of monstrosity, Genette speaks of the narrator's "jalousie" in recounting the entire *Recherche* "comme s'il ne supportait pas de laisser à un autre la moindre part de son privilège narratif" [as though he couldn't bear to leave to another the least part of his narrating privilege] (1972, 250). Some progress is apparent in Muller's understanding of the pluralism—"*les* voix narratives"—of this voice; but Muller's purpose is to ascribe each of these voices to a subjectivity—"le protagoniste," "le héros," "le narrateur," "l'auteur," "le romancier," and "l'écrivain"—again reducing voice to an emanation of identity.

Recently, however, we have learned to understand voice apart from its service to subjecthood. Formulating this myth of voice as presence, Derrida wrote, "Aucune conscience n'est possible sans la voix; la voix *est* la conscience" [No awareness is possible without voice; voice *is* awareness] (1967, 89). This apparent presence-to-itself of consciousness, argues Derrida, is undone by the temporal spacing of voice, penetrated by deferral. Inscribed by "différance," voice is made available for analysis apart from any contingent status as vehicle of presence. Bakhtin similarly revises voice in the novel, arguing for a heteroglossia of many voices there where scholarly tradition has reduced "a symphonic (orchestrated) theme . . . to the piano keyboard" (263). Stylistic analysis has thus tended to create false wholes, false substitutes premised upon the false unity of individual speech: the screen of "an authorial individuality in language" (264). Instead, Bakhtin's "internal dialogism" (326) resituates voice as an index not of singular presence, but as the site of vigorous opposition, the struggle between "one's own and another's word." No longer "a direct, single-voiced vehicle for expression," "construed simply as a thing that articulates the intention of the person uttering it" (354), the utterance has been disconnected from subjectivity.

An instance of the displacement of character by voice might be read in Beckett's trilogy, beginning with a voice that seems to be Molloy's, or, in the second part, Molloy's double, Moran. As the trilogy continues, character and existence become increasingly doubtful; Malone, who had seemed to be the creator of Molloy and Moran, comes to seem as imaginary as they did. "As for the uncertain, nameless, floundering narrative voice" of the trilogy's final work, *L'innommable*, writes Calinescu, "the reader is at a loss to say whether it is one broken voice or several" (1987, 310). Such a shift from voice as an emanation of the singularity of character to an implicit reversal, voice or voices in conflict with singular consciousness, seems to bespeak a postmodern character: a self evacuated and replaced by a profusion of voices.[8]

We are now in a position to turn to questions of voice as an intimation of what becomes of selfhood in Proust, looking at two polar moments in which voice, on the one hand, and feeling, response, affect—the substance of interiority—on the other, are conjugated in different ways. An early scene presents the hero filled with affect but unable to give coherent voice or expression in discourse. Staging the hero's confused attempt to formulate a language able to render his "impressions," the scene depicts his reaction to a little tile-roofed shed on the bank of the Montjouvain swamp, discovered after an energetic struggle with wind and rain. His impression is of confused light and reflection as the sun's gilded surfaces, washed by rain, are reflected in the sky, on the trees, and on the wall and roof of the shed. "Voyant sur l'eau et à la face du mur un pâle sourire répondre au sourire du ciel" [Seeing upon the water and on the surface of the wall a pallid smile responding to the smiling sky], says the narrator, he exclaims in a surge of enthusiasm, "Zut, zut, zut, zut" [Gosh, gosh, gosh, gosh] (I, 153). As he himself admits, however, these "mots opaques" fail to convey his "ravissement." The failure here to find voice marks a moment of searing affect, of incoherent, Dionysian (Raimond 53) communion with the scene.

Mirroring this scene is a much-later episode in which voice emerges in profusion, driven, however, by an absence rather than an excess of response—and rather than conveying an inner self, eclipsing and substituting for interiority. Returning to Paris after years in a sanatorium, the narrator looks out upon a line of trees when his train stops in the countryside. Unable to respond to the play of light and shadow upon their trunks, he pronounces to himself a bitter discourse of resignation. "Arbres, pensai-je, vous n'avez plus rien à me dire, mon coeur refroidi ne vous entend plus" [Trees, I thought, you no longer have anything to say to me. My heart, grown cold, no longer hears you] (IV, 433). His apostrophe to the trees goes on to document the narrator's cold, failed response: "Je suis pourtant ici en pleine nature, eh bien, c'est avec froideur, avec ennui que mes yeux constatent la ligne qui sépare votre front lumineux de votre tronc d'ombre" [I am in the midst of nature; but it is with indifference, with boredom that my eyes register the line separating your luminous brow from your shadowy trunk]. As the train moves on, the narrator continues to observe indifferently the play of the setting sun's light on windows and houses. He compares the coldness of these "diverses constatations" to the indifferent remarks he might have made to a lady strolling with him in a garden, when, "par politesse pour la dame, pour dire quelque chose" [out of politeness for the lady, so as to say something], he might have pointed out its various features. In closing lines he continues to refer to these observations as a discourse he might have made to someone accompanying him on the train: "Je me signalais à moi-même comme à quelqu'un qui m'eût accompagné et qui eût été capable d'en tirer plus de plaisir que moi, les reflets de feu dans les vitres et la transparence rose de la maison" [I indicated to myself as to someone who might have been traveling with me and might be able to extract from them more pleasure than I, the flame-like reflections in the windowpanes and the pink transparency of the house] (IV, 434).

Out of failed response, out of an inner blankness, emerges a chorus of discoursing voices, beginning with a voice that unnecessarily narrates its own condition to itself. The self is fractured into different speakers, beginning with a superfluous narrator producing a superfluous listener, continuing to be figured as a gentleman stroller making polite observations to an accompanying lady, and ending finally as an explicit division of the self into traveler and traveling companion. Even this companion, however, takes cold notice of the observations: "il avait pris connaissance de ces couleurs sans aucune espèce d'allégresse" [he had taken note of the colors without any kind of joy]. Such a multiplication of speakers and voices produces an excess of discourse in a profusion that seems empty and sterile, the superfluous product of a failure, the absence of an engaged self. The voices are bored, detached, and factitious, a profusion of sterile discourses substituting for affect.

Another moment of inner fracture and division marked by the emergence of voice is the moment the narrator fails, curiously enough, to recognize his own writing when his article at last comes out in the *Figaro*. He reads the opening lines of his *Figaro* article with indignation—"Cela, c'était trop fort. J'enverrais une protestation" [This was really too much. I would write and protest] (IV, 148)—that someone has stolen his work, realizing only belatedly that it is in search of precisely this, his own writing and voice, that he opens the *Figaro* so eagerly every morning. We rarely hear him quote himself, as Moore points out; that is, we hear nothing but his ubiquitous narrating voice, and rarely his voice as we hear those of speaking characters. In fact, it is their voices that inform him of his own state—"comme les trompettes du Jugement"—when the duchesse de Guermantes at the final "matinée" calls him "mon plus vieil ami" [my oldest friend], and the prince's nephew remarks, "Vous qui êtes un vieux Parisien" [You, an old Parisian] (IV, 506).

Returning to the summer-afternoon reading scene of *Combray*, we are now in a position to identify a further model of selfhood replaced by voice. These afternoons have been, suggests the narrator, "vidés par moi des incidents médiocres de mon existence personnelle que j'y avais remplacés par une vie d'aventures et d'aspirations étranges" [carefully emptied by me of the mediocre incidents of my personal existence, which I had replaced with a life of strange adventures and aspirations] (I, 87); the reading self would seem to be emptied of its "existence personnelle," "replaced" by the narrating voice of the fiction being read. Such an emptying-out of the self in favor of a fictive narrating voice offers a model of what may be at work in the *Recherche*'s construction of a subject. The self now emptied and replaced by the immanence of voice, an image of selfhood's interiority is rendered as the "screen" of the narrator's awareness, or "espèce d'écran diapré d'états différents que . . . déployait simultanément ma conscience" [sort of screen dappled with different states . . . which my consciousness simultaneously unfolded] (I, 83).

Juxtaposed on the screen of awareness are qualitatively different fragments of selfhood, running, says the narrator, "des aspirations les plus profondément cachées en moi-même jusqu'à la vision tout extérieure de l'horizon que j'avais . . . sous les yeux" [from my most deeply hidden aspirations to the wholly external vision of the horizon spread out before my eyes] (I, 83). Differences of inner and outer topography, from the innerness of subjectivity to the most far-away otherness, the horizon of the outside world, are flattened to the "screen" of awareness. Awareness becomes a screen of simultaneously juxtaposed images, collapsed—like the topography of doorknobs and curtains in the magic lantern passage—and flattened to the immanence of a screen. Voice, it would seem, becomes the textual equivalent of a screen, the expulsion and flattening of interiority to immanence.

In a strangely pre-postmodern observation, Blanchot notices that interiority, in Proust, is cancelled as it is "unfolded without," unfolded as image: "il n'y a plus d'intériorité, car tout ce qui est intérieur s'y déploie au dehors, y prend la forme d'une image" [interiority no longer exists, for all that is interior unfolds without, taking there the form of an image] (22). Blanchot, however, then retreats from this postmodern understanding of the image as the exteriorization of what used to be "subjectivity." Meaning and depth, having been evacuated, flattened into image, are restored when Blanchot argues that the image in itself is "sans signification, mais appelant la profondeur de tout sens possible" [without signification, but calling for the profundity of all possible meanings] (22). We cannot ignore here, however, an implicit depthlessness of the self, whose most inner aspirations are flatly juxtaposed on the same plane as the outer horizon. The very notion of selfhood as depth, character, opacity, has been excavated and unfolded as immanence, voice, evoking the "immanence" of Hassan's "patina of thought" now lying over all of experience in a colonization by thought. Similarly, Baudrillard's "obscene" involves the collapse of distinction between inner and outer, private and public, the dissolution of the "scène," or public stage itself; all is unfolded without, in an "obscene" revelation or flattening of difference.

Understanding the narrating voice now as the absence of self, as the screen-surface of a hollow, departed interiority, we are in a position to reread the voyeurism of the *Recherche*. Contributing to the impression of a certain flat, screen-like depthlessness is Marcel's passivity and failure to respond, particularly acute in his voyeuristic observation of the intimate and scandalous scenarios of others. As understood by Freud in his argument for the vicissitudes undergone by instincts, voyeurism involves its apparent reversal, a vicarious exhibitionistic pleasure in which the observer imagines him- or herself in the position of the observed. Such a reversal is certainly suggested, for instance, when the narrator sees Gilberte for the first time behind the hawthorne hedge. Initially, all the narrator's senses are concentrated in

ce regard qui n'est pas que le porte-parole des yeux, mais à la fenêtre duquel se penchent tous les sens, anxieux et pétrifiés, le regard qui voudrait toucher, capturer, emmener le corps qu'il regarde et l'âme avec lui. (I, 139)

that gaze which is not merely the messenger of the eyes, but from whose window all the senses lean, anxious and petrified, a gaze eager to touch, capture, and bear off the body it is looking at, and the soul with it.

But there ensues a second gaze, the narrator tells us: "un second regard, inconsciemment supplicateur, qui tâchait de la forcer à faire attention à moi, à me connaître" [a second, unconsciously imploring look, that tried to force her to pay attention to me, to see, to know me]. Such a shift in the narrator's gaze seems consonant with Freud's claim for the reversal implicit in voyeurism. In this reversal, the original, gazed-at object seems somehow to draw the looker's subjectivity. This subjectivity now transferred to and invested in the object, the original looker now, in effect, gazes back upon him- or herself, construing a new object in the place of the original subject. The Freudian gaze is thus, implicitly, also its own reversal, the desire for passivity—to be gazed upon, to be "objectified" by a new gaze.[9] Gilberte's refusal to see him, to endorse the voyeuristic scenario by construing him as the object of *her* gaze, frustrates the narrator as "une preuve d'outrageant mépris" [evidence of outrageous contempt].

Later voyeuristic episodes, however—the sadistic lesbian exchange at Montjouvain between Mademoiselle Vinteuil and her friend, the homosexual encounter of the baron de Charlus and Jupien in the Guermantes's courtyard, the brothel whipping of the Baron in *Le temps retrouvé*, even the narrator's evening at the Opéra [10]—suggest an increased passivity that never reaches the Freudian phase of reversal. Instead, such fascination would seem to derive, as Bersani puts it, from "Marcel's exhilarated shock . . . at discovering his own absence from the world" (401). The narrator is not so much the "objectified" original subject of Freudian voyeurism as he is absent—an absence that, as Baudrillard suggests, is in itself fascinating: "l'homme est fasciné par ce qui l'exclut. . . . Son absence le fascine, comme de voir sans être vu" [man is fascinated by what excludes him. . . . His absence itself fascinates him, like seeing without being seen] (1969, 170). "C'est en se caressant elle-même" [It's in caressing herself], continues Baudrillard, "c'est par la manoeuvre autoérotique que la stripteaseuse évoque au mieux le désir" [it's with her autoerotic movement that the strip-teaser most effectively arouses desire] (1972, 106). Such claims suggest a revised understanding of voyeurism in which one's own absence from the world is beheld as *spectacle*, and as such, fascinating, mesmerizing. It is the release from desire, from its appetitive appropriations, that allows the world to be beheld as pure image, spectacle, that restores the ability to *see*, producing "an unprecedented visibility of past appearances" (Bersani 419). This release from desire might produce, however, perhaps not restfulness and indifference as Bersani argues, but fascination. It is when the self has no further desiring investments in the world that the world becomes fascinating spectacle: the moment one has, like Lukacs's tragic figure, left the stage. "La fascination," writes Baudrillard,

est une passion nihiliste par excellence, c'est la passion propre au mode de disparition. Nous sommes fascinés par toutes les formes de disparition, de notre disparition. Mélancoliques et fascinés, telle est notre situation générale dans une ère de transparence involontaire. (1981, 231)

is a surpassingly nihilistic passion, it's the particular passion of the mode of disappearance. We are fascinated by all forms of disappearance, of our own disappearance. Melancholic and fascinated: such is our general situation in an era of involuntary transparence.

The narrator's voyeurism might thus be an index of his own departure, his own "disparition"—and a rereading of voyeuristic scenes in the novel suggests not Freud's subject/object reversals, but Baudrillard's absence of engagement, the melancholic fascination of a failure to engage selfhood. The Montjouvain scene, for instance, is introduced by the narrator as a source of intellectual knowledge, an "impression" later leading to what he calls "l'idée que je me suis faite du sadisme" [the idea I had formulated of sadism] (I, 157). The narrator's reaction to the scene is thus strangely constative, objective, that of a dispassionate observer, his response simply "Je savais maintenant, pour toutes les souffrances que pendant sa vie M. Vinteuil avait supportées à cause de sa fille, ce qu'après la mort il avait reçu d'elle en salaire" [I knew now what reward M. Vinteuil, in return for all the suffering he had endured in his lifetime on account of his daughter, had received from her after his death] (I, 161). All affect seems to be missing—no shock or sympathy for the pathos of Vinteuil's death from anxiety over his daughter, merely the somewhat clinical observation of Mlle Vinteuil's struggle to overcome her own instinctive virtue, scruples, and tenderness for sensual pleasure: "Et je comprenais combien elle l'eût désiré en voyant combien il lui était impossible d'y réussir" [And I understood how greatly she must have longed for such an escape when I saw how impossible it was for her to succeed] (I, 162). This "spectacle" of Montjouvain, witnessed by a narrator who remains an indifferent, unengaged onlooker, is confirmed much later in his reaction to Albertine's claim that the "demoiselles Vinteuil," as Charlus calls them, were virtual big sisters to her. The narrator realizes that at the time of Montjouvain, he believed he was only contemplating "un spectacle curieux et divertissant" [a curious and entertaining spectacle], certainly a strangely dispassionate assessment of the scene. Now, however, with Albertine's admission, he understands that this "spectacle curieux et divertissant" has opened up for him "la voie funeste . . . du Savoir" [the fatal path of Knowledge] (III, 500). Both at the moment of its occurence, when Montjouvain is "spectacle," and later, when it is retrospectively recognized as the initiation to a certain sexual knowledge, the scene is beheld by a surprisingly contemplative, spectating hero.

The narrator as dispassionate, withdrawn spectator is again apparent in the homosexual encounter of the Baron and Jupien, which he links to "un obscur ressouvenir de la scène de Montjouvain" [a dim memory of the scene at Montjouvain] (III, 9). The theatricality and spectacle of both scenarios is suggested in an explicit mention of their "imprudent" and "unlikely" "mise en scène." The mise en scène of the Baron and Jupien fascinates the narrator for its very exclusion of him, the danger, imprudence and challenge it offers—"comme si de telles révélations ne devaient être la récompense que d'un acte plein de risques" [as if such revelations were only to be the reward of an act full of risk], and he undertakes the comic, dangerous circumnavigation of the courtyard inspired by his recent reading of explorations and voyages in the Boer Wars (III, 10). The very riskiness of spying on the Baron and Jupien, with its implicit exclusion of the narrator, would seem to be what draws his fascination. But such fascination remains constative, unengaged, for there is otherwise no affective response—no visceral response of surprise, shock, desire. From the "violent" noises he overhears, the narrator merely notes, "j'en conclus plus tard qu'il y a une chose aussi bruyante que la souffrance, c'est le plaisir" [I concluded from this later on that there is another thing as clamorous as pain, namely pleasure] (III, 11): again, a surprisingly tranquil, contemplative, indifferent assessment of the spectacle.

The same contemplative distance will be maintained when the narrator watches an even more violent mise en scène, the sadomasochistic scenarios staged by Jupien for the Baron's pleasure. The hero registers no surprise when, upon hearing "je vous en supplie, grâce, grâce, pitié, détachez-moi, ne me frappez pas si fort. . . . Je vous baise les pieds, je m'humilie, je ne recommencerai pas. Ayez pitié" [I beseech you, mercy, have pity, untie me, don't beat me so hard . . . I kiss your feet, I abase myself, I won't do it again. Have pity] (IV, 394), he beholds, bruised and bloody, Charlus. Rather than registering astonishment, however, the narrator's account continues to document action: "Tout d'un coup la porte s'ouvrit . . ." [Suddenly, the door opened . . .]. There follows a succession of unlikely scenarios, none of which seems to provoke any response in Marcel the observer. Charlus complains that the cruelty and debauchery of his tormenter lack conviction; a priest leaves a room with a soldier, provoking only the indifferent observation, "c'était cette chose si rare, et en France absolument exceptionnelle, qu'est un mauvais prêtre" [it was that rare and in France altogether exceptional thing, a bad priest] (IV, 407–8). Jupien mentions a client who had to reschedule his appointment that day in order to allow for his daughter's wedding; a young man "en smoking" asks for an appointment with Léon for the following morning and is told it will depend on how long the abbey keeps him; the narrator even realizes that during bombing raids Jupien's clients, abandoning themselves to the darkness of the streets and subway, forego preliminaries and accede directly to furtive pleasures (IV, 413). The narrator's only response, however, is to observe in an aside to Jupien that his brothel is "plus qu'une maison de fous, puisque la folie des aliénés qui y habitent est mise en scène, reconstituée, visible. C'est un vrai pandemonium" [worse than a madhouse, since the madness of the lunatics who inhabit it is enacted, reconstructed, visible—it is a veritable pandemonium] (IV, 411). Yet in spite of what the narrator himself points to as its mad, spectacular theatricality, Jupien's brothel fails to provoke affect or response in him.

The narrator's failure to respond is the more apparent in his subsequent remarks upon the absence of affect on the part of Jupien's young employees, as he wonders what might have brought Jupien's young men to acts which, he claims, "avaient dû leur inspirer au début une vive répugnance" [must in the beginning have inspired in them a lively disgust] (IV, 415). Given his own supposition, why has *he* not felt "une vive répugnance" or surprise, the very affects whose absence he observes in others? The narrator continues to detail an astonishment he ascribes to onlookers of perverse practices, but which he has not seemed to feel himself:

Ainsi quand nous étudions certaines périodes de l'histoire ancienne, nous sommes étonnés de voir des êtres individuellement bons participer sans scrupule à des assassinats en masse, à des sacrifices humains, qui leur semblaient probablement des choses naturelles. (IV, 416)

Thus when we study certain periods of ancient history, we are astonished to see individually good beings participate without scruple in mass assassinations or human sacrifices which probably seemed to them natural things.

The affect that is the object of Marcel's dispassionate, clinical observations but which he himself fails to register—surprise and repugnance—is displaced, postponed, and ascribed to future historians.

Many of the most pathetic and dramatic scenarios in the novel are thus flattened to the indifference and remoteness of spectacle, of a mise en scène. The pathos of Swann's love affair is dismissed in the narrator's curious aside, "comme quand j'avais complaisamment écouté le récit des amours de Swann" [as when I had complacently listened to the account of Swann's love affairs] (III, 500)—a "complacence" that is startling in light of Swann's anguish. Included in the collection of flattened dramas is Marcel's tormented relationship with Albertine, voyeuristic in that his fascination with the possibility of Albertine's lesbianism is the fascination of his own absolute exclusion as male from Albertine's erotic life. It is in its moments of greatest likelihood that Albertine's possible lesbianism is most mesmerizing for Marcel, most irresistible; it is when she claims that Mlle Vinteuil and her friend were virtual big sisters to her that Marcel tells his mother, "il faut absolument que j'épouse Albertine" [I absolutely must marry Albertine]. Marcel's jealousy then becomes the expression of his voyeurism, provoked by fantastic visionary scenes of his own exclusion from Albertine's erotic pleasure with others.

Understanding Marcel's jealousy as essentially voyeuristic and thus an expression of his own flattened interiority puts us in a position to reread the Albertine volumes. Generally understood as a climactic story of jealous anguish and suffering by such critics as Beckett, for whom there existed no greater depiction of that "desert of loneliness and recrimination men call love" (1931, 54), the Albertine affair certainly suggests extreme despair. It furthermore offers a final opportunity in which some pathos, as an emanation of selfhood, might be recovered. Yet in thinking back on the story, we somehow feel curiously detached from the account of the narrator's suffering. Is it that we are as lacking in affect and response as Marcel himself—or that something in the way the Albertine anguish is depicted has anesthetized any spontaneous, instinctive sympathy on the reader's part? Perhaps the narrator is as absent from the scene of his own suffering as he is from those of others. In his discussion of such an "absent narrator," Gene Moore points to a sort of quashing of the self in favor of the demands of analysis. This subordination of a sense of self comes about through the use of fragmented or partial selves as examples of the working of universal laws (610). Partitioned into "ma jalousie," "ma souffrance," this fractured self is thus acted upon by greater laws and functions as instruments for registering independent forces. But the narrator's incessant analysis of his jealousy as an entity of its own eventually distances both himself and us from it. This analysis involves assertions such as "la jalousie est de ces maladies intermittentes dont la cause est capricieuse, impérative, toujours identique chez le même malade, parfois entièrement différente chez un autre" [Jealousy is one of those intermittent ailments whose cause is capricious, arbitrary, always identical in the same patient, sometimes entirely different in another] (III, 539); "la jalousie est généralement partielle, à localisations intermittentes" [jealousy is generally partial, intermittent and localised] (III, 730). In making jealousy an object of study, the narrator saps the pathos of jealousy's suffering.

Such relentless analysis, numbing our spontaneous sympathy for the narrator, is not only of interest for the partial, fragmented selves it produces, however, but for its own impact on the narrative. Understanding the *Recherche*'s "monsieur qui dit 'je'" as a postmodern, fractured Beckettian subject or self would provide an explanation for what has often been called the "modal incompatibility" of the narrative. The contradiction between the "fluidity" of the first sections of the *Recherche* and the "discontinuité croissante" of the Albertine volumes, with their obsessive analysis and hypothesizing, has preoccupied critics, who have struggled to reconcile this apparent incompatibility. Genette, for instance, argues that it is a function of the recounting narrator's memory; as he gets closer to his own narrating present, his memory becomes "à la fois plus sélective et plus monstrueusement grossissante" [simultaneously more selective and more monstrously expansive]. Other critics, however, emphasize the incompatability between "récit," or story, and moralizing "traité" or tract, pointing out that the *Recherche*'s "récit" is heavily overvoiced by the moralizer's general laws and all suspense destroyed (Rogers 148).

Progress is apparent in Ellison's suggestion that such moralizer's "mastery" may be illusory. In his analysis of critical views on this "incompatability," Ellison explains the distinction between "récit" and "traité" by reading their "contradiction" as a tension between symbolic discourse (the actions of the believing, desiring hero) and allegorical (the disabused narration of the knowing narrator, or the narrator who *believes* he now knows) (133). "Proleptic technique in the *Recherche*," writes Ellison, "derives from the transformation of the hypothetical into the factual." Ellison suggests this is a perverse effort to impose narrative control "at the expense of the essence of the allegorical sign—which is unknowable." The narrator thus "falsifies the basis of his argument and gains an illusory mastery" (131).

We need to look further at this movement from the hypothetical to the factual. With Ellison's suggestion that this assertive "factual" may bespeak an *illusory* knowledge and a false mastery, the problematic gap between hero and narrator narrows. Perhaps these maxims pronounced by an authoritative voice—destroying suspense, in Rogers's claim—are not necessarily so destructive after all; the recounting voice's very immanence suggests that its authoritative maxims may not be so removed from the hero's actions. The narrator's arrogance in handing down truths from above in the "plus tard, j'ai compris" [later on, I understood] formula—of which his moralizer's maxims are one expression—perhaps betrays an ongoing struggle to cope with, to understand, and to explain, his own experiences. His maxims might then be read as transparently overconfident assertions of mastery on the part of a postmodern self unable to domesticate his own "histoire." In elevating its incoherences to the status of universal, preexisting laws, the narrator (somewhat pathetically) justifies his own failed control.

We need, then, to look further at the obsessive analysis of the *Recherche* narration, to ask whether the narrator's declarative maxims should be read with more suspicion—whether there might be a link between hypothesizing and moralizing, and whether the maxims might be the trace of the ultimate failure of analysis. The narrator's hypothesizing efforts organize much of *La prisonnière*, according to Malcolm Bowie's analogy of the jealous lover as researcher, sustained by the scientific aspect of the narrator's inquiry: his efforts to "speculate and construe," the development of a "debate between the inductive and hypothetico-deductive methods" (55). In Bowie's argument, the power of *La prisonnière* lies in the extended "dialogue that goes on between scientist and tormented lover," far more developed than the mere exchange of incidental allusions or lexical borrowings. Bowie furthermore suggests that this involves a "comedy of misapplied intellect" (50), in which the narrator "brings powerful instruments to bear upon trivial subjects" (61).

These hypothesizing scientific efforts, however, may not suggest the power of the investigating mind, but rather the reverse—the ineptness of hypothesizing, its comic futility. Pointing to the narrator's "two-hypothesis" tendency, in which mutually contradictory, conflict- ing hypotheses are elaborated in succession, Bowie claims that "this is the moment at which the speculative intelligence breaks out, moves on, takes risks." Yet in one of the first examples of such conflicting hypothesizing Bowie cites, the baffled narrator eventually asks in be- wilderment, "Laquelle des deux hypothèses étaient la vraie?" [Which of these two hypotheses was the correct one?] (III, 863). Hypothe- sizing would seem merely to produce, not overcome, mystification. Caught in such "circularities and double-binds," argues Bowie, the narrator realizes that the only way out of such confused hypothesizing "would be to make no hypothesis at all." At such moments he fanta- sizes a perfectly accessible, transparent world open to "experimental observation" (54)—as in the dreams of omnipresence in Albertine's life, a "state of total intelligence" (55) or ideal experimental conditions of observation. Such perfect access to Albertine's inner life and past, writes Bowie, "would relieve him of the anxious need to speculate and construe" (55). There may, however, be another variation of the de- sire for "no hypothesis at all," another solution to the narrator's "anx- ious need to speculate and construe" and thus a way out of his endless hypothesizing. And that solution is not perfect, total access to Alber- tine, but the formulation of totalizing maxims, of proclamations that by "fiat" arrest and preempt the speculative hypothesizing effort. A paradigm of this possible solution to hypothesizing might be read in the narrator's despairing image of all the people Albertine has ush- ered from the edges of his imagination, "où je ne me souciais pas d'eux" [where I took no notice of them], into his heart, producing ever-increasing uncertainties, an ever greater body of material to be mastered through hypotheses. This image, however, announcing the ever-greater need for ever-more hypotheses, is immediately followed by the famous maxim, "L'amour, c'est l'espace et le temps rendus sensibles au coeur" [Love is space and time made perceptible to the heart] (III, 887). Rather than the hypothesizer's dream of perfect ob- servation, which would eliminate the need for hypothesizing, the nar-

rator resorts instead to the abrogation of hypothesizing through maxims, arresting speculative reasoning with the imposition of a universal law.

Might this movement, from hypothesis and speculation to their foreclosure in maxim, be paradigmatic? Does anything in the narrator's hypothesizing effort foretell its futility and eventual abdication? Criticism has long implied as much. Rivière was among the first to notice Proust's dislike of obscurity—if the narrator doesn't know enough to flesh out his characters, he hypothesizes, says Rivière: "faute de mieux, il les peuplera de ses hypothèses" [for lack of anything better, he'll people them with his hypotheses] (quoted in Fokkema and Ibsch 1988, 14). Rivière's "faute de mieux," however, implies a gulf between Marcel's knowledge and the character proper, and specifies a gap that later receives more explicitly skeptical treatment as the gulf between speculating narrator and elusive character is increasingly recognized as decisive. The narrator speculates as to why the Guermantes treat their cousin Madame de Gallardon with such disdain: "peut-être parce qu'elle était ennuyeuse, ou parce qu'elle était méchante, ou parce qu'elle était d'une branche inférieure, ou peut-être sans aucune raison" [perhaps because she was boring, or because she was disagreeable, or because she was from an inferior branch of the family, or perhaps for no reason at all] (I, 323). The narrator's hypothesizing thus ends in what Ibsch notes as a surprisingly anticlimactic statement ("peut-être sans aucune raison") expressing "doubt over the possibility of a sufficient explanation" (McHale 145). The narrator realizes, it seems, that there simply may not be a sufficient explanation for the Guermantes's coldness toward their cousin.

Nevertheless, critics are determined to maintain the distinction between Proust as a modernist and the postmodernists; in Proust, runs one claim, "the principle of looking for an explanation is being maintained. The convention that an attempt at causal explanation must be made in any case was to be abolished only by the Postmodernists" (McHale 145). Yet such an "anticlimax," the possibility that there may be no reason at all, is more decisively threatening to the hypothetical process than McHale suggests. The very gratuitousness of the final possibility, "peut-être sans aucune raison," subverts the dignified process of analysis. The critical claim that there may not be a "sufficient explanation" does not convey the extent to which analysis is being dismissed here, in its foolish and futile effort to explain where there simply may not be "any reason."

Could, then, the narrator's hypothesizing be not so much "an attempt at causal explanation" as, by its very accumulations and excess,

a demonstration of the failure of hypotheses? Françoise's enigmatic behavior teaches the narrator, as he says, that

une personne n'est pas, comme j'avais cru, claire et immobile devant nous, avec ses qualités, ses défauts, ses projets, ses intentions à notre égard . . . , mais est une ombre où nous ne pouvons jamais pénétrer, pour laquelle il n'existe pas de connaissance directe, au sujet de quoi nous nous faisons des croyances nombreuses . . . une ombre où nous pouvons tour à tour imaginer avec autant de vraisemblance que brillent la haine et l'amour. (II, 367)

a person is not, as I had believed, transparent and motionless before us, with his merits, his defects, his plans, his intentions with regard to ourselves . . . , but is a shadow we can never penetrate, of which there can be no such thing as direct knowledge, and on whose account we form countless beliefs . . . a shadow in which we can alternately imagine, with equal likelihood, that there burns hatred and love.

The motives of others are consistently unfathomable: his father doesn't respect pacts; Gilberte is like the eternally changing government of an unstable country; Marcel cannot understand Saint-Loup's gentle request that a journalist put out his cigar, followed by a slap entirely alien to such politeness (II, 478). Nor does Marcel understand Saint-Loup's friendship for him.

Against such a background, Marcel's collection of hypotheses seems all the more futile. Returning with his grandmother after her "petite attaque" on the Champs-Elysées, he notices that his mother refuses to look at her, and offers the following speculations.

Peut-être fut-ce pour que celle-ci ne s'attristât pas en pensant que sa vue avait pu inquiéter sa fille. Peut-être par crainte d'une douleur trop forte qu'elle n'osa pas affronter. Peut-être par respect, parce qu'elle ne croyait pas qu'il lui fût permis sans impiété de constater la trace de quelque affaiblissement intellectuel dans le visage vénéré. Peut-être pour mieux garder plus tard intacte l'image du vrai visage de sa mère, rayonnant d'esprit et de bonté. Ainsi montèrent-elles l'une à côté de l'autre, ma grand-mère à demi cachée dans sa mantille, ma mère détournant les yeux. (II, 615)

Perhaps this was in order that my grandmother might not be saddened by the thought that the sight of her might have alarmed her daughter. Perhaps out of fear of a grief so piercing that she dared not face it. Perhaps out of respect, because she did not feel it permissible for her without impiety to notice the trace of any mental enfeeblement on those revered features. Perhaps to be better able later to preserve intact the memory of the true face of her mother, radiant with wisdom and goodness. Thus they went up side by side, my grandmother half-hidden in her shawl, my mother averting her eyes.

Similarly, Marcel hypothesizes over the presence of the Baron's two footmen behind the door when he emerges from trampling the Baron's hat. Their "démarche nonchalante" implies they happened to be there "en passant pour leur service." Three other explanations are then entertained by the narrator: that the Baron received guests who made him feel it necessary to post his men behind the door as a "secours voisin" [reinforcements posted close at hand]; that the footmen listened behind the door out of curiosity; and the third, that the entire scenario had been planned and executed by the Baron, who had asked them to listen "par amour du spectacle" [out of a love of spectacle] (II, 847).

Such profusions of hypotheses would only seem to proclaim the futility of hypothesizing, the failure of the epistemological effort, as an example from the Albertine context demonstrates. Albertine claims she ran into a woman a week ago, but that there was not and will never be anything between them. The narrator knows the woman hasn't been to Paris for ten months, and that, had he been outside at that particular moment, his senses would have told him Albertine hadn't met the woman. This hypothesis, that he would have seen the truth, had he been there, "n'est pas invraisemblable" [is not unlikely]—yet, "est-ce bien sûr encore?" [even so, is that certain?], he asks; and his hypothesis is immediately swept aside by the knowledge that the witness of the senses would have yielded to an attempt "à comprendre par quelle illusion d'optique je n'avais pas aperçu la dame" [to understand by what optical illusion I had failed to perceive the lady]. Thus is hypothesizing demonstrably futile—and the turn to maxims not only implicitly prepared, but enacted as the narrator immediately formulates one: "le monde des astres est moins difficile à connaître que les actions réelles des êtres" [the stellar universe is not as difficult to know as the real actions of other people] (III, 696).

The "factual," masterful proclamations of the narrator's "traité" may thus be an attempt to impose truth from above, to create a world through legislation, once epistemological efforts are shown to be futile. The helpless and arbitrary product of hypothesizing may thus be not knowledge and illumination but the imposition of maxims: the very impossibility of knowing produces shrill proclamations of universal laws. This might be as subtle as comparing the blank pages of his indifferent writing efforts to the fatefulness and destiny of a card hand, implicitly ascribing his weakness of will and discipline to a higher order of necessity, "fate": "Ce qui finissait toujours par sortir de mes efforts, c'était une page blanche, vierge de toute écriture, inéluctable comme cette carte forcée que dans certains tours on finit fatalement par tirer" [what invariably emerged from all my efforts was a virgin page, undefiled by any writing, as ineluctable as that forced card which in certain tricks one is fatefully made to draw] (II, 447).

More often, however, the appeal to a universal order occurs in the more legislative form of a maxim. The fact that such proclamations occur frequently in contexts suggesting uncertainty and the impossibility of knowing throws into question their assertiveness. It is often in the context of all that escapes knowledge that the narrator makes his most "knowing" claims. Paradigmatic of this tendency is the confession or at least recognition of his own ignorance ("Je sentais qu'une partie de la vie d'Albertine m'échappait" [I felt that part of Albertine's life escaped me]), followed by a maxim ("L'amour, dans l'anxiété douloureuse comme dans le désir heureux, est l'exigence d'un tout") [Love, in its painful anxiety as in its happy desire, is the demand for a whole] (III, 614). When Albertine claims Andrée wants to show her the Buttes-Chaumont, the narrator is unable to decide whether Albertine is lying about never having been there. His bewilderment itself then produces the maxim, "Car la vérité change tellement pour nous que les autres ont peine à s'y reconnaître" [For the truth changes to such an extent for each of us, that other people have difficulty in recognizing what it is] (III, 529). Much later, Mme Bontemps claims that three years ago, Albertine insisted on going often to the Buttes-Chaumont. Remembering that Albertine had told him she'd never been there, the narrator's breath catches and a maxim follows: "La réalité est le plus habile des ennemis. Elle prononce ses attaques sur le point de notre coeur où nous ne les attendions pas, et où nous n'avions pas préparé de défense" [Reality is the most cunning of enemies. It delivers its attacks at the point in our hearts where we were least expecting them and where we have prepared no defense] (III, 890).

The impossibility of interpreting Albertine's momentary absences during an outing or sudden shifts of mood generate suspicions that she's talked to someone, or has been reluctantly obliged to change a plan, mysteries that produce the maxim "La réalité n'est jamais qu'une amorce à un inconnu sur la voie duquel nous ne pouvons aller bien loin" [Reality is never more than the first step towards an unknown along the road to which we can never progress very far] (III, 534). Albertine's baffling, quixotic qualities force the helpless claim, "A chaque fois une jeune fille ressemble si peu à ce qu'elle était la fois précédente . . . que la stabilité de nature que nous lui prêtons n'est que fictive et pour la commodité du langage" [Each time, a girl so little resembles what she was the time before . . . that the stability of nature which we ascribe to her is purely fictitious and a convention of speech] (III, 573). In the context of Andrée's as well as Albertine's undecidable lies over going to the Verdurins when Mlle Vinteuil and her friend might be there, the narrator declares, "La souffrance dans

l'amour cesse par instants, mais pour reprendre d'une façon différente" [The suffering of love ceases from time to time, but only to
resume in a different form] (III, 610). Resolving to go to the Verdurins in order to discover whom Albertine might have wanted to see
there, the narrator follows this uncertainty with the declaration that
he's reached the point where "une femme ne sert plus pour nous que
de transition avec une autre femme" [a woman no longer serves any
purpose for us except as a transition to another woman] (III, 674).
The tiny clues in Albertine's "récit," which is suspicious "soit par insuffisance . . . de petits faits, soit par excès" lead the narrator to dé-
clare, "Le vraisemblable, malgré l'idée que se fait le menteur, n'est pas
du tout le vrai" [Plausibility, notwithstanding the liar's conviction, is
by no means the same as truth] (III, 684).

Further maxims produced by Albertine's mystery are prompted by
Charlus's indication, at the Verdurins, that the two "demoiselles Vinteuil," expected, had not come after all. The narrator notices that "ce
n'était pas mon premier doute relatif à la vertu d'Albertine que les
paroles de M. de Charlus venaient d'éveiller en moi" [it was not the
first doubt as to Albertine's virtue that M. de Charlus's words had
awakened in me] (III, 728)—there are already many other doubts.
And, from this idea of doubts and uncertainty about Albertine's virtue, the narrator passes to a maxim: "A chaque nouveau fait on croit
que la mesure est comble, qu'on ne pourra pas le supporter, puis on
lui trouve tout de même de la place . . . on finit par ne plus s'occuper
de lui" [Each new fact makes us feel that the limit has been reached,
that we cannot bear it; then we manage to find room for it all the
same . . . and end by paying no further attention to it] (III, 728).
Listening to Vinteuil's septet, Marcel wonders—"comme on interroge
de nouveau une souffrance interne"—whether Albertine has or has
not seen Mlle Vinteuil lately, "car c'est en moi que se passaient les
actions possibles d'Albertine" [for it was in myself that Albertine's possible actions occurred]. The uncertainty of Albertine's relations with
Mlle Vinteuil then produces the maxim, "De tous les êtres que nous
connaissons, nous possédons un double" [For everyone we know we
possess a double] (III, 757).

The narrator eventually reaches a point at which his maxims themselves become riddled with hypotheses, suggesting the uncertainty of
even the most declarative statements, and implicitly testifying to the
mystery that continues to mine the most assertive proclamations. He
proclaims that jealousy arouses "un certain penchant à mentir chez la
femme que nous aimons" [a certain tendency to lie in the woman we
love]. However, within the very maxim that the beloved lies once she
discovers her lover's jealousy, more hypotheses are produced: "Elle

ment . . . soit qu'elle ait pitié, ou peur, ou se dérobe instinctivement par une fuite symétrique à nos investigations" [She lies . . . whether from pity, or from fear, or because she instinctively eludes us in a flight that is symmetrical with our investigations] (III, 597). The assertion itself is thus riddled with uncertainty, as if hypothesizing has now invaded and proliferates within the maxims themselves: the very proclamations that seem intended to put an end to hypothesizing.

The failure of his efforts to ascribe his difficulties to universal truths is implied toward the end of *La prisonnière*, when the narrator thinks of Albertine's vivacity in the face of an irresistible temptation, one example being her impatience to go to a vacant apartment belonging to Andrée's grandmother. The narrator realizes that this apartment he'd never thought about now has "une horrible beauté" and pronounces a maxim that implies the error of proclaiming maxims; for a statement of knowledge, a maxim or a "découverte scientifique," can never be adequate to the material it claims to explain: "L'inconnu de la vie des êtres est comme celui de la nature, que chaque découverte scientifique ne fait que reculer mais n'annule pas" [The unknown element in the lives of other people is like that of nature, which each new scientific discovery merely reduces but does not abolish] (III, 893). This maxim thus proclaims the delusion of believing one is in a position to pronounce maxims.

An indication of the explosion of hypotheses under the impact of the Albertine mystery is the curious turning of multiple hypothesizing upon the narrator himself. Resolving to keep Albertine from Trocadéro and the lesbian Léa and her friends, but momentarily baffled as to how to do so, the narrator opens his hands, looks at them, and cracks his knuckles. He then offers two hypotheses for his action. Either it offers a momentary escape, a relaxation from the problem of thwarting the Trocadéro plan, or it represents precisely the contrary, an effort to keep his body flexed and prepared as somehow "une arme d'où partirait le coup qui séparerait Albertine de Léa et de ses deux amies" [a weapon from which would depart the shot that would separate Albertine from Léa and her two friends] (III, 654). Intriguingly, however, the conflicting hypotheses—the use of his body as an *escape* from the problem, or as precisely its solution—between which it is impossible to decide, flout the analytic process in producing such contradictory possibilities. Analysis is further perverted in that so decisive a failure is produced when it is applied to the narrator himself. If hypothesizing cannot help the narrator uncover his own motives, how can it yield Albertine's?

Noticing Albertine's grammatical irregularities, the "brusques sautes de syntaxe" with which, in a discussion about women, Albertine's "je" becomes "elle" and the action described suddenly "une chose qu'elle avait aperçue en promeneuse innocente, et nullement accomplie" [something she had witnessed as an innocent passerby, not a thing that she herself had done] (III, 659), the narrator perceives such jolts as dodges, escapes from implication in dubious acts. Similarly, however, the narrator's own maxims would seem to betray such evasion, following as they do the same syntactical leaps—in his case, however, "je" becomes "on," and his own helplessness elevated to the status of universal laws. Such slippage from hypothesizing to maxims would be, then, not the difference between the mystified hero and the knowing narrator, but the need to abrogate the futility of his investigative efforts by proclaiming the universality of his own circumstances.

Such a shift from a primarily epistemological inquiry to ontological "fiat" is consonant with McHale's analysis of the shift from a modern to postmodern literary mode; McHale understands this shift as the movement from an epistemological "dominant," with such prevailing concerns as how one can know the world, to an ontological dominant, when the question becomes, What worlds are there to know? But the Proustian narrator's "fiats" would seem to take ontology a step further; rather than searching out these "worlds," the narrator abdicates, helplessly construing the "world" of fragments of his own helplessness. Marcel's "anxieuses hypothèses, perpétuellement remaniées" only suggest the impossibility of hypothesizing, its uselessness, its ineptitude. Entangled in quantities of futile hypotheses, Marcel only produces more questions in an ironic and perverse backfiring of their very purpose: to produce knowledge. The narrator's moralizing "truths" emerge as a patent cover for his own failure to understand and master the world through knowledge; unable to "know" the world, he elevates his lack of knowledge to the level of universal truth and imposes it by maxim.

Such a revised understanding of Marcel's voyeurism and maxims as a pattern not of engagement, domination, and mastery, but as the fascination of his own absence and an index of failed control enables us to review Bersani's claim that Marcel's writing of his story is a "redemptive replication of damaged experience," experience somehow fractured by desire. Bersani suggests that the quest for essences is narcissistic, the quest for the self's own desires—and is, as such, tormented, fractured by desire. Art, or writing, is the ability to see the world as appearance liberated from the encumbrance of essences, of truth; art is not the capture of essence, but the *release* from the appetitive, appropriative *hunger* for essences. It is the collapse of the world as reflecting, porous image of the self, invested with meaning; it restores the world to its original differences and opacity, its original

Otherness, the world liberated from the appropriations and disfigurations of desire. These disfigurations are such, argues Bersani, that the sun image at the close of *Sodome et Gomorrhe*, the "bloody sacrifice of all joy," is in fact the sacrifice of the spectacle itself, for the symbolic and desiring imagination has appropriated and thereby disfigured the world. In order to write, however, Marcel will need to relinquish desire's investments in the world. "The return to the past in literature," argues Bersani, "means a certain loss of Marcel as an actor *in* that past and, as a result, an unprecedented visibility of past appearances" (419). The sacrifice of action, runs this Bersani argument, is thus the recuperation of vision. Bersani thus suggests that the "reappearance of the world" in Marcel's book is a way of correcting the original appropriation of desire, a return to the opacity of the world: "a kind of posthumous responsiveness to surfaces, a redefining reenactment of Marcel's interest in the world" (419). As we have seen, however, Marcel's behavior toward the world is characterized not so much by desire, with its aggressive appropriations and disfigurations of the world, but by voyeuristic fascination. The moment Bersani locates as Marcel's return to the past in literature, the moment Marcel is no longer an actor in that past, may in fact be situated much earlier; Marcel has always already contemplated the world as the theatrical spectacle of his own absence—an absence indexed by increasingly futile hypothesizing, and ultimately certified by maxims which, by ontological "fiat," elevate his own helpless distance from the world by ascribing to it the indisputability of universal truth.

Notes

1. In asserting that the hero of Proust's *Recherche* is no longer a character, Lyotard proposes a somewhat cautious and conventional substitute; the hero is now "the inner consciousness of time." Underlying unity is thus banished on the level of character, but recuperated as idea (1986, 33–34).

2. Critics who have observed this difference include Picon, who remarks of the *Recherche* "je," "combien plus vaste et clairvoyant que le 'il' de *Jean Santeuil*, qui, lui, a l'étroitesse du personnage biographique" [how much vaster and more clairvoyant than the "he" of *Jean Santeuil*, who has the "narrowness" of a biographical character] (30). De Lattre also refers to a "je qui ne peut plus être pris pour un il" [an I who can no longer be taken for a he] (I, 130).

3. The hero/narrator dichotomy is argued, for instance, by Muller's "deux moments de réflexion": "un où le Narrateur n'a pas encore compris 'les leçons de la vie' et un autre, où il est revenu de ses erreurs et où il partage la croyance de son auteur" [one in which the Narrator hasn't yet understood "life's lessons" and another in which he has overcome his errors and shares the belief of his author] (46). Similarly, Ricoeur claims the narrator's voice is scarcely discernable until what Ricoeur calls "la grande visitation"; following

the Guermantes matinée's accounts of involuntary memory, however, it is the narrator's voice that dominates (199). Genette argues for a more rigorous distinction between hero and narrator: "la voix de l'erreur et de la tribulation ne pouvait s'identifier à celle de la connaissance et de la sagesse" [the voice of error and of tribulation cannot be identified with that of knowledge and wisdom] (1972, 260).

4. Gene Moore argues that the "petit tortillard" episode is peculiarly postmodern in its lack of a totalizing, governing narrative paradigm. Narrative material is organized not by time, but by the technology of the timetable, as segments of disjointed memories are evoked by names along the itinerary ("Postmodernism and 'le petit tortillard,'" MLA Convention, Washington, DC, 28 December 1990).

5. The confusion between an authorial "je" and a fictive "je" is apparent in Proust's inscription to Madame Sheikévitch: "Mais j'aimerais mieux vous présenter les personnages que vous ne connaissez pas encore, celui surtout qui joue le plus grand rôle et amène la péripétie, Albertine. Vous la verrez quand elle n'est encore qu'une jeune fille en fleurs à l'ombre de laquelle je passe de si bonnes heures à Balbec. Puis quand je la soupçonne sur des riens . . . " [But I would prefer to introduce you to the characters you don't yet know, particularly the one who plays the greatest rôle and brings about the peripety, Albertine. You'll see her when she's still but a young girl in bloom, in whose shade I spend such agreeable hours at Balbec. Then when, prompted by trivial details, I suspect her . . .] (Letter to Madame Sheikévitch, 1915; quoted in Genette 1982, 293).

6. Marcel Proust, Letter to René Blum, le 5, 6 ou 7 novembre 1913, in Kolb, ed. (vol. XII).

7. Other critical positions on the narrator/author cohabitation within the *Recherche*'s "je" include Brée's argument, extended by Genette, that Proust's use of first-person narration in the *Recherche* is a deliberate esthetic distancing device, an artifice prepared through the exercise of third-person narration in *Jean Santeuil*. The *Recherche*'s "je" is thus not the return to Proust's own, but the calculated contrivance of a highly deliberate, rehearsed intention (Brée 1950, 15, and Genette 1972, 255).

8. Hans Bertens argues for just such an understanding of selfhood replaced by a plethora of voices.

9. Robert Con Davis offers an insightful analysis of Freud's and Lacan's positions on voyeurism, detailing the passage from Freud's "seeing" to Lacan's "Gaze."

10. The implicit voyeurism of the "soirée à l'Opéra" episode has been pointed out by Candace Lang.

Chapter 3
Memory, Neurology, and Narration

The previous chapter's anxious narrating voice, culminating in the helpless, pathetic "fiats" of shrill maxims, invites further scrutiny and skepticism of the "gnarus," or narrator as "one who knows." Compromised by futile efforts to control what the narrator doesn't know, narration as the knowledgeable, masterful display of memory's contents demands revision. Further investigation of the *Recherche* narration might proceed, then, by turning to alternative models of memory— beginning with that alternative provided, for instance, by neurology. Provoking dramatic revisions in theories of the workings of memory, recent neurological advances argue for a mechanism surprisingly akin to that of fiction-writing: a mechanism in which the role of the imagination is far more significant than has been thought, and calls into question the essentialist notion of memory as a fixed record, re-called, as Freud believed, in a variety of imperfect ways. Theorizing memory as the ongoing reorganization or recategorization of material, neuroscientist Gerald Edelman implies there may be no such thing as a specific, fixed memory. Instead, memory may work in relationships, in structural networks signifying differentially, rather than in the retrieval of isolated core facts. Fueled by the imagination, these relationships interact to produce constantly changing scenarios rather than static memories. Memory, it seems, may resemble nothing so much as an inventive, incessantly revised fiction. The *Recherche* narration, now no longer credible as the masterly account of a knowledgeable, remembering narrator, might nonetheless be shown to be "remembrance"—but through its very forgetfulness, invention, and repetition.

Narration and neurology? What interdisciplinary leaps are being made here? "Science," concludes Cynthia Ozick in a meditation on

Snow's two cultures, "teeming and multiform, is about how the earth and the heavens and the microbes and the insects and our mammalian bodies are constructed, but literature is about the meaning of the finished construction" (51). Science is about construction, literature about the meaning of that construction: a comfortable distinction increasingly untenable. Such formerly unbridgeable realms as science and literature increasingly find their way to each other in newly elaborated "passages" (Serres) establishing provisional and specific exchanges. "Rare, complex and local," writes Paulson, "they have partial application and are not steps on a hypothetical pathway to generalized knowledge or universal method" (36). Prompted, for instance, by Serres's claim that noise is anything that interferes with the transmission of a message, Paulson resituates literature not so much as Arnold's rather static repository of the "best that has been thought or said," but as noise: as what perturbs, interrupts, and interferes with the circulation of ideas—an argument that reanimates the fixed literary object of knowledge and consumption.

The idea of a "passage" between science and art is invoked more ambitiously in Calinescu's argument for a redrawing of "frameworks of reference." Such inclusive frameworks suggest a more aggressive reorganizing and redrawing of boundaries, abolishing the need for passages between discrete fields as the fields are redrawn to overlap. "Once science's claims to total reproducibility, absolute uniqueness of truth and total predictability were shown to be untenable," suggests Calinescu, "it became possible to discover that the differences among various kinds of human experiences are unbridgeable only within certain frames of reference, and that such frames are not intrinsically preferable to others" (1983, 275). Redesigning "more broadly postmodern frames" would thus render apparent "highly significant common features." While the notion of a frame continues to suggest boundaries and borders, or limits, we might imagine such frames as baroque, constructed precisely of what ruptures and spills beyond them, of transgressions, contradictions and "passages."

A point of entry here is provided not only by the polemics intimated by Paulson and Calinescu in their urging of exploratory new "passages" and redesigned "frameworks," but in their structural models as well. Paulson's move away from literature as object, repository, receptacle toward more dynamic models of interference, interruption—the derouting rather than transmission of ideas—offers a suggestive beginning for an effort to understand shifts, revisions, and recombinations in the process of narration. And Calinescu's "boundaries" and "frameworks" provide not only a figure for this effort of rupturing and redesigning frames, but situate us squarely within neurology, as well; for Edelman's theory argues that cell specialization occurs only once boundaries—frameworks—have formed among groupings of cells. Conjugating narration and neurology with the help of such intermediate domains as psychoanalysis and historiography, this chapter will use principles of separation and rupture as well as of contiguity and alliance to establish a postmodern "framework of reference."

Edelman's breakthrough may be the discovery that memory is not so much the retrieval of fixed facts as it is the ability to reorganize information. One important organizational category, for instance, is contextual association. We remember a loved one's face not in isolation, but in association with specific temporal contexts or networks of activity: walking the dog, reading the newspaper. Edelman's theory demonstrates this importance of contextual association on the molecular level and works up, showing that function is largely determined by context and history at different levels of brain activity, even to the complex work of memory itself.

Opposing the stance that neuronal function in the brain is genetically determined, or programmed, Edelman argues that the function of different neurons is decided by the cell's context and history as it develops. His dramatic discovery shows that cell specialization is largely a function of where cells happen to be when cell groups begin to form. This collecting of cells into groups is carried out by cell adhesion molecules, or CAMs, on the cell surface. Their selective stickiness will bind them only to cells with the same kind of CAM. Since the position of each cell during embryonic development is not under genetic control, the formation of cellular groups, in collections established by the CAMs, is a matter of the cell's chance context: the randomness of where it happens to be when the CAMs go to work. Borders among cellular groups are established once their respective cells don't adhere to each other. And Edelman has discovered that cell specialization occurs after the formation of these borders, when cells on one side of the border become one kind, and on the other side of the border another.

Having thus shown the importance of context and history in cellular differentiation and organization, Edelman goes on to argue that context and history are decisive in brain function as well. The importance of context, which, through the CAMs, creates diversity in brain development before birth, continues after birth: no longer in the emergence of neuronal groups, but in the strengthening of their pattern. Repeated stimuli strengthen internal connections of the neuronal group. Future stimuli then select the group with the most advanced, developed, connections, the neuronal group best prepared to receive and organize them.

At yet higher levels, organizing takes place through maps, or collections of neuronal groups. These maps maintain relationships either between sensory receptors and neural groups in the brain, or between neural brain groups alone. Maps "speak" back and forth to each other, and their function is the final part of Edelman's theory. They work to help the organism cope with its environment, their purpose being to organize perceptions in ways that permit the organism to act appropriately. As the organism's environment changes, so do its mappings in order to permit it to adapt. The more abstract remappings are constantly checked against new sensory information. Brain maps thus file different information according to adaptive needs. In an essay on Edelman's theory, Israel Rosenfield gives the example of a spy who, in a music hall listening to "Casta Diva," suddenly overhears the remark "Nine o'clock tomorrow night" (1986, 26). One set of maps allows him to file away the useful professional information of the assignation; another allows him to enjoy "Casta Diva." The two bits of information are thus categorized differently. Later, the spy may have forgotten the overheard assignation time. Annoyed, he hums "Casta Diva" and suddenly remembers the nine o'clock meeting—a recategorization of the two bits of information that demonstrates the power of context, or temporal contiguity, in the workings of memory. The spy may also see a poster for a nine o'clock movie and suddenly remember the nine o'clock assignation, suggesting a recategorization of the information according to similarity.

But such patterns of recategorization—one according to contiguity, or metonymy, the other according to identity, or similarity—seem to work differently according to different phases of development. It would seem that an originally undifferentiated experience of the world, a sort of "metaphoric totality" implied by Piaget and by Lacan's "imaginary," eventually moves through a metonymic phase of identifying the components comprising the whole, as in Klein's perception of "part objects" and the attendant affective values they produce. From such mental operations identifying contiguous parts, relationships among those parts are then perceived, such as synecdochic links between part and whole. Hayden White thus speaks of a "continuity between an early naturally 'metaphoric' phase in the child's mode of relating to the world and the kind of 'ironic' manipulation of alternative modes of classifying and manipulating phenomena attained to by the 'rational' adult" (1978, 7).

We realize, then, that such metonymic or habitual associations are at the origin of the very development of an ability to "metaphorize," or perceive equivalences among totalities—the spy's ability to remember the nine o'clock assignation, for instance, when prompted by a poster advertising a nine o'clock movie. Metaphoric relationships may seem more esthetically compelling than the chance contingency of metonymic relationships—but further investigation of metaphor suggests its own necessary origin in a sort of metonymy, the barrage of repeated contextual association. In order to be able to associate a nine o'clock movie listing with a nine o'clock assignation, the concept of "nine o'clock" must first be developed through habitual association, through context: the child's initial understanding that nine o'clock comes every day after eight o'clock and before ten o'clock. Invoking Piaget, White presents this categorically:

Only because of the possibility of apprehending relationships of contiguity is this process of symbolization, and a fortiori, of thought itself, rendered possible. . . . With the onset of a consciousness of contiguity—what we would call metonymic capability—a radical transformation is effected without which the "group of displacements" necessary for symbolization, speech and thought would be impossible. (White 1978, 8)

Displacement precedes and renders possible symbolization. In neurological terms, we develop the ability to categorize only through a barrage of repeated stimuli—through "habit," context, association—which strengthens neuronal connections, such that future stimuli then "select" the neuronal routes most prepared to process them. Once associative, contiguous relationships are established, metaphoric thought, symbolization—the manipulation and reorganization of contiguities—becomes possible.

These associations, one according to context, the other according to kind or similarity, evoke the linguistic categories of metonymic and metaphoric association established by Jakobson, developed by Lacan into a veritable mechanics of the unconscious and by White into the very terms by which we understand history. The significance of Edelman's work is that such organizing principles, claimed by linguistic, psychoanalytic, and literary theory, now have a molecular, biological basis: brain maps categorize sensory data according to context as well as kind, that is, according to both metonymic and metaphoric principles. Edelman argues that "remembrance" occurs when brain maps respond to a stimulus in ways necessarily different from those of our first encounter, producing recategorization—as when the spy "remembers" the nine o'clock assignation upon seeing a poster for a nine o'clock movie. We develop skills at categorizing, learning to exploit new, surprising ways of organizing information, both categorizing and recategorizing material.

The neurological categorization of stimuli finds further resonance in White's work on a larger sort of categorization, the writing of history. Operating on this vaster scale, White analyzes the ways in which the "processing" of history works according to certain categorizations. The very act with which the historian turns his or her attention to the past, argues White, is "prefigurative" in its implicit delimiting and defining of an object of consciousness: a "prefiguration" which evokes the neurological preparedness of the mental apparatus whose very *perception* of stimuli is immediately an initial categorization. In a bold move, White asserts that this prefiguration is poetic "inasmuch as it is precognitive and precritical," but that it is also poetically prefigurative of the "*concepts* [the historian] will use to *identify the objects* that inhabit that domain" (1973, 30–31). "In the poetic act which precedes the formal analysis of the field," suggests White, "the historian both creates his object of analysis and predetermines the modality of the conceptual strategies he will use to explain it" (30–31). White goes on to argue that the writing of history can implicitly be understood as conforming to various "modes" of historical consciousness, "modes" based on the "prefigurative strategy which informs each of them" (1973, xi)—metaphor, metonymy, synecdoche, and irony. Thus, the very act of perception with which the historian approaches his or her material is already constitutive of that material: a "prefiguration" that finds a neurological counterpart in Edelman's claim that the act of perception itself is an implicit selection of a certain neuronal pathway and thus a particular categorization of the perceived material. There is no perception, Edelman and White seem to suggest, whether historic or neurological, that isn't "prefigurative."

This implicit claim for a sort of "poetics" of perception, whether neurological or historic, opens up the framework of literature. A "passage" from neurology to literature is sketched in Rosenfield's discussion of Edelman's theory when Rosenfield cites Proust's peculiarly poetic episodes of involuntary memory as examples of neurological recategorization.[1] These moments are not simply "vivid imaginations of the past," suggests Rosenfield, but "a mixture of past and present." "They represent a categorization, a generalization . . . of past and present events" (1988, 83). The presence of powerful joy indicates a change in the emotional value and significance of such "memories" for the narrator; for "these recollections *now* have a new meaning and therefore are not really the past events in themselves vividly recalled." Thus, the "past," "what we take to be a collection of recollections, is really a new creation" (1988, 84). This new creation is empowered by the present context, the physical sensation of an uneven paving-stone, a starched napkin, or the clinking of a spoon, provoking a powerful "recategorization" of a remembered moment. An originally trivial sensation is, through "involuntary memory," recategorized, suddenly imbued with significance and colored by joy. Rosenfield emphasizes the importance of the rememberer's present context and its bearing upon the "memory": "since context must, of necessity, constantly change, there can never be a fixed, or absolute, memory. Memory without the present cannot exist" (1988, 80). This emphasis on the present perspective of the rememberer resituates memory as an activity fundamentally of the present, rather than a recall or return of—or to—the past.

But Rosenfield's "passage" here from neurology to Proust remains quite specific and local, precisely a "passage" between two realms, what he calls a "literary interlude" in his book on memory. The implications of Edelman's work, however, are far vaster and encourage a more ambitious and integrated "framing" effort. Proust's moments of involuntary memory may indeed be examples of "recategorization," but only the most sensational and visible—whereas the "framing" of neurology and narration offers more subtle and intricate possibilities. Edelman's theory of memory implies that perception is to some degree creation—in that perceptions are "processed" differently by each brain—and that memory, as the recontextualizing of these creations, is largely a function of the imagination, which constantly revises old perceptions. Creation and imagination? We are squarely in the realm of fiction. Memory, as the working and reworking of material created by perception and revised by the imagination—as an act of creation and revision—suggests the endless rewriting of an ongoing fiction. Would the behavior of fiction then provide a model for the behavior of memory? Memory, we realize, is synchronic; the act of remembering is not self-reflexive. While it yields past accounts of its objects, it does not yield past accounts of itself. We remember something, in a transitive act with a direct object; we don't remember ourselves remembering. Assessing the revisionary process of memory thus demands a diachronic record over which change may be traced—and legitimizes a turn to fiction as a model for patterns of creation and revision, the very dynamic, Edelman suggests, of memory.

Examining fiction for patterns of creation and revision, for its inner diachrony, takes us to questions of narration; for Edelman's demonstration that memory is subject to the same principles of creation and revision as fiction points to memory as an ongoing process rather than a fixed record, as a narration rather than a narrative. Memory as process would thus have startling implications for the act itself of *narrating* as process, both memory and narration now reanimated as incessant revision rather than fixed record. This would involve thinking not only of memory as a far more dynamic remembering, but of narration as, similarly, the more active narrat*ing*, restoring to each the dynamism of a present participle. As Proust's narrator suggests, "Entre le moindre point de notre passé et tous les autres un riche réseau de souvenirs ne laisse que le choix des communications" [Between the slightest point of our past and all the others a rich network of memories produces a multitude of communicating paths to choose from] (IV, 607). The processes of narrative and memory may be precisely the, endless exploration of the various possibilities of this network of communications, the endless combinations and permutations Edelman calls "recontextualization."

The act itself of narrating, or "narration," is isolated by Genette from its two products, "histoire" and "récit," effectively eliminating the confusion between duration of the telling and duration of the told. Now seen as an "acte producteur," narration is studied for its transitivity, the effects it produces; and the terms of Genette's investigation are thus situated primarily in the interaction between "histoire" and "récit" as he studies the way one rearranges the other through variations in "ordre," "fréquence," and "durée" (1972). Nevertheless, Genette's understanding of narration as an "acte producteur," emphasizing the products of this act rather than the "act" itself, effectively repeats the old tendency to bypass and neglect it as an *act* with internal vicissitudes and duration of its own. This continues in Genette's later revision, *Nouveaux discours du récit*, where narration is still essentially seen as an "acte producteur," though now producing both "histoire" and "récit" simultaneously ("l'acte narratif instaurant, [inventant] *à la fois* l'histoire et son récit") [the narrative act *simultaneously* instantiating (inventing) the story and its account] (1983, 11); narration is still scrutinized for its product, its transitivity, rather than for itself.

Other critics have gone on to focus on yet a further product of the narrating act, the exchange or transference through which a complicity or coercion is played out between teller and listener: the listener's implication or sullying through his or her very association with the telling. The idea of a narrative "contract" defining the relationship between teller and listener is studied in Brooks's discussions of Maupassant's "Une ruse," where the ruse is ultimately suggested as the doctor's "sullying" of a young bride by recounting an unwelcome story of another woman's infidelity, providing in sinister explanation, that he is at her disposal, should she similarly require his services

(217) Brooks also traces such "contamination" in Balzac's "Facino Cane," where the reader inherits, with Facino's unexpected death, a story "he doesn't know what to do with" (220), and in *Le Colonel Chabert*, where Chabert's efforts to transact his story of burial alive fail utterly, for—Chabert's wife and fortune now another's—no one wants to listen to an unwelcome voice from the grave. Brooks also cites the sullying narrative contract of Clamence's querulous, garrulous confession in Camus's *La chute*. Stakes of life and death attend the narrative contract between Scheherezade and the sultan, where her nocturnal tales must succeed in their effort of intellectual coercion if she is not to be executed at dawn.

By contrast, however, relatively little attention has been accorded narration outside its effects, outside the transitivity of its consequences. Hence flat critical assertions that the narration of the *Recherche* is accomplished in "la durée d'un éclair" [the duration of a flash of lightning] (Genette): "L'acte de narration de Marcel ne porte aucune marque de durée, ni de division: il est instantané. Le présent du narrateur . . . est un moment unique et sans progression" [Marcel's act of narration bears no mark of duration, nor of division; it is instantaneous. The narrator's present . . . is a unique moment without progression] (1972, 234). "The sense of narrative 'durée,'" writes Moore, "is . . . minimal" (610). Even when duration of the narrating act is admitted, it presumes a bland, undifferentiated expanse, what Steel calls a "featureless band of time" (166). The act of narration is assumed to wreak no change upon *what* is narrated, and the narrator's position of final knowledge and mastery is unquestioned: "il sait tout, mais ne peut le dire que dans le temps" [he knows everything, but can only say it within time] (60) asserts Tadié, and Ricoeur argues for a "narrateur qui n'oublie rien" [a narrator who forgets nothing] (1985, 193). The act of narration, however, as Edelman's theory and the Proustian text demonstrate, is anything but a stable, authoritative recounting of knowledge, the patient accumulation of information Paulson argues against. It is a wandering itinerary, repeatedly revising itself, as subject to the interferences of temporal duration as the events that it recounts.

This work of revision, or recontextualization, is visible in the strange incidence of an anecdote that occurs twice in the narration of the *Recherche*.[2] Interestingly, the anecdote in both cases is presented not as event, but as remembered event. Even within the dramatic present of events sustained by the narration, the episode in each case is given through a moment of reverie, a parenthesis in the (remembered) action. In the first telling, the narrator Marcel thinks back to the meanderings of a little local train, saying that while the conductor cries out "Doncières, Grattevast, Maineville," he'll record what the beach or garrison town evokes for him (III, 463). The second time the memory is presented, its status as memory is again signaled; the narrator explains at some length that this particular memory arose through the desultory movement of his "rêveries":

Je ne sais pourquoi le cours de mes rêveries, qui avait suivi jusque-là des souvenirs de musique, se détourna sur ceux qui en ont été, à notre époque, les meilleurs exécutants, et parmi lesquels, le surfaisant un peu, je faisais figurer Morel. Aussitôt ma pensée fit un brusque crochet, et c'est au caractère de Morel . . . que je me mis à songer. (III, 668)

I don't know why the course of my reveries, which had hitherto followed musical memories, turned now to those men who have been the best performers of music in our day, and among whom, slightly exaggerating his gifts, I included Morel. At once my thinking took a sharp turn, and it was Morel's character . . . that I began to ponder.

In both instances, then, the text specifies that the episode is memory, not event; that even within the action of the narrative—the action remembered by a reminiscing narrator—this particular episode consists of a *memory* remembered. For a book claiming to be composed of recollection, to draw its inspiration and impetus from the triggering power of involuntary memory, the doubly mnemonic status of this anecdote (remembered action *within* a narrative of remembered action) bears a singularly paradigmatic significance. Furthermore, the fact that this doubly remembered anecdote is repeated provides a curiously visible, even conspicuous, instance of the mechanics of the recounting narrator's memory. If the first account is doubly remembered, the recurrence of the anecdote has a sort of triply remembered thickness; we begin not with perception, but with remembrance itself—recontextualization in Edelman's terms—and go on to yet further recontextualizations.

The episode is first encountered in *Sodome et Gomorrhe* and centers around Morel's claim to Charlus that he needs evenings free for algebra classes. The narration details Charlus's interrogation and Morel's responses. What about coming to see the Baron afterward? Impossible, claims Morel, the classes often run very late. When Charlus objects that one can just as easily learn algebra from a book, Morel even agrees, confessing that he doesn't, in fact, understand much of what goes on in the class. Charlus, triumphant ("Alors?"), adds the final point that algebra is useless for a violinist, but Morel is obstinate; he likes it, and it relieves his "neurasthénie" (III, 464).

The narrative then turns to a particular late evening in which Morel refuses to see the Baron, and recounts his night in the sumptuous Maineville brothel at the invitation of the Prince de Guermantes.

> En tous cas Morel, quelque objection qu'on fît, réservait certaines heures tardives, que ce fût à cause de l'algèbre ou du violon. Une fois ce ne fut ni l'un ni l'autre mais le Prince de Guermantes qui . . . lui offrit cinquante francs pour passer la nuit ensemble dans la maison de femmes de Maineville. (III, 464)

> In any case Morel, whatever the objection raised, reserved certain late hours for himself, whether for algebra or for the violin. Once it was for neither, but for the Prince de Guermantes who . . . offered him fifty francs to spend the night with him in the brothel at Maineville.

The Baron gets wind of this plan, and in a jealous rage bribes the keeper of the brothel into hiding him in the room next to Morel's—where Morel reclines, lifeless, surrounded by three women, pale, terrified, without strength to lift his glass of champagne; for he, in turn, hearing that a gentleman has paid a sizable sum to observe him, guesses the Baron's presence and intentions. The unsolved algebra mystery lies in contiguous proximity, then, to the account of an evening that was not a mystery at all, to Morel's chagrin.

The same anecdote of the mysterious algebra classes is repeated in *La prisonnière*, where Morel again agrees to be at the Baron's complete disposal on the condition that he have evenings free, "car il désirait pouvoir après le dîner aller suivre un cours d'algèbre" [for he wished to be able after dinner to attend an algebra class] (III, 668–69). Again, the Baron asks to see him afterward, Morel insists this would be impossible, the class often runs very late. Charlus claims one can just as easily learn algebra from a book and Morel agrees, "car on ne comprend rien à un cours d'algèbre" [for one doesn't understand a thing in an algebra class]. Charlus continues to protest, claiming algebra is useless for a violinist—"Morel riposta qu'elle était une distraction pour passer le temps et combattre la neurasthénie" [Morel retorted that it was a distraction to help pass the time and to fight his neurasthenia] (III, 668).

This second account of the algebra interest, however, while more detailed and developed than the first, only renders the "image enténébrée" of Morel's evenings more inscrutable; for, rehearsing the same details, the second telling adds the enigmatic, confounding fact that Morel often busied himself at the Baron's solving equations (III, 669). Could Morel really be studying algebra? Charlus is not convinced, and this version goes on to develop his bewilderment in the face of an array of unsavory possibilities.

C'était peut-être une coucherie avec une femme, ou, si Morel cherchait à gag-
ner de l'argent par des moyens louches et s'était affilié à la police secrète, une
expédition avec des agents de la sûreté, et qui sait? Pis encore, l'attente d'un
gigolo dont on pourra avoir besoin dans une maison de prostitution. (III,
668–9)

It was perhaps some affair with a woman, or, if Morel was seeking to earn
money in shady ways and had joined the secret police, an expedition with
detectives, and who knows? Worse yet, an engagement with a gigolo whose
services might be needed in a brothel.

The episode closes upon Charlus's enduring uncertainty as to what
Morel was truly up to; for the Baron is too busy with other dis-
tractions, and never discovers "ce qu'étaient, au vrai, ces mystérieux
et inéluctable cours d'algèbre qui ne se donnaient que la nuit" [what
actually were these mysterious and inevitable algebra classes given
only at night] (III, 669).

More interesting, however, than Charlus's eternal bafflement is the
narrative's description of it, which offers an example of what Edelman
calls contextualization. The initial (*Sodome et Gomorrhe*) account, in
turning afterward to a brothel scene, cast Morel's mysterious algebra
classes into contiguity with illicit erotic activity, maintaining, we recall,
that the algebra was not an alibi for the brothel visit. The association
of algebra and the brothel is contextual, not causal—metonymic, not
metaphoric. In the second (*La prisonnière*) account, however, this
chance contextual relationship has contracted significance, suddenly
become meaningful; the literal and contiguous "brothel" of the first
telling has here been swallowed up by the Baron's musings, his theories, absorbed as one of his possible versions of Morel's nocturnal activity: indeed, as the most threatening explanation of Morel's algebra
interest ("Pis encore, l'attente d'un gigolo dont on pourra avoir besoin
dans une maison de prostitution"). The brothel scenario has become,
for the Baron, the fearful possible answer, the explanation of the algebra mystery, having moved from a contiguous, proximate status in
the first telling to a metaphoric relation in the second account. From
algebra-studying *and* brothel-going as contiguous examples of Morel's
evening activities in the first account, the relation becomes predicative
in the Baron's jealous imagination: for Morel, he suspects, algebra-
studying *is* brothel-going.[3]

This change from the first to the second account of the same episode powerfully argues for the importance of contiguity, of temporal
context, of metonymic, proximate association: the significance that
proximity may contract among different elements in the workings of
a "memory," whether biological or narrative. Edelman's theory, as we
have seen, argues for the decisiveness of such contiguity in cell spe-

cialization. The chance position of a cell during embryonic development is crucial in determining the eventual function of that cell as CAMs create borders within which specialization occurs. Contiguity goes on to play an essential role in the function of memory; the power of such temporal contiguity in the work of memory is one of the implications of Edelman's theory. Certainly, the notion of context suggests as much—that we "remember" a friend's face not so much because we are able instantly to isolate it in the clutter of memory, but because the map of its temporal context yields a network of associations in which it functions.

The importance of temporal contiguity in the work of memory is confirmed by experiments with amnesiacs, who have lost the ability to reconstruct temporal context. They remain able to recognize general categories even as they forget their own association with them; they recognize hats as hats, for instance, but are unable to identify their own—to remember the temporal contiguities that link them to their hats. Similarly, in one study, an amnesiac isolated in a closed room was unable to remember what month it was; when the curtains were opened and he looked out upon trees in full leaf and a passerby in a light dress, he exclaimed, "By golly, it must be July or August." He was able to deduce the summer month, but not recall his own contextual participation within it. Having lost his grasp of temporal context, he could not retain other information dependent on temporal associations. The ability to categorize according to temporal contiguity would thus seem to be a crucial function of memory—indeed, perhaps *the* function.

Such a resounding validation of chance association, of the power of temporal contiguity—one of the most daring assertions of Edelman's theory—has important implications for critical work on Proust. When Genette demonstrated that many of Proust's metaphors are in fact prompted by metonymic associations, Paul de Man argued that such descriptive analysis did not address the logical tensions that oppose metaphor to metonymy. His and subsequent arguments have tended instead to emphasize the difference between the two, repeating Proust's own gesture of privileging the power of metaphoric association as necessary, while consigning metonymic, or chance association, to a lesser elegance: to see contingency and chance as more esthetically shaky relationships. De Man's celebrated reading calls into question the Proustian text's esthetic claims for metaphor by demonstrating that a particular metaphor is in fact a metonymy: a relationship of chance contiguity, as well as of habit: the cliché, or habitual association of the expression, "torrent d'activité" (1979, 66–67). This "deconstruction" of metaphor as in fact "merely" metonymy establishes an implicit hierarchy and suggests that the text is unable to live up to its ambitious esthetic claims; having proclaimed its foundation in metaphor, runs de Man's argument, the text in fact "deteriorates" into metonymic associations. Ellison goes further in his discussion of the "seductiveness" of metonymy pretending to be metaphor. Metaphor is two-tiered, glittering, "seductive": an outward ornamentation that fools the naïve reader (Swann) into believing it contains truth and an inner core of slippage, difference, vanishing (1984, 25–27). We are close here to the Lacanian notion of metonymy as delay, postponement, and deferral: the slippage by which closure can never be complete—as in the revisions or "recategorizations" of the Proustian text, where rewritings only produce increased bafflement.

But metonymy, it would seem, is just as "necessary" neurologically as metaphor originally claimed to be esthetically. Context and contiguity, relationships of chance, structure the workings of the brain from the level of cell adhesion molecules to the complex function of memory itself. Metonymy governs the operation of the mind as much, if not more so, than metaphor; indeed, we have just observed that an originally metonymic relationship can, in the narrative "memory," reappear as a necessary or metaphoric bond. Ellison argues for such an evolution in his discussion of Proust's "Journées de lecture," where metonymies are shown to acquire the necessary links of metaphor. Proust's depiction of secluded garden scenes of childhood reading emphasizes that what is later remembered nostalgically is not the book itself, but instead the very disruptions of the reading act:

le jeu pour lequel un ami venait nous chercher au passage le plus intéressant l'abeille ou le rayon de soleil gênants qui nous forçaient à lever les yeux de la page ou à changer de place, les provisions de goûter qu'on nous avait fait emporter et que nous laissions à côté de nous sur le banc . . . (1971, 160)

the game for which a friend came to fetch me at the most interesting passage, the troublesome bee or shaft of sunlight which forced me to look up from the page or to change my position, the provisions for tea which I had been made to bring and which I had left beside me on the seat, untouched . . . (1988, 195)

"It is this remembrance," notes Ellison, "—of what for the young boy was mere contingent distraction—that now becomes the necessary chain of associative phenomena granting access to the essence of past time" (90).

There are further examples of such evolution—from contingency to necessity, metonymy to metaphor—in the Proustian text. The narrator, listening to the hiccups of the heater, realizes that while they have no connection to his memories of Doncières, the association of these memories with the water heater over the course of one long afternoon has established a bond.

Mais sa rencontre prolongée avec eux en moi, cet après-midi, allait lui faire contracter avec eux une affinité telle que, chaque fois que (un peu) déshabitué de lui, j'entendrais de nouveau le chauffage central, il me les rappellerait. (III, 642–43)

But its prolonged encounter with them in my thoughts that afternoon was to give it so lasting an affinity with them that, each time I had fallen out of the habit and heard the central heating again, it would bring them back to me.

    This pattern of narrative contiguity and association recontextualized later as a more necessary bond is further apparent in the two deaths of the grandmother and Bergotte. A context of proximity or association is established through Bergotte's bodily presence in the household of the grandmother's death agony, where he visits the narrator every day, even though—in an explicit comparison—he suffers, runs speculation, from the same illness as the grandmother. The chapter on the grandmother's death then turns to a description of Bergotte's "acheminement vers la mort" [slow progress toward death] (II, 622). Already Bergotte can scarcely see and has difficulty talking, troubles that afflict the grandmother as well. Bergotte's contiguity here with the grandmother's illness later becomes, in the description of his death, a full "recategorization" of hers. In fact, Bergotte's death is announced by an explicit reference to the grandmother's: "Nous avons vu, au moment de la mort de ma grand-mère, que sa vieillesse fatiguée aimait le repos" [We have seen, at the time of my grandmother's death, that her weary old age loved repose] (III, 689). Both deaths are long prepared by illness, brought on by a "crise d'urémie." The similarities continue as a parade of doctors begins, including in each case a doctor particularly proud to display his wit before a literary patient. Both the grandmother and Bergotte, however, eventually rebel at the host of doctors. Attempts to combat the illness with drugs seem in each case only to hasten death, Bergotte patently dying of an overdose on a day in which "il s'était ainsi confié à un de ces amis (ami? ennemi?) trop puissant" [he had thus entrusted himself to one of these too-powerful friends (friend? enemy?)]. Drugs may also have hastened the grandmother's death, according to the narrator's speculations that, in giving morphine for her pain, "nous ne faisions que l'exaspérer davantage, hâtant peut-être l'heure où la captive serait dévorée" [we merely exacerbated it further, hastening perhaps the moment when the captive would be devoured] (II, 618).

An even larger pattern of "recategorization" is explicit in the narrator's discussion of love affairs as successive recontextualizations of the same original paradigm. Realizing that his love for Albertine was already "inscribed" in his love for Gilberte, the narrator argues that the memory of past loves is also "la prophétie de nos amours nouvelles . . . les amours suivantes, leurs particularités étant calquées sur les précédentes" [the prophecy of our new loves . . . the later loves with their particularities being patterned after the earlier] (IV, 486–87)—and goes so far as to suggest that the extended account of his suffering over Albertine is a recategorization of Swann's tormented love for Odette: "mon amour pour Albertine avait répété, avec de grandes variations, l'amour de Swann pour Odette" [my love for Albertine had, with important variations, repeated the love of Swann for Odette] (IV, 593).[4]

Recategorization is not only at work as narrative pattern in the *Recherche*, but thematized as the suffering produced by the rupture and severing of old categorizations. The painful dismembering of old and establishing of new categorizations, as Proust suggests in anguished passages on the narrator's first trip to Balbec, attends any exposure to new stimuli such as the alien, high ceilings of his room in the "Grand Hôtel." That the anguish arising from the rupture of habit produces a climate of suffering fertile to creativity is repeatedly suggested, however. It is demonstrated by Bergotte, whose cycle of writing, riches, women, suffering, and writing turns "les caresses en or, et l'or en caresses" [caresses into gold, and gold into caresses] according to "cette circulation de l'argent que nous donnons à des femmes, qui à cause de cela nous rendent malheureux, c'est-à-dire nous permettent d'écrire des livres" [this circulation of the money we give to women who because of that make us unhappy, which is to say permit us to write books] (IV, 487). This fertility of suffering is noticed by de Man, who refers to "a mood of distrust which, as the later story of Marcel's relationship with Albertine makes clear, produces rather than paralyzes interpretative discourse" (58)—and by Beckett, who discusses the triadic structure of habit, suffering, and creation. Thinking of Françoise's suggestion that a proper, well-behaved secretary to arrange his papers would be so much more helpful than "cette fille qui lui fait perdre tout son temps" [this girl who makes him waste all his time], the narrator realizes that "En me faisant perdre mon temps, en me faisant du chagrin, Albertine m'avait peut-être été plus utile" [by making me waste my time, by making me unhappy, Albertine had perhaps been more useful to me] (IV, 947). And the narrator concludes, "Les années heureuses sont les années perdues, on attend une souffrance pour travailler" [The happy years are the lost years, one must wait to suffer before one can work] (III, 488).

Such recategorization—involving the disconnecting of old associations or categorizations and their reorganization in new ways—is implied in Lacan's work on metonymy and metaphor, as Chaitin argues. In efforts to correct the perception that Lacan privileged metaphor over metonymy, Gallop and Chaitin return to Lacan's algorithms to demonstrate that the "plus" sign defining the metaphoric function must be read as containing within it the "minus" sign of the metonymic function. Metaphor comes about by "crossing the bar" of metonymy, adding a vertical stroke to the horizontal "minus" sign. This works, explains Chaitin, because "any metaphor is, or contains, an implicit predication" (1000), as when "the sunset of life" is implicitly understood to mean "old age is the sunset of life" (1001). But an implicit predication is a metonymy: "the juxtaposition of two or more signifiers whose signified is a latent signifier." Chaitin cites Quintilian's example of the metonymy "thirty sails," where, implicitly, "thirty sails are a fleet"; fleet is the latent meaning produced by the contiguity of "thirty" and "sails." Significantly for our discussion here of context and contiguity, Chaitin notes the importance of "linearity," "that is, the general rule that the juxtaposition of signifiers in a chain is taken to be meaningful" (1001). Meaning is produced by juxtaposition, proximity, and context, as when "thirty" placed next to "sails" acquires a new, composite signification. Similarly, in the Proust passages, algebra-studying is thrown into proximity with brothel-going, acquiring the potential for a sudden new composite meaning, a meaning derived from contiguity. This new composite meaning is apparent in the Baron's suspicious ruminations of the second episode, speculations linking, in his mind, Morel's mysterious nocturnal activity with brothels. Contiguity has become predication, in the Baron's suspicions; the combination of algebra-studying and brothel-going implies Morel's illicit sexual behavior, creating the metonymy of two activities whose signified is a latent signifier: sexual treachery. Studying algebra becomes, in the Baron's suspicions, a pretext or alibi for—which is to say, an attribute of—Morel's infidelities.

Such rearrangement of meaning is possible, Chaitin points out, because of another property of signifying systems. In addition to the linearity that allows significance to arise from contiguity, signifying systems are also capable of emptying out meaning so as to create new signifying chains, new couplings of subject and attributes. Once this disconnecting of subject and predicate has occurred in the going-underground of the subject, argues Chaitin on behalf of Lacan, new, creative, even "untoward" combinations can be established. Citing the Hugo line—"sa gerbe n'était ni avare ni haineuse" [his sheaf was neither avaricious nor spiteful]—used by Lacan to illustrate metaphor, Chaitin writes, "the sheaf has been emptied of its connections with crops, fields, agriculture, nature and so on, and has been reconnected to attributes which belong to human beings such as Boaz, that is, avarice and spite" (1003).

This progression—the emptying of meaning so as to proceed to the recombining of meaning—implies that metonymy is indeed the substructure, or necessary operation, of metaphor. Such a substructure argues against the privileging of metaphor over metonymy—we need, says Gallop, "to recognize the horizontal line in metaphor's cross, the bar of metonymy, which is fundamentally intricated in metaphor" (132). In her polemic against metaphoric privilege, Gallop cites Irigaray's accusation of "the privilege of metaphor (quasi solid) over metonymy (which has much more to do with fluids)" (Irigaray 108, quoted in Gallop 127); for Irigaray argues that science has neglected the study of fluids in favor of the study of solids, and goes on to suggest, via assertions linking the feminine to fluidity, that psychoanalysis has neglected feminine sexuality. More pertinent here, however, is Irigaray's linking of metonymy with fluidity and its attendant notions of porousness, seepage, hemorrhage, and entropy: images that suggest not only a seeping-out of attributes, but a seeping-in. Such an understanding of the inherent fluidity or instability of metonymy would then carry over into the metaphoric structure, importing with it a slippery, destabilizing tendency that would undermine the decisiveness of the metaphoric connection, or "plus" sign. This instability would be particularly pertinent and visible over the evolution of a narrative as understood here, with its incessant contextualizations and recontextualizations.

Such an understanding of metonymy perhaps not so much as a definitive or decisive severing, but as flows and seepages, as entropies, brings us back to the notion of neurological "contextualization." The metonymy of algebra as an attribute of sexual treachery, we remember, occurs when the Baron muses suspiciously in the *second* account of Morel's algebra interest. A "contextualization" that may influence this retelling of the anecdote—and perhaps explain the Baron's increased mystification—is that, in *La prisonnière*, where the algebra anecdote recurs, the narrator is recounting his own increasingly similar circumstances, tormented and bewildered by Albertine's enigmatic sexuality. For between the two accounts, Albertine has confessed that the lesbian Mademoiselle Vinteuil and her lover were virtual "big sisters" to her. The narrator's depiction of his own baffled circumstances, his own context of bewilderment, may well inform his account of Charlus's helpless speculations; indeed, the second account of Morel's algebra interest is given, perhaps significantly, while the narrator waits for Albertine to respond to his summons and return from the matinée at Trocadéro, where the lesbian Léa, as Marcel has just discovered, is to perform.

The context of summoning Albertine from a potential lesbian encounter with its Morelian climate of "tenebrous" sexual behavior throws new light upon the apparent whimsical ramblings of the narrator's thoughts as he waits for Albertine. From thoughts of music, the narrator's own "rêveries" turn to the finest musicians of his day, among them Morel—and thence to certain "singularités . . . de caractère," including the elusive "image enténébrée" of Morel's leisure activities. The itinerary of this "rêverie" would seem to be defined by the bafflement of the narrator's own Charlus-like efforts to fathom Albertine's behavior. His own current context of recounting the story of a sexually elusive Albertine produces a new, more inscrutable account, or "recontextualization," of Morel's algebra mystery. The apparent capriciousness of his "rêveries"—which, having wandered among musical memories, move to performers, including Morel, before taking a sudden turn to "certain peculiarities of [Morel's] character"— finds a contextual explanation; it is within the context of an extremely Morel-like, unfathomable Albertine that Morel's algebra interest is "recontextualized" as even more unfathomable. As Edelman points out, crucial to the act of remembering is the present of the rememberer: the significance of each "memory" depends on present context (80). The context *from* which the narrator recounts—his own helpless speculations over enigmatic Albertine—may well contaminate, or seep, into his account of Charlus's suspicions. Similarly, as the narrator notices early on in describing garden-reading scenes of Combray, his own observer's position—his own observing awareness—intervenes as an inescapable "aura" preventing direct contact with the observed:

Quand je voyais un objet extérieur, la conscience que je le voyais restait entre moi et lui, le bordait d'un mince liséré spirituel qui m'empêchait de jamais toucher directement sa matière; elle se volatilisait en quelque sorte avant que je prisse contact avec elle, comme un corps incandescent qu'on approche d'un object mouillé ne touche pas son humidité parce qu'il se fait toujours précéder d'une zone d'évaporation. (I, 83)

When I saw an external object, my awareness that I was seeing it remained between myself and it, surrounding it with a thin spiritual border that pre-

vented me from ever touching its substance directly; it would somehow evaporate before I could make contact with it, in the way that an incandescent body brought into proximity with something wet never actually touches its moisture, since it is always preceded by a zone of evaporation.

But such seepage may work both ways. The narrator's new account of Charlus's baffled context, shaped perhaps by the narrator's present account, in *La prisonnière*, of his own increasing bewilderment, may, in turn, seep back into Marcel's narration. Indeed, we haven't seen the last of algebra in the *Recherche*. Contextual influence—metonymy's capacity both to contract and to sever associations—is particularly apparent in the evolution of the algebra image. Once new metonymic bonds have established algebra as an attribute of sexual treachery, for example, it is clear that algebra can no longer retain its *own* attributes; having become a marker or attribute for sexual illicitness, algebra can no longer lay claim to its own austere atmosphere of chaste, disembodied, intellectual abstraction. Just as algebra became, in *Sodome et Gomorrhe*, an attribute or quality of sexual mystery—the outward sign of Morel's suspected infidelities—so the predication is reversed later on, when sexual illicitness flows back into algebra, becoming itself a property or attribute of algebra. When we notice an increasing association of Albertine and algebra, then, we can no longer inscribe the old algebraic attributes of purity, austerity, and chastity, but now attach to algebra a highly charged atmosphere of sexual mystery.

Thus, in *La prisonnière*, algebra, originally a literal, metonymic, contiguous activity—the putative direct object of Morel's evenings—increasingly appears as figural, as metaphor. Algebra becomes a metaphor for enigmatic sexuality, the mystery of an "algebraic Albertine" in an example of Chaitin's "untoward" recombinant metaphors, rendered possible by the operations of a metonymic substructure. Algebra, Morel's contiguous object and grammatical direct object, becomes Albertine's predicate; for the narrator increasingly details himself as forced into Charlus's suspicious, helpless uncertainty before an inscrutable "algebra" that is Albertine, a mask of abstraction he is unable to decipher. A letter from Albertine prompts the thought of how bloodless and abstract is this "translation" of a personality: "j'étais tout de même déçu du peu qu'il y a d'une personne dans une lettre" [I was nevertheless disappointed over how little there is of a person in a letter] (IV, 37). A letter appears to the narrator as dessicated as algebraic signs:

une lettre où même de la personne il reste très peu, comme dans les lettres de l'algèbre il ne reste plus la détermination des chiffres de l'arithmétique, lesquels déjà ne contiennent plus les qualités des fruits ou des fleurs additionnés. (IV, 37)

a letter in which even of the person very little remains, as in algebraic letters there no longer remains the precise value of the arithmetical figures, which themselves no longer contain the qualities of the fruit or flowers that they enumerate.

The tip of Albertine's nose is an "extrait algébrique" wreaking emotional turmoil: "Ce petit bout de museau, ce signe où se résume la personnalité permanente d'une femme, cet extrait algébrique, cette constante, cela suffit pour qu'un homme . . . ne puisse disposer d'une seule de ses soirées" [This little tip of nose, this sign epitomizing the permanent personality of a woman, this algebraic excerpt, this constant factor, is sufficient to keep a man . . . from disposing of a single one of his evenings] (IV, 24). An "algèbre de la sensibilité" forces the narrator to recognize his own desire in Albertine's apparent lesbian inclinations, but the more vivid his own desires have been, the greater now their torment for him as he perceives their energy in Albertine—"Comme si," he says, "dans cet algèbre de la sensibilité ils reparaissaient avec le même coefficient, mais avec le signe moins au lieu du signe plus" [as though in this algebra of sensibility they reappeared with the same coefficient but with a minus instead of a plus sign] (IV, 98). Eventually, what Albertine might have done, says the narrator, with the little laundress Aimé claims to have interviewed, "ne m'était plus signifié que par des abbréviations quasi-algébriques qui ne me représentaient plus rien" [was no longer indicated to me by anything but quasi-algebraic abbreviations which no longer represented anything for me] (IV, 109)—but, however, for the "reconnecting" of the current of his suffering, searing his heart "a hundred times an hour." In his fruitless efforts to interpret an enigmatic Albertine, the narrator refers to "l'équation approximative à cette inconnue qu'était pour moi la pensée d'Albertine" [the approximate equation of that unknown which Albertine's thought was for me] (III, 850). Reflecting this obsessive algebra context is what Beckett freely cites as a direct quotation: "'My imagination provided equations for the unknown in this algebra of desire'" (1931, 55). The narratives of *La prisonnière* and *La fugitive* may even be read as the narrator's extended attempt to write an algebraic equation himself, to write the equation that will yield the solution to Albertine's sexual mystery, the equation that will derive the unknown.

Context, then, the very present of the narration, seems in part to be responsive to, if not at times determined by, its direct object: the told, which, as we see in the algebra case, seeps back into and shapes the context of the telling, the narrating present. Narration emerges as an act of the moment, re-creating and redefining itself instant by instant, each moment of narration inflected by its own object. From a model of subject directing or manipulating object, as Morel solves algebra equations and Marcel sequesters Albertine, those objects in turn shape and direct the narration itself; the recounted material seeps back into the "instance de narration" (Genette). In a prescient observation, the narrator even implies that his own contextual association with Swann's story, the very proximity of listening to it, may generate its recontextualization as his own; thus the entire mystery of Albertine's surreptitious activities might be produced by a fearful and unfounded analogy with, or recontextualization of, Odette.

Je pensais alors à tout ce que j'avais appris de l'amour de Swann pour Odette, de la façon dont Swann avait été joué toute sa vie. Au fond, si je veux y penser, l'hypothèse qui me fit peu à peu construire tout le caractère d'Albertine et d'interpréter douloureusement chaque moment d'une vie que je ne pouvais pas contrôler toute entière, ce fut le souvenir, l'idée fixe du caractère de Mme Swann, tel qu'on m'avait raconté qu'il était. Ces récits contribuèrent à faire que, dans l'avenir, mon imagination faisait le jeu de supposer qu'Albertine aurait pu, au lieu d'être la bonne jeune fille qu'elle était, avoir la même immoralité, la même faculté de tromperie qu'une ancienne grue, et je pensais à toutes les souffrances qui m'auraient attendu dans ce cas si j'avais jamais dû l'aimer. (III, 199–200)

I thought then of all that I had learned about Swann's love for Odette, of the way in which Swann had been deceived all his life. In fact, when I think of it, the hypothesis that made me gradually construe the whole of Albertine's character and painfully interpret every moment of a life that I could not control in its entirety, was the memory, the conviction of Mme Swann's character, as it had been recounted to me. These accounts contributed towards the fact that, in the future, my imagination toyed with the idea that Albertine might, instead of being the good girl that she was, have had the same immorality, the same capacity for deceit as a former prostitute, and I thought of all the suffering that would in that case have been in store for me if I should ever have loved her.

Intriguingly, such "recontextualization" of Odette in *La prisonnière*, the increasingly tormented account of the narrator's bewilderment over Albertine's past and sexual inclinations, is confirmed when Françoise finds among the narrator's papers the "récit relatif à Swann et à l'impossibilité où il était de se passer d'Odette" [a story about Swann and the impossibility of his doing without Odette] (III, 868).

Such a dynamic model of the power of context in metonymic disconnecting and reconnecting, seepage and exchange, in many ways finds further resonance in the dynamics of transference, as understood by Lacan. Transference is the ever-present context within which the psychoanalytic exercise is played out. Beginning with this new emphasis on the active, unfolding present of the exchange, we might trace a shift in the understanding of this "present" since Freud. The

Freudian unconscious was to be uncovered and deciphered in his famous archaeological metaphor, a mysterious territory to be mapped
and colonized ("Where id was, there ego shall be" [XXII: 80]). For
Lacan, as Felman points out, the shift from Freud was to emphasize
the position of the observer. Freud decentered the subject, resituating
the observed; Lacan pursues this decentering by resituating the observer. As Felman puts it, "Freud . . . emphasizes the revolutionized
observed—the resulting revolutionized image of the human mind; Lacan brings out the implication of the revolutionized scientific *status of
the observer.*" The observed, for Lacan, is "pulled," shaped, determined by the observer, who in turn is pulled and shaped by the object
of observation—in Felman's metaphor, the working of "contradictory
gravitational pulls" (1987, 65).

The essential exercise of analysis becomes, for Lacan, not so much
the uncovering or conquering of obscure territory, but the dynamic
exchange of transference—a shift from a metaphorics of geography,
space, to a metaphorics of time: the incessantly present temporality
of transferential exchange. Such a shift is consonant with the new
neurological understanding of memory not as a fixed record to be uncovered, but as a constantly evolving, moment-by-moment contextualization realized differently according to different "presents." Lacan, in
fact, at times implicitly argues against the Freudian understanding of
a fixed past, which is particularly apparent in a certain slippage of his
use of the word "histoire." "Ce que nous apprenons au sujet à reconnaître comme son inconscient, c'est son histoire" [What we teach the
subject to recognize as his unconscious is his history] (1966, 139), he
writes in an apparently Freudian claim. But Lacan's sentence goes on
subtly to modify the word "histoire": "—C'est-à-dire que nous l'aidons
à parfaire *l'historisation actuelle* des faits qui ont déterminé déjà dans
son existence un certain nombre de 'tournants' historiques" [That's to
say that we help the subject to complete the *present historization* of facts
which have already determined in his existence a certain number of
historical "turning points"] (my emphasis). The word "histoire" becomes "l'historisation actuelle," with a new emphasis on the present
within which the exercise of "historization" takes place; history and
the past are resituated—recontextualized—as constructions within
the present, a putting-into-history of determining "faits." This emphasis on the past not as opposed to the present but occurring instead
within the present is repeatedly implied by Lacan. He speaks of "le
sujet comme 'gewesend,' c'est-à-dire comme étant celui qui a ainsi été"
[the subject as "having-been," which is to say as being the one who has
been thus] (1966, 132)—the present participle "étant" read as a construction of the present moment: "Dans l'unité interne de cette tem-

poralisation, l'étant marque la convergence des ayant été" [In the internal unity of this temporalization, the "being" marks the convergence of all the "having beens"]. Such slippage from history toward its reconstruction in the present is also apparent in the shift depicted in the claim that "l'historicité fondamentale de l'événement que nous retenons suffit pour concevoir la possibilité d'une reproduction subjective du passé dans le présent" [the fundamental historicity of the event that we retain suffices to conceive the possibility of a subjective reproduction of the past in the present] (1966, 168); the notion of the "historicity" of any event "retained" becomes instead a "reproduction" within the present.

Lacan explores the implications of such "presentness" of a past necessarily, subjectively *reconstructed* by going on to suggest that the reality of this past, its truth or falseness, is not the most "troublesome" aspect of the problem of the past. "Car la vérité de cette révélation, c'est la parole présente qui en témoigne dans la réalité actuelle et qui la fonde au nom de cette réalité" [For the truth of this revelation is the present speech which bears witness to it in present reality and which founds it in the name of this reality] (1966, 132). The truth of revelations made in the psychoanalytic exercise does not thus lie in any "objective" or imaginative status they might have, but insofar as they obtain through "la parole *présente*" within "la réalité *actuelle*." "Ce qui se réalise dans mon histoire," argues Lacan,

n'est pas le passé défini de ce qui fut puisqu'il n'est plus, ni même le parfait de ce qui a été dans ce que je suis, mais le futur antérieur de ce que j'aurai été pour ce que je suis en train de devenir. (1966, 181)

is not the past definite of what was since it is no longer, nor even the perfect past of what has been in what I am, but the future anterior of what I will have been for what I am in the process of becoming.

History is no longer a return to the past, but a construction of the past from the perspective of the present; it is "those structures of the past that emerge as having been significant for the self now being constructed" (Smith 107). Symmetrically, the future is no longer an objective geographical territory-to-come, but a "futur antérieur," a projection cast from within the present context of "ce que je suis en train de devenir." The past, history, and future become speculative emanations based in the very situated, present becoming of the subject.

Like Morel, Charlus, and Marcel, we also have a pressing equation to solve. We have been working with memory and with fiction. Just what is the relation between the two, and what equation will define this relationship? It is tempting to suggest that each is a metaphor for the other, each implicitly analogical, comparative—just different enough to preserve the tension of metaphor: the difference between literal and figural meaning. For necessary to the function of metaphor is the knowledge that it is being used figurally. Thus, saying "memory is fiction" would normally be understood analogically as the claim that memory is *like* fiction. But this is not doing justice to Edelman's theory, which is far more daring in its implication that memory *is* fiction; not the analogical, metaphorical "is," understood as "is like," but the literal "is" of a tautology, of a mathematical equation, the "is" of "equals": memory equals fiction. Does this mean that the tautology is reversible, that fiction equals, "is," memory? We have seen that the behavior of fiction seems to be the behavior of memory; both unfold according to principles of creation and revision. Todorov seems to suggest the idea of a narrative "memory" when he argues that narrative transformation—the time engaged by the narrative—carries out a "same-but-different" process: the end bound to the beginning, but somehow "different" from it (1971, 241). Narrative transformation, he suggests, is thus accomplished by the conjugation of what Ricoeur calls resemblance and difference: elements implied in Edelman's account of memory's constant "recategorization," where the diachronic work of memory produces endless variation.

Metonymy and its constant slippage may indeed be the "motor" of narrative, as Jakobson and Genette ("le parcours métonymique [est] la dimension proprement prosaïque du discours") [the metonymic trajectory [is] the properly prosaic dimension of discourse] (61) have claimed—but now, suggests Edelman, of memory as well. In assessing the importance of being able to organize experience, Peter Brooks notes how urgent it is for us to be able to "make sense," and that narrative, as the ordering of meaning in time, answers that need (285). But the effort to make *sense*, Edelman's theory now suggests, is always preceded by the surreptitious preliminary activity of *making* sense: literally producing it, creating it, writing and rewriting it, such that memory's "history" is constantly being ficted and reficted. Proust's text endorses such an equation of memory and fiction explicitly, claiming that "l'arbitraire du souvenir [est] presque aussi absolu que celui de l'imagination" [the arbitrariness of memory [is] almost as absolute as that of the imagination] (II, 666). Later, thinking of the images of Balbec that prompt him to go back for a second visit, the narrator realizes that these remembered images are as wrong, as off, as deceptive, as the images of the imagination: "Les images choisies par le souvenir sont aussi arbitraires, aussi étroites, aussi insaisissables, que celles que l'imagination avait formées et la réalité détruites" [The images chosen by memory are as arbitrary, as narrow, as elusive as those which the imagination had formed and reality has destroyed] (III, 149). Referring to his surprise each time he sees the faces of Gilberte, Madame de Guermantes, or Albertine after an interval, the narrator wonders, "Ne prouvait-il pas combien un souvenir ne se prolonge que dans une direction divergente de l'impression avec laquelle il a coincidé d'abord et de laquelle il s'èloigne de plus en plus?" [Did this not prove that a memory is prolonged only in a direction diverging from the impression with which it originally coincided but from which it increasingly departs?] (IV, 489).

If indeed memory is necessarily ficted, the status of autobiography as genre, long in question, becomes increasingly problematic—for autobiography's "fictedness" (entailing the collapse of all claims to recount a "true" or "historic" past) now seems neurologically necessary. Such "fictedness" has been embraced in the autobiographical writing of many of the "nouveaux romanciers." The turn to autobiography in the 1980s by these masters of experimentation in fiction, explorers of fiction's endless possibilities, would seem to suggest that this long exercise has prepared them for what might be the supreme fiction: autobiography. One thinks of Sarraute's memoir *Enfance*; Robbe-Grillet's claim in his autobiography *Le Miroir qui revient*, "Je n'ai jamais parlé d'autre chose que de moi" [I have never spoken of anything but myself] (10); Butor's autobiographical-poetic collections, *Envois* and *Exprès*. As Frank Kermode remarks in his review of *Enfance*, whether memories are faithful to "what really happened" is now incidental to the autobiographer. What matters is the synchronic import, the affective value those "memories" have for the "rememberer." Kermode cites Sarraute's debate with her alter ego, who suggests that before discussing an illustration in a children's book, the writer should really make sure the illustration is indeed in that book. The writer refuses, saying "Non, à quoi bon? Ce qui est certain, c'est que cette image est restée liée à ce livre" [No, what's the point? What is certain is that this image for me remains linked to the book] (47–48).

Edelman's theory, suggesting that the work of memory may be the work of fiction, thus implies the collapse of Snow's and Ozick's distinctions: scientific theory is literary theory, neurological memory is fiction. But is this really so new? We recall that a theory itself, whatever it may attempt to explain, never claims to be more than an ambitious fiction, a hopeful construct of what may be—and that this ambitious fiction is the closest we'll ever get to reality. Thinking of the wildflowers of his childhood, Proust's narrator realizes in a nostalgic passage that the flowers he sees today for the first time don't seem to him to be real—and muses that perhaps reality only takes shape in the memory (I, 182). What he doesn't go on to say, however, but what his narration enacts—with neurology's interdisciplinary substantiation—is that perhaps memory itself only takes shape as fiction. As the *Recherche* narration has always already shown, the very object that eludes capture by neurology's ambitious theory—memory—is as ficted as theory itself.

Notes

1. The invocation of Proust in analyses of scientific studies of memory has become quite trendy. Other recent examples include a discussion of scientific advances that emphasize the importance of network, associative activity in memory, but that nonetheless, in contrast to the implications of Edelman's work, argue for the "laying down" of static, unchanging "memories" (Hilts). This more conservative work suggests the traditional operation of memory as a "retrieval" function, while Edelman's research would seem to point to memory as a far more dynamic, inventive, imaginative process. Another discussion, citing memory loss with advancing age, also asserts the value of re-creating the original environment in the retention of memory (an unwitting reference to what Proust called "involuntary memory"). Proust's madeleine scene is then invoked as an example of such "recreation" (Suplee). I am grateful to Bernie Levinson and Kathleen Micham, respectively, for passing these articles on to me.

2. A possible biographical explanation for this twice-told anecdote in the *Recherche* is that Proust died while working on the third typescript of *La prisonnière*, where the anecdote recurs; *La prisonnière* was thus not published for another year, during which Proust's brother Robert and Jacques Rivière reviewed the typescript (Robert). It is certainly possible, then, that Proust, had he lived to see publication of the volume, would have noticed the repeated material and removed it. Since the material remains, however, in the last autograph typescript of *La prisonnière*, its "recontextualization" and thus implications for duration and vicissitudes within the act of narration itself cannot be dismissed.

3. Though his discussion of inadvertently repeated material in Proust's *Recherche* does not include the algebra anecdote, Philip Kolb theorizes that the repetitions "represent conscious efforts to improve style, or material, or both" (1936, 262). Kolb thus understands an implicit progression to be at work: a notion I develop here as a movement from chance proximity to "recontextualization" as "necessary" association.

4. Yet a further "love affair" recategorization is implied by Charles Blondel, who points to the "triple répétition" of the old duc de Guermantes's jealous infatuation with Madame de Forcheville (Odette): "Le vieillard, imitant dans ce dernier amour la manière de ceux qu'il avait eus autrefois, séquestrait sa maîtresse, au point que, si mon amour pour Albertine avait répété, avec de grandes variations, l'amour de Swann pour Odette, l'amour de M. de Guermantes rappelait celui que j'avais eu pour Albertine" [The old man, imitating in this final love the pattern of those that he had had in the past, sequestered his mistress to such an extent that, if my love for Albertine had, with important variations, repeated the love of Swann for Odette, M. de Guermantes's

love for Odette in turn recalled my own for Albertine] (IV, 593; quoted in Blondel, 121). Blondel's discussion, however, scrutinizes a certain repetition of action on the level of character and behavior; I am concerned here to examine "recontextualizations" within the act of narration. These "recontextualizations" point to an imperative to reconcieve the narrating act.

Chapter 4
Marcel's "Ecriture Féminine"

Leaving the narrating voice to turn to its product, the "world" represented in the *Recherche*, this chapter draws on elaborations of the
"feminine" as that "space" in the text that subverts narrative mastery
and questions representations of sexual difference. What follows,
then, is an interrogation of the possessive apostrophe in my chapter
title: the mark of appropriation, defining "Marcel" as possessor and
master of an "écriture féminine." But in the peculiar (subjective-
objective genitive) grammar of this construction, "Marcel" might
equally be read as the object of an "écriture féminine": a reversal suggesting the putting into "écriture féminine" of Marcel, in which the
aspiring writer narrating the *Recherche* is himself the one written.
Such an ambiguity, the always-possible chiasmus or reversal of subject
and object, destabilizes the position of each; like Hegel's master and
slave, each both usurps and depends upon the position of the other
for its own. In Paul de Man's terms, the possessive apostrophe is properly unreadable, refusing to decide between two conflicting power relationships; each term is unstable as subject or object, possessor or
possession, master or mastered.

Its unreadability, however, is precisely what makes such an illegible
title appropriate here, for I would like to restore the title's occulted
reversibility—and overturn the assumptions of a critical tradition that
has tended to repeat Marcel's claims for mastery rather than question
them. The eruption of what might be read—or unread—as an "écriture féminine" in the Proustian text ultimately explodes the mark of
possession, refusing to be annexed and domesticated within Marcel's
narrative discourse. This refusal transgresses the confident subject/
object notions of narrator and narrated, speaker and speech, writer
and written, overturning the implicit claim to mastery that structures

these relationships. Marcel's failure in the position of possessing sub-ject throws into question not only his own "authority," but, as well, the claims of a critical tradition that has repeated his "authoritative" as-sertions, thereby endorsing the shaky hierarchy of the subject/object distinction.

My use of "écriture féminine" within a canonical male-authored text may be less—or more—scandalous when qualified here as a criti-cal rather than polemical move. Originally the call to "write the body" as the only authentic means to "write the feminine," "écriture fémi-nine"'s claims have subsequently been questioned, beginning with its source, the very speaking or writing subject herself. Is she speaking herself as subject or speaking for herself as object? As Shoshana Fel-man asks when Irigaray argues the impossibility of "speaking woman" within the Aristotelian, logocentric structures of Western discourse, "Is she speaking the language of men, or the silence of women? Is she speaking as a woman or in the place of the (silent) woman, for the woman, in the name of the woman? Is it enough to be a woman in order to speak as a woman?" (1975, 3). Felman points to Irigaray's repetition of the "oppressive gesture" that has reduced woman to something "spoken for," a representation (4). The inevitable fall into representation by which the speaking subject becomes an object "spo-ken for" is pursued by Ann Rosalind Jones's suggestion that the effort to "speak the body" fails to recognize that the body itself is always already mediated, enmeshed in representation; "the notion of a fe-male reality," as Rita Felski further puts it, "is itself mediated by ideological and discursive systems that are neither innocent nor trans-parent" (28). "Ecriture féminine" would seem to stand now as the failure to "speak" the unmediated body, instead speaking "for" the body inevitably mediated by representation. But even as it "bespeaks" representation, however, "écriture féminine" marks the point of fail-ure of representation's confident tautologies, the moment at which a text's mimetic illusions dissolve. Used here as a writing that literally "dissolves"—in the idiom of the Proustian text's "ices" episode—nar-rative claims, "écriture féminine" confounds Marcel's and his critics' attempts to domesticate it as representation: representation under-stood, as Alice Jardine puts it, as "the sorting out of identity and difference . . . the process of analysis: naming, controlling, remem-bering, understanding" (118). It will be used to explore a "space coded as feminine" in which definitions and differences no longer retain an illusory stability, and in which the very category of the "feminine" dissolves in sexual ambiguity and oscillation.[1] What is in question is the possibility of mimetic closure—whether a text can close around that which it claims to represent, to "control." His own claims and those of his critics notwithstanding, Marcel's own confident "écriture féminine" too unstably slips toward its reversal, the writing of Marcel by an "écriture féminine."

Such questions of mastery and closure arise particularly in *La prisonnière* and *Albertine disparue*, perhaps the more so since the discovery of a dramatically different autograph typescript of *Albertine disparue*, published in 1987 by Grasset. The apparent "aporia" posed by Gallimard's and Grasset's conflicting texts seems only to confirm Proust's "postmodern" undecidability in obliging us to choose between conflicting endings, as in Fowles's *The French Lieutenant's Woman*, to the Albertine story. But such irreconcilably different endings are ultimately consonant with what, I argue, is Albertine's *own* eternal undecidability; the very existence of such conflicting, contradictory endings to her story of sexual undecidability only further figures—in fact, in a curious oxymoron, establishes the definitive undecidability of—Albertine herself. Such "undecidability," however, is established well before Albertine's death. Intriguingly, no matter what the edition of *Albertine disparue*, Albertine has always already, in *La prisonnière*, overturned all attempts to derive a coherent narrative that would explain her mysterious sexual past and inclinations, confining her within a history. Narrative tensions culminate in a scene in which Marcel's writerly mastery is explicitly subverted by the eruption of an "écriture féminine" and his encounter with a discourse that cannot be confined by his authorial efforts: one that usurps the idiom he is most confident he masters, overturning the narcissistic, mimetic structures of writer/written, speaker/speech, inside/outside, male/female, heterosexual/homosexual. This leads to the dissolution of the founding paradigm of representation itself: the hierarchical difference between semiosis and mimesis, source of meaning and its reflection.

Sequestering Albertine in his Paris apartment, Marcel undertakes an investigation that, in the original Gallimard edition, will perforce be twofold: the second investigation, in *Albertine disparue*, rendered necessary by the failure of the first, recounted in *La prisonnière*. Between the two investigations, Albertine flees her captivity and is killed. Marcel, convinced that her death will now loosen tongues, renews his efforts at detection—and, as critics have tended to argue, finally succeeds. "True knowledge of Albertine's wayward activities comes in an ironical series of retrospective messages," suggests Ellison (182); "the hero makes an 'objective' discovery of her hidden life and of the essence of the true Albertine," maintains Black (185).[2]

In fact, however, Marcel never manages to establish the definitive truth of Albertine—and critical claims are undermined by what remains inconclusive evidence. The resistant ambiguity of a text that has been construed to state assertive claims to "truth," "knowledge," "objectivity," "discovery," and "essence" argues for further scrutiny.[3] Such belief in the hero's narrative mastery implies excessive confidence in the male hero's role as detective and narrator, in his capacity to elaborate a coherent history.

A review of Marcel's efforts will uncover the tenuousness of such conclusions, for each of his informants' claims erodes in the face of reasons each may have to lie. When, after Albertine's death, Marcel delegates Aimé to conduct his detective mission in Balbec, Aimé extracts the fact that Albertine frequently shut herself up in a bathhouse with an elegant friend, as well as with younger girls. This seems definitive evidence of a lesbian past, until Marcel remembers his grandmother's remark about the keeper of the bathhouse, the source of this information: "c'est une femme qui doit avoir la maladie du mensonge" [she's a woman who must suffer from the disease of mendacity] (IV, 101), for she recounted an unlikely story to the grandmother's friend Mme de Villeparisis. Is the keeper of the bathhouse lying to Aimé about Albertine?

Marcel resolves anew to establish some certainty by sending Aimé to Nice, where he discovers a little laundress who claims her caresses so transported Albertine that, saying, "Ah! Tu me mets aux anges" [Oh! It's too heavenly] (IV, 106), Albertine bit her arm—and the little laundress shows Aimé the mark. Once again, however, this apparently incontrovertible piece of evidence is undone by the possibility that Aimé himself is lying: a possibility critics have neglected, in spite of Marcel's own speculation that Aimé, wanting something to show for Marcel's payments, had fabricated the little laundress and her claim rather than return empty-handed. Furthermore, in the very passage in which Marcel justifies his choice of Aimé as deputy, he also lists qualities that arouse suspicion of Aimé's integrity.

Aimé me parut bien choisi. Il appartenait à cette catégorie de gens du peuple soucieux de leur intérêt, fidèles à ceux qu'ils servent, indifférents à toute espèce de morale, . . . aussi incapables d'indiscrétion . . . que dépourvus de scrupules. (IV, 74)

Aimé seemed to me to be a good choice. He belonged to that category of working-class people keenly aware of their own advantage, loyal to those they serve and indifferent to any form of morality, . . . as incapable of indiscretion . . . as they are devoid of scruples.

Marcel thus claims that Aimé has his complete confidence even as he tells us Aimé is utterly unscrupulous.

In yet another example of the undecidable lies produced by the very attempt to discover the truth of Albertine's lies, Albertine's friend Andrée makes what would seem to be, once again, a decisive revelation. Andrée claims that the evening Marcel returned to the apartment with flowers, she and Albertine were nearly surprised together, and invented the story of Albertine's dislike of the syringa scent to force Marcel to the kitchen, giving themselves more time to recover their composure. Once more, however, the critical tradition has ignored the possibility that the informant herself might have reason to lie. Marcel speculates that Andrée might be jealous because, he says, "j'avais eu des relations avec Albertine et qu'elle m'enviait peut-être—croyant que je me jugeais à cause de cela plus favorisé qu'elle—un avantage qu'elle n'avait peut-être pas obtenu, ni même souhaité" [I had had relations with Albertine and she envied me, perhaps—believing that I therefore considered myself more favored than she—an advantage she herself had perhaps not obtained, nor even desired] (IV, 183). Andrée's jealousy would also prompt her claim that Albertine enjoyed relations with girls provided by Morel (IV, 179).

But Marcel's bewilderment is not only induced by his failure to discover whether Albertine has a lesbian past and inclinations; it is provoked, as well, by his failure to imagine—to grasp, possess—the lesbian possibility. "L'histoire de Gomorrhe," writes McGinnis, "est une histoire non-racontée" [Gomorrah's is an untold history] (94). The destruction of Gomorrah in fire and brimstone for "sin" analogous to that of Sodom can only be supposed; Gomorrah's only history is speculation deriving from its association with Sodom. For the narrator, female homosexuality is not only unknown, it is "too unknown": unknowable. "Cet amour entre femmes était quelque chose de trop inconnu, dont rien ne permettait d'imaginer avec certitude, avec justesse, les plaisirs, la qualité" [This love between women was something too unknown, whose pleasures and nature nothing enabled me to imagine with certainty, with precision] (III, 887). Lesbians, it would seem to the narrator, inhabit a space beyond appropriation by the imagination—they are not specular "others," as women are to men, defined in relation to men, but absolutely "Other," entirely outside the specular sexual economy.[4]

This desire that is "too unknown" also confounds the Baron de Charlus, who discovers that his young male lover Morel is attracted to women, but not as a man—rather, Morel desires women with the desire of women for each other (III, 720–21). Charlus, like Marcel, is confounded by a lesbian desire that not only arouses his jealousy, but stymies his understanding:

Le baron . . . se sentait torturé par une inquiétude de l'intelligence autant que du coeur, devant ce double mystère, où il y avait à la fois de l'agrandissement de sa jalousie et de l'insuffisance d'une définition. (III, 721)

The Baron . . . felt himself tormented by an anxiety of the mind as well as of the heart, confronted with this double mystery in which the arousal of his jealousy was combined with the sudden inadequacy of a definition.

This "sudden inadequacy of a definition," the failure to "grasp" lesbian desire in the confines of a definition, implies that for Charlus as well as the narrator, lesbian desire is absolutely Other, "too unknown." Charlus, however, has further reason to be mystified by his male lover's sapphic attraction to women. The "adequacy" of definitions accounts for heterosexual attraction across the sexes and homosexual attraction within them. But—in a chiasmus that conveys the *Recherche*'s sexual ambiguity—that the Baron's homosexual lover should desire women as a lesbian explodes the grid of definitions, in a crisscrossing of sexual identity, difference and inclination. Is Morel— a male lesbian—hetero- or homosexual? Is he a man or a woman?

Albertine's ambiguous sexuality provokes the same questions, of course, for, beyond the mystery of her sexual inclinations, her sexual identity itself is as unclear as Morel's. Much has been said of her "male" attributes, beginning with her feminized male name.[5] Proust himself suggested she was a "transposed" man, according to Gide:

Il dit se reprocher cette "indécision" qui l'a fait, pour nourrir la partie hétérosexuelle de son livre, transposer "à l'ombre des jeunes filles" tout ce que ses souvenirs homosexuels lui proposaient de gracieux, de tendre et de charmant, de sorte qu'il ne lui reste plus pour *Sodome* que du grotesque et de l'abjet. (I, 694)

He reproached in himself this "indecision" which led him, in developing the heterosexual parts of his book, to transpose to "the shadow of young girls" all that his homosexual memories suggested as gracious, tender and charming—with the result that nothing was left him for *Sodome* but the grotesque and abject.

It is largely agreed that after the death of his former chauffeur and valet Alfred Agostinelli, Proust put aside his work on *Le côté de Guermantes* to write what became *La prisonnière*, retrospectively preparing Albertine's role in the novel by inserting her presence among the "little band" of *A l'ombre des jeunes filles en fleurs*, her Paris visit to Marcel in *Sodome et Gomorrhe*, and Marcel's second stay in Balbec with her.[6] Agostinelli had fled Paris for Nice just as *Du côté de chez Swann* was published, and Proust's searing, impassioned telegrams of instructions to Nahmias, sent to retrieve Agostinelli, leave no doubt as to his sentiments at a time when, as he wrote to a friend, his chagrin precluded any enjoyment of Swann's success[7], nor does a September 1914 letter: "J'aimais vraiment Alfred. Ce n'est pas assez de dire que je l'aimais, je l'adorais" [I truly loved Alfred. It's not enough to say I loved him, I adored him].[8] Proust's own efforts only too poignantly anticipate his narrator's in the face of Albertine's flight and eventual death, leaving Albertine's sexual identity forever unclear; as Harold March was driven to claim in an attempt to resolve the question, "Albertine is not a man, she is not a woman" (180).

With the publication of Grasset's *Albertine disparue* in 1987, Albertine's suspected lesbianism would appear to be definitively confirmed. Such at least is the narrator's reaction upon reading Mme Bontemps' telegram announcing Albertine's accident and death. The original, Gallimard edition telegram read "Elle a été jetée par son cheval contre un arbre pendant une promenade" [She was thrown from her horse against a tree while riding]; the Grasset edition adds, "qu'elle faisait au bord de la Vivonne" [by the banks of the Vivonne]. The narrator interprets Albertine's presence in the proximity of Montjouvain, following upon her claim in the little tram to friendship with Mlle Vinteuil, as conclusive evidence of her homosexuality; hence the omission, in the Grasset edition, of the narrator's post-mortem inquest. Such a conviction, however, is based upon the narrator's *interpretation* of information given in the telegram, not upon fact, as Reginald McGinnis points out. McGinnis, however, cedes to the Grasset editors' claim that, in contrast to the persistent uncertainties detailed in the Gallimard edition, the narrator's conviction of Albertine's lesbianism is not subsequently overturned in the Grasset text. But, argues McGinnis, "savoir la fuite d'Albertine 'du côté de Gomorrhe', ce n'est ni s'insinuer à Gomorrhe ni éclaircir la vérité sur sa vie. C'est savoir seulement que celle dont la vie est restée inconnue est morte du côté de l'inconnu" [knowing of Albertine's flight to "the Gomorrah way" is neither to explain Gomorrah nor to illuminate the truth of her life. It's only to know that she whose life remains unknown died by way of the unknown] (101). Thus, the resolution of Albertine's mystery occurs in the context of an even greater mystery, that of Gomorrah; the certainty of Albertine's lesbianism pales before the far greater uncertainty—the "unknowability"—of lesbianism itself.

Such recognition of Gomorrah's residual "unknowability" is an important critical step. Even so, however, the tendency to domesticate Gomorrah recurs on another level when its "unknowability" is recuperated as a necessary step in Marcel's "apprentissage." Thus, the figure of sexual "inversion" *pre*figures Marcel's itinerary from error to knowledge. It is with Albertine, asserts McGinnis, "que le narrateur connaît l'obscurité la plus complète, la confusion la plus totale. Et c'est en ce sens-là que l'épisode d'Albertine prépare la révélation de la vérité" [that the narrator knows mystery at its most complete, confusion at its deepest. And it's in this sense that the Albertine episode prepares the revelation of truth] (102). If Marcel becomes a writer, runs McGinnis's argument, "c'est qu'il a su profiter des mensonges de la vie pour atteindre une vérité romanesque" [it's that he knew how to benefit from life's lies to reach a fictional truth] (103). But the *interpretive* nature of the narrator's conviction remains, however, as does the baffling "insuffisance d'une définition," the intellectual "unknowability" of Gomorrah. To recuperate such absolute refusal of intelligibility as a necessary step along the narrator's positivist itinerary toward enlightenment is to repeat the appropriative gesture of earlier critical claims: those asserting that Marcel arrives at "definitive knowledge" of Albertine's lesbian past by espousing the dubitable assertions of Marcel's (Gallimard-edition) informants.

In both cases, however, the argument for or against Albertine's imputed lesbianism rests on there being a difference between historic and fictive acts, such that it would be possible to establish certain assertions as truth, history, and others as falsehoods, fictions. In an intimation, however, of the overturning of genres underway (and genders, as Albertine later demonstrates), the text makes it impossible to decide between truth and falsehood, history and fiction. Albertine herself dissolves the difference, for even when she tells the truth her assertions refuse to align into an intelligible account. Truth, for her, is just as incoherent, just as resistant to history's organizational efforts, as falsehood. As Marcel is forced to observe, "Elle était si changeante d'ailleurs que même en me disant chaque fois la vérité sur ce que, par exemple, elle pensait des gens, eût dit chaque fois des choses différentes" [She was so inconsistent that, even in telling me the truth every time about, for instance, what she thought of other people, she would say something different every time] (III, 605). Truth, "history," like fiction and falsehood, is a collection of unrelated, self-contradicting episodes, each erasing and replacing the last in the "bloc-notes" ("notepad") (III, 601) that is Albertine: a "bloc-notes" refusing all narrative progression, whether historic or fictive.[9] "Il était incroyable," Marcel tells us, "à quel point sa vie était successive, et fugitifs ses plus grands désirs" [It was incredible how spasmodic her life was, how fugitive her greatest desires] (III, 910). Albertine's mystery is perhaps nothing more than her congenital inconstancy, provoking Marcel to anxious hermeneutic efforts where there is merely picaresque succession. She confounds both historical and fictive progression; thus, any claim to "knowledge" of Albertine's sexual truth would impose an artificial difference upon genres she herself scrambles, arbitrarily decreeing certain claims as truth, history, and others as falsehoods, fictions. The sexing of Albertine's desire as hetero- or homoerotic—a judgment based on the conviction that she is consistently either telling the truth or lying—remains blocked by her willful dissolution of generic difference.

In fact, Marcel himself, in intermittent moments of lucidity, has periodically confessed the enduring uncertainty of his "knowledge," the shakiness of his narratorial mastery. He realizes as early as *Sodome*, "Pour Albertine, je sentais que je n'apprendrais jamais rien, qu'entre la multiciplicité entremêlée des détails réels et des faits mensongers je n'arriverais jamais à me débrouiller. Et que ce serait toujours ainsi" [As for Albertine, I felt that I would never discover anything, that, out of that tangled mass of factual details and falsehoods, I would never unravel the truth; and that it would always be so] (III, 131). Then in *La prisonnière* we read "Moitié par ma jalousie, moitié par ignorance . . . j'avais réglé à mon insu cette partie de cache-cache où Albertine m'échapperait toujours" [Partly out of jealousy, partly out of ignorance of such joys . . . I had unknowingly settled the outcome of this game of hide and seek in which Albertine would always elude me] (III, 533). Some pages further comes the remark, "tout cela, dont je n'ai jamais su si c'était vrai" [all this, of which I never discovered the truth] (III, 564). Much later is the admission, "Combien peu d'ailleurs, je savais, je saurais jamais de cette histoire d'Albertine, la seule histoire qui m'eût particulièrement intéressé" [How little, besides, did I know, would I ever know, of this story of Albertine, the only story that would particularly have interested me] (IV, 193). Marcel's final helpless, bewildered question in the Venice episode of Gallimard's *Albertine disparue* only too painfully puts the status of his investigation: "Et encore même sur Albertine étais-je sûr de savoir quelque chose?" (IV, 228) [And even, as for Albertine, could I be sure of knowing anything?] (IV, 228). Marcel's efforts to annex Albertine's story, to derive the narrative of her sexual past, collapse in an endlessly unanswered question, one that returns the inquisition to its source, searching no longer for knowledge of Albertine's "otherness," but doubting the position of knower himself in a dissolution of the power structure of those polarities. Marcel's imperialistic attempts to grasp the "truth" backfire in a fracturing of the subject; his question falls back upon himself to divide and bewilder its own—now highly ironized—"author."

That Albertine's sexual identity should thus be as unstable and elusive as her sexual desires has provoked tremendous anxiety among critics, baffled, like Charlus, before such "inadequacy of a definition" and anxious to colonize an undecidable terrain with the grid of sexual difference and definition.[10] Symptomatic of this anxiety is critical response to a scene in which Marcel's efforts to master Albertine's story, to "author" her sexual truth, are overturned as the narrator himself becomes the one mastered—the one "written."

The long story of knowledge's quest and failure, its ironic falling-back upon the would-be knower, is anticipated by the eruption of an "écriture féminine" early in *La prisonnière*: a scene that seals Marcel's failure to confine Albertine. Particularly subversive in this episode is that it is not Marcel the writer who writes, but rather is "written," confounding the attempt to locate "authority"; that the "written" piece is not in writing, but spoken, defying stylistic difference and definition; and that the desire "spoken" is both male and female, hetero- and homosexual, blocking the assignment of sexual identity and preference. Locating "writer" and "written," subject and object, master and mastered, inside and outside, speech and writing, male and female, hetero- and homoerotic desire thus becomes an uncertain and ironized enterprise. Such polarities—and the power relations they assume—dissolve in a passage that has fascinated and eluded critics, who repeatedly attempt to straighten out the "differences" confounded by and cohabiting this discourse.

Culminating in Albertine's eloquent and extravagant plea for ices in molded architectural shapes, this subversive episode is initiated by an indication of the danger that peddlers' poetic street cries, heard from within the apartment, constitute for Marcel's tenuous mastery of Albertine in their arousal of Albertine's desire. Marcel reflects on their significance as a symbol of the vibrant and restive street life circulating beneath Albertine's window:

J'entendais en eux comme le symbole de l'atmosphère du dehors, de la dangereuse vie remuante au sein de laquelle je ne la laissais circuler que sous ma tutelle, dans un prolongement extérieur de la séquestration, d'où je la retirais à l'heure que je voulais pour la faire rentrer auprès de moi. (III,633)

I heard in them a sort of symbol of the atmosphere outside, of the dangerous stirring life through whose midst I did not allow her to circulate save under my tutelage, in an external prolongation of her sequestration, and from which I withdrew her at the hour of my choosing to make her return home to my side.

The threat of this sensual "outside" is apparently domesticated by Marcel's confidence that his sequestration of Albertine is elastic and expandable, allowing her to circulate outside in a prolongation of the inner space of his dominance: "outside" is merely the extension of inside, annexed by Marcel's mastery.

These claims for mimetic control—the absorption of what is "other," "outside," as one's own in a closed narcissistic space—develop when Marcel appropriates Albertine's highly figural discourse as his own ("Sans moi elle ne parlerait pas ainsi, elle a subi profondément mon influence. . . . Elle est mon oeuvre") [But for me she wouldn't speak thus, she has profoundly experienced my influence. . . . She is my creation] (III, 636). The episode will close symmetrically with Marcel's restatement of such claims for mastery; Albertine's eloquence is "une preuve que j'avais du pouvoir sur elle, qu'elle m'aimait" [a proof that I had power over her, that she loved me] (III, 638). Marcel's closed mimetic circle appears intact, the episode contained within his mirrored assertions of power over Albertine. Her discourse is his own in a confident tautology.[11]

Such assertions of possession and mastery are repeated by critics, who argue similarly that outside (discourse) is a specular reflection of inside (subject) in a narcissistic, tautological space. The passage has thus been read on the register of author and text as an example of Proust's control, symptomatic of a confident distance that allows him to mock the excesses of his own style. A "Proustian self-pastiche," Albertine's exaggerated metaphors would point to what is "mièvre" and "convenu" (Genette) in Proust's own stylistic instrument. In this demonstration of authorial mastery, claims Emily Eells, Proust shows his reader he is "maître de ses moyens, peut se moquer de lui-même" [master of his means, able to make fun of himself] (117). Jean Milly repeats the inscription of authorial mastery ("Proust démontre simplement qu'il sait s'imiter, prendre de la distance par rapport à lui-même dans un exercice imposé" [Proust simply demonstrates that he is able to imitate himself, to establish a distance from himself in an imposed exercise] (149)). This "distance" is also read as that of mastery by Lejeune, who places a "Proust-narrator" in the analyst's position of interpreter: listening, analyzing and intimating that he understands Albertine's discourse (136). Even when the mirror is seen to cast back the distorted reflection of caricature, as for Richard, the implicit mockery posed by such amplification goes unnoticed. Riffaterre comes closer to noticing the subversiveness of the reflection itself in a scene in which "the text authors its author in turn." But he nonetheless concludes with the (authored) author's power intact: "The author becomes child to the textual figment born of his desire; playing Pygmalion to Albertine's Galatea, he puts himself back in the position of the suckling babe" (1987, 384–85). In Riffaterre's claim, the author "authors" himself into the powerful, domineering position of the demanding child. The recurrent image of "Proust au miroir" (Eells, Lejeune) is symptomatic of the critical tradition's tendency to close the space of mastery and possession. It suggests an anxious and persistent critical need to domesticate this passage by ascribing it to Proust's stylistic mastery—repeating on the level of author and text the narrator's narcissistic claim that Albertine's eloquence is a demonstration of his own power.

What must be asked, however, is how far the mimetic tautology extends—can specularity close upon itself, or is it inevitably self-subversive? To what extent does such specularity, to post-Lacanian readers, necessarily produce a fractured subject? Even more pertinent is the question of why critics have repeated Marcel's insistence on the mimetic value—Albertine's discourse as a reflection of his own "authorial" control—of the passage. The question of mastery, of power, is more complicated—more subverted—than the critical tradition has understood, and more implicated in its own study of the question. For between Marcel's two mirrored claims for control, the episode carries out their subversion as Albertine breaches the confines of specularity. Countering Marcel's confident understanding of outside as a prolongation of inside, Albertine's desire, instead, imports the outside, violating her sequestration with its sounds and presence ("Elle voulait successivement tout ce qu'elle entendait crier") [She wanted successively all the things she heard cried] (III, 633). Her gesture of appropriation is literalized as ingestion when she goes on to create an entire "géographie pittoresque" of sculpted ices, which, she says, "je regarde d'abord et dont je convertis ensuite les monuments de framboise ou de vanille en fraîcheur dans mon gosier" [I look at first and whose raspberry or vanilla monuments I convert into coolness in my gullet] (III, 636). Exemplifying the critical perspective on Albertine's figured discourse, Milly reads it as confirmation of Marcel's mastery, claiming that Albertine's talk of going out is adroitly deflected by Marcel's insistence on ices: "Albertine, habilement vaincue sur le plan pratique, se trouve enfermée dans le cercle de la parole" [Albertine, handily defeated in practical terms, finds herself enclosed in the circle of speech] (144). What Milly and others have neglected is that Albertine's appropriation of that "parole" will rupture the confines of the "circle" that is her sequestration, her specular role and the arena of criticism's illusory mastery of sexual difference.

The eruption of outside within inside, the invasion of intimate tranquil space of an alien and threatening "other," continues as Marcel recognizes that his own tutelage has produced, he says, "ces paroles du genre de celles qu'elle prétendait dues uniquement à mon influence, à la constante cohabitation avec moi" [these words of the kind that she maintained were due entirely to my influence, to constant cohabitation with me] (III, 636). But Marcel's sentence goes on to qualify Albertine's "speech" as somehow out of context, transgressive, menacing—his own, yet other:

ces paroles que, pourtant, je n'aurais jamais dites, comme si quelque défense m'était faite par quelqu'un d'inconnu de jamais user dans la conversation de formes littéraires. (III, 636)

these words, however, that I would never have uttered, as though I had been somehow forbidden by an unknown authority ever to use literary forms in conversation.

For Marcel, Albertine transgresses a "sacred" distinction in her use, "en parlant, des images si écrites et qui me semblaient réservées pour un autre usage plus sacré et que j'ignorais encore" [in speaking, of such "bookish" images as seemed to me to be reserved for another, more sacred use of which I was as yet unaware] (III, 636). However, Marcel himself, as a literary young man, commits the same stylistic indiscretion, as we know from, among other instances, a conversation with the Duchesse de Guermantes in which he claims that on another occasion she resembled "une espèce de grande fleur de sang, un rubis en flammes" [a sort of great blood-flower, a flaming ruby] in her red dress: an exaggeratedly literary image indulgently mocked by M. de Bréauté, "qui faisait tiédir sous son monocle un sourire indulgent pour cet amphigouri de l'intellectuel" [who warmed beneath his monocle an indulgent smile for this intellectual's rigmarole] (III, 547). Marcel's haste to disclaim an idiom that is precisely his own—coupled with his opening and closing assertions that, to the contrary, it *is* his own—suggests the tenuousness and confusion of his discrete categories, and ironizes his preoccupation as to whose discourse Albertine pronounces. It is both hers and Marcel's, in a scrambling that ironizes any claims for "authority."

Thus Marcel himself transgresses the "rules" of his own stuffy stylistics in his insistence on the difference between speech and writing. Yet his claims for stylistic "difference" are repeated in critical work on this passage, as critics reproduce Marcel's anxious attempt to preserve a shaky typology. Gaubert, for example, deepens the absolute difference between the two as not one of degree, but of essence ("nature"). His claim is that Albertine's discourse bears too great a truth value, refers too explicitly to her secret life, to be conversational—for it is *writing* that explores the most unique, secret realm of each person (185–87). But the critical tendency to define and differentiate appears in its most anxious form in discussions of the erotic resonance of Albertine's figural discourse. Symbols of phallic obsession are repertoried: the "obelisks," "Vendome columns," "votive columns," "erect pylons," and "pillars" of Albertine's ice-cream architecture which, for Eells, Lejeune, Milly, and Richard, "represent" a fellatio phantasm. Riffaterre, in fact, develops an entire "deep throat" intertextual network, including, for instance, Envy's ingestion of the snake in Giotto's allegory (382–83). Such readings impose a heterosexual desire upon the text, rewriting it as a male phantasm of feminine desire—repeating Marcel's own narcissistic error of reading Albertine's discourse mimetically as the reflexion of his own. As Milly notices without developing the implications of such coexistence, however, symbols of a penetrable or curvaceous female body are equally present in the same architectural descriptions: "temples," "églises," "rochers," "montagnes," "monuments."[12] The need to identify the sexuality of such ambiguous desire is suggested by Lejeune's contorted claim,

Proust a essayé de faire exprimer par Albertine, sous le biais de la succion d'un univers en glace, le rapport oral d'une homosexuelle avec le corps de l'autre, mais il n'a pu s'empêcher ici encore de parler en homosexuel masculin. (135)

Through Albertine, Proust tried indirectly to express, via the suction of a universe of ices, the oral relationship of one female homosexual with the body of another; but even here he was unable to avoid speaking as a male homosexual.

Albertine's desire resists being gendered as either male or female, while its undecidable object prevents its identification as homo- or heterosexual.

Part of the phallic-phantasm argument includes pointing to the eroticism of the depicted "succion"; however, the passage specifies that Albertine's desire does not run to suction, but to *dissolution*. She evokes "obélisques" only to "melt" them: "dont je ferai fondre le granit rose au fond de ma gorge" [whose pink granite I shall melt in the depths of my throat] (III, 636). "Je me charge avec mes lèvres de détruire, pilier par pilier, ces églises vénitiennes" [I take upon myself to destroy with my lips, pillar by pillar, these Venetian churches], imagines Albertine voluptuously, and, summarily, "tous ces monuments passeront de leur place de pierre dans ma poitrine où leur fraîcheur fondante palpite déjà" [all these monuments will pass from their stony state into my chest, where their melting coolness already throbs] (III, 637). The dissolving of boundaries, read by critics as more erotic than subversive, has been understood as a depicted rather than a signifying act, as mimesis rather than semiosis. Beyond the level of depiction, however, the passage scrambles gender and sexual categories to "signify" the very "dissolution" of representation. For if

Albertine's phallic symbols initially might be claimed to evoke a heterosexual desire, they conclude with a symmetrical reference to
Montjouvain and the lesbian Mlle Vinteuil ("Mais tenez, même sans
glaces, rien n'est excitant et ne donne soif comme les annonces des
sources thermales. A Montjouvain, chez Mademoiselle Vinteuil . . . ")
[But say, even without ices, nothing is so exciting or makes one so
thirsty as the advertisements for thermal springs. At Montjouvain, at
Mademoiselle Vinteuil's . . .] (III, 637). The passage refuses to stabilize as the expression of a desire either male or female, either het-
ero- or homoerotic, in a subversive indeterminacy that "dissolves"
such distinctions.

What can be ascribed to such desire, however, is its energy, the "volupté cruelle" of its exuberant images of destruction ("des postillons,
des voyageurs, des chaises de poste sur lesquels ma langue se charge
de faire rouler de glaciales avalanches qui les engloutiront") [postill-
ions, travelers, post-chaises over which my tongue busies itself rolling
freezing avalanches that will swallow them up] (III, 637). In discussions of this erotic outburst, critics invariably point to its sadistic
gestures, as, for instance, the "castration" suggested by Albertine's description of tiny figures swallowed up in avalanches—again betraying
critical preoccupation with the passage as representation. Even on the
level of representation, however, this image of castration participates
in the general effacing of sexual difference, thus subverting representation's sexual paradigms. More significant is that critical attention to
the scene depicted has failed to notice what takes place in the language of depiction itself: Albertine's arousal through the sensuality of
her own eloquence. As Marcel himself observes,

Elle sentit que je trouvais que c'était bien dit et elle continua, en s'arrêtant un
instant, quand sa comparaison était réussie, pour rire de son beau rire qui
m'était si cruel parce qu'il était si voluptueux. (III, 636)

She sensed that I thought it was well expressed and continued, pausing for a
moment when her comparison was successful to laugh that beautiful laugh of
hers which was so cruel to me because it was so voluptuous.

As Albertine goes on, evoking the coolness of raspberry sherbet in
her throat, her voluptuous laugh explodes again—provoked, as a
dismayed and mystified Marcel observes, by the equally possible, undecidable causes of eloquence or sexual pleasure ("jouissance"). A
threatening equation of eloquence and eroticism takes shape:

Et ici le rire profond éclata, soit de satisfaction de si bien parler, soit par
moquerie d'elle-même de s'exprimer par images si suivies, soit, hélas! par

volupté physique de sentir en elle quelque chose de si bon, de si frais, qui lui causait l'équivalent d'une jouissance. (III, 636)

And here the deep laugh burst out, whether in satisfaction at speaking so well, or in self-mockery for using such sustained images, or, alas! in voluptuously feeling inside herself something so good, so cool, as to be equivalent for her to a sexual pleasure.

The autoeroticism of Albertine's arousal through the "voluptuousness" of her own stylistic extravagance explains Marcel's dismay. Erupting within the inner space of his mastery is Albertine's erotic independence, symptomatic of a sexual history that lies outside Marcel's control. Albertine's auto-arousal through her own eloquence suggests again that the power of the passage lies not in the scene represented, but in the activity of language itself as it offers a strange "equivalent" to desire. Her lexical "pleasure" here culminates in an "écriture féminine": a metaphorical language that "speaks" bodily desire in an idiom only "equivalent" to sexual pleasure. The accumulation of sexual and stylistic ambiguities—Albertine's undecidable sex, her undecidable inclinations, the undecidable spoken or written idiom of her discourse—points to a blockage of representation. The uncertain relation of a voluptuous language to a voluptuous body (Marcel can only speak of "equivalence") confirms the inherent mystification of a relation that can only be metaphorical, of speech that can only be "equivalent" to the body. "The feminine," as Sharon Willis has put it, "is not other than the perpetual translation effect—body to language—body and language always missing each other" (83). The elusiveness of this "écriture féminine," its charge of a desire that can only be approximate to a bodily desire, continues in its transgressive context as a written yet also spoken idiom. Writing and speech simultaneously each displace the other, each "equivalent" to the other and to the bodily desire each "embodies" discursively. Marcel's insistent categorizations of written and conversational idioms are here undone by an "écriture féminine" that scrambles spoken as well as written idioms, male as well as female gendering, hetero- as well as homoerotic sexing.[13]

Another symptom of the anxiety generated in the critical tradition by this episode has been the insistent preoccupation with the "excess," the extravagance of such a discourse. Milly refers to the "décalage de l'expression par rapport au contenu" [the gap between expression and its contents] (137), suggesting a slippage or loss of equivalence: a breaching of the mimetic repetition of meaning as form in which form no longer repeats its contents. Richard goes further in referring to the "baroquisme excessif" of Albertine's discourse, pointing to the extravagant energy with which it eludes the framing confines of narrative, its history and teleology.[14] Critics have failed to recognize the performative value, however, of such extravagance. Albertine's final images no longer merely exceed stylistic containment in their extravagant desire for fantastic ice-cream shapes, but actively carry out the dissolution of boundaries. The cool sensuality of ices reminds Albertine of Montjouvain and her lesbian friend Mlle Vinteuil, for when Albertine was visiting, as good ices were not to be had in the area, the girls would sit in the garden drinking different mineral waters. "Nous faisions dans le jardin notre tour de France" [We used to make our own tour of France in the garden], says Albertine, "en buvant chaque jour une autre eau minérale gazeuse" [by drinking a different mineral water every day] (III, 637). The innerness of the garden is the vastness of the country itself in Albertine's audacious tautology: an ambitious equation that collapses all sequestering barriers. Marcel's elastic and megalomanic conception of Albertine's sequestration—outside as inside, as the extension of the mastered space of his apartment—is overturned by Albertine's effortless reversal: inside (the Montjouvain garden) is outside (France) in a breaching of boundaries. Albertine's overturning of the "distinctions" of gender and genre are complete.

Marcel's interruption and reclaiming of discursive control at this point ("mais entendre parler de Montjouvain m' était trop pénible, je l'interrompais") [but to hear her speak of Montjouvain was too painful for me, and I interrupted her] (III, 637), his reassertion of narrative mastery of Albertine, will fail, however: a failure that traditional criticism, having placed its confidence in the male hero's narratorial powers, has invariably read as success. This failure culminates in a reversal whereby the nonnarratable (Albertine) transgressively narrates the narrator, speaks the speaker, writes the writer: her "écriture féminine" appropriates Marcel's idiom to express a sensuality that resists all representation, a desire that cannot be annexed by narrative. Collapsed in this exuberant destruction of stylistic—and sexual—representations is the confident critical premise that mastery of this passage is mastery of representation, mastery of the mimetic reflection. Critics differ only in their convictions as to what is represented: a male homosexual discourse in the guise of a lesbian discourse (Lejeune); Marcel's own great work to come in the architectures of churches, temples (Milly); sexual phantasms in the phallic imagery of obelisks, pillars, and so forth (Eells, Milly, Riffaterre); and, for many critics of this passage, Proust's own discourse in this extravagant parody, a self-representation that apparently closes the mimetic model. However, Marcel the narrator's claims for mastery and their ironic failure only too undecidably implicate Marcel the author. Can any one (sexed, desiring) subject—that is, a representation—claim control of a passage that dissolves representation: that destroys the possibility of representing sexuality and desire? Critical confidence that a representational tautology can be established (Albertine's figures "representing" something else) is unquestioned. The need to identify the origin of the reflecting or mimetic side of the equation has led critics to ignore the fact that such a representational relationship is distorted and reworked in a chiasmus of properties that produces undecidable ambiguities. Representation is forestalled by the eruption in the text of an undecidable "equivalence," blocking any unquestioned passage from origin or power source to its own mimetic reflection. Beyond the threshold of ambiguity announced by the idea of "equivalence," the equations are rewritten against the logic of representation: male is undecidably female, heterosexual desire is undecidably homosexual, Marcel (Proust) the writer is undecidably Marcel the narrator, speech is undecidably writing, inner mastery is undecidably outside "other." In the oscillation of undecidable equivalences put into play by the text, "écriture féminine" exceeds its assigned, confined position as mimetic reflection—and dissolves imposed differences of genre and gender, dissolving the possibility of representation itself.

Notes

1. The feminine as radically subversive is developed in Jardine's interrogation of Lacan's *Encore*, where Lacan's speculations on the "feminine" take shape as a metonymic series of substitutions including the notions of supplementarity, of the "true," the Real, the unconscious, and God. Lacan stops short of naming feminine jouissance as "writing," a connection that will be completed by Michèle de Montrelay—but it is precisely the implications of the feminine for "writing" that suggest my use here of "écriture féminine" as beyond representation, including any representation of the feminine itself. Intriguingly, Stephen Melville points out *Encore*'s peculiar and anxious relationship to writing; noting that the *Encore* meditations are made in Lacan's knowledge that his "séminaires" have become an "écriture," Melville writes, "what is happening is that Lacan is discovering himself to be read, exposed beyond the reach of his voice, his signifiers not waiting upon his 'dire'" (367). See also Sarah Kofman's use of feminine "jouissance" as undecidable oscillation in "Ça cloche" (111).
2. One might trace, however, increasing critical suspicion that Albertine's truth may ultimately elude the narrator, beginning with Ellison himself, who refers to the "delusion" of Marcel's possession of Albertine (182). Jefferson Humphries discusses Albertine as an inaccessible, gnostic "otherness," or lack that must be mourned, while Kristin Ross elaborates a Lacanian allegory in which Albertine occupies the inaccessible space of Lacan's "real."
3. Malcolm Bowie offers a recent example of this tendency to impose definition upon the text when he claims that the "joy" Marcel ultimately ex-

periences might "fittingly be called knowledge" (64). The remark he refers to, however—"une joie pareille à une certitude" [a joy similar to a certainty]—subtly preserves (in the ambiguity of the word "pareille") the difference between "joy" and "certainty," and refuses to yoke them in a tautology. Later in this discussion, I will argue that the term "equivalent" produces a similarly ambiguous, undecidable relationship between the ideas it links.

4. Monique Wittig advances the argument that lesbians are not women— that is, not defined in specular terms as "Others" to men.

5. An extensive discussion of Albertine's "transposed" sexuality is provided by Justin O'Brien.

6. This argument for a "post hoc" insertion in the text of an Albertine inspired by Agostinelli is advanced by Bardèche (II, 74), and echoed by Tadié (287) and Ellison (136).

7. Marcel Proust, Letter to Louis de Robert, early December 1913, letter 173 of *Correspondance de Marcel Proust 1913*.

8. Marcel Proust, Letter to Reynaldo Hahn, October 1914, *Lettres retrouvées*: 107; quoted in Tadié, 283.

9. The Moncrieff and Kilmartin translation of the *Recherche* renders "bloc-notes" as "diary," losing the willful opposition to successive temporal order suggested by "bloc-notes": a "note-pad" whose top sheet exists in isolation both from preceeding, torn-off sheets and from those that lie beneath.

10. Symptomatic of this anxiety is the energy with which sides are taken on the question of Proust's own sexual inclinations. O'Brien, for example, quotes a French psychologist who claims Proust was not homosexual, but that his narrator was merely interested in discovering and curing Albertine's vice (935). O'Brien also cites Levin's 1949 claim in his introduction to *Letters of Marcel Proust* that Albertine indeed honors Agostinelli's memory in her association with cars and planes, but that Proust's letters offer evidence of his attraction to women. O'Brien then makes his own heated contribution to the debate: "The early date of Dr. Nicholas' study does not excuse his blindness to the special reasons for Proust's interest in homosexuality. Such an error, made by a medical-psychologist in 1931 is quite as serious as that by a specialist in Modern European literature made in 1949" (935). Although this eagerness to assign sexual definition and inclination has lately become more nuanced, as in Bowie's recent discussion of elements of bisexuality in Proust's narrative (Morel as a bisexual, for instance, as well as the narrator's "indefinite capacity for bisexual phantasy" [81]), it persists in attempting to domesticate, through such labeling, the subversion at work in the text's representations of sexuality: a subversion, I argue here, that threatens the possibility of representation itself.

11. In another context, Marcel seems more wary of the dangers of such appropriation of another's discourse. As Rosemary Lloyd points out, Marcel, longing for a letter from Gilberte, suddenly realizes that his own hopeful epistolary construction cancels the very possibility of enjoying the *otherness* of such a letter as, he says, "quelque chose qui ne vînt pas de moi, quelque chose de réel, de nouveau, un bonheur extérieur à mon esprit, indépendant de ma volonté, vraiment donné par l'amour" [something that had not originated from me, something real, something new, a happiness external to my mind, independent of my will, truly given out of love] (I, 402; quoted in Lloyd, 349).

12. Interestingly, Milly claims that earlier versions of the passage contained "essentiellement des symboles masculins," while the feminine "symbols" were

inserted afterward, possibly as late as 1922 (144): an addition that implies, I would argue, a deliberate intention to maintain sexual ambiguity in the passage.

13. The hysteria of Albertine's discourse is apparent, not least in its confusion of gendered distinctions; as Juliet Mitchell has written, "the hysteric's voice is the woman's masculine language." The concept of hysteria, however, seems inadequate to account for the subversion at work in this passage—for hysteria, as one response to cultural impositions of sexual identity, implies their persistence; sexual differences are simultaneously assumed, "put on," in a testimonial to the power of such representations. Albertine's discourse, however, seems to dissolve such representations in a refusal to stabilize as emanating from either a male or female subject, to express either hetero- or homoerotic desire. Rather than assuming both, in the hysterical paradigm, the text assumes neither.

14. The "baroque" excess of another "écriture féminine" in the novel— Gilberte's extravagant and misleading signature on her telegram to Marcel in Venice—was suggested to me by Alan Astro.

Chapter 5
Figuration and Resistance

Representation now questioned from within its own mimetic forms, as the preceding chapter argues, we will need to look more closely at the work of figuration, and particularly at the text's claims for it. For representation's resistance, opened up through Albertine's overturning of narratorial claims, provokes further questions as to the putative purposes and behavior of figuration. An investigation of such considerations takes us to the climactic final pages of the *Recherche* and the question of whether Marcel is ready to write at the conclusion of his narration—to uncertainties that haunt the very proclamation of his authorial intentions. His technique, the triumphant answer to his "tâtonnements" [gropings], is to be metaphor, the stylistic device that corresponds to involuntary memory in yoking temporally remote moments and thus provides the tool that is to be his means to "the past recaptured." Yet, after the anguish of the Albertine captivity, one would think the very notion of capture would provoke reluctance, hesitation, and ambivalences on the narrator's part, for it was precisely captivity that drained Albertine of her charm. "Une fois captif chez moi l'oiseau que j'avais vu un soir . . . avait perdu toutes ses couleurs . . . avait peu à peu perdu sa beauté" [Once a captive in my house, the bird that I had seen one evening . . . had lost all her colors . . . had gradually lost her beauty] (III, 678). Her very presence as "la grise prisonnière, réduite à son terne elle-même" [the gray captive, reduced to her dull self] cramps the play of his imagination, "mon seul organe," he realizes, "pour jouir de la beauté" [my only organ with which to enjoy beauty] (IV, 450). Desire, he sees, is always "le désir d'autre chose" (Lacan 1966, 277). It demands distance and resistance, a space permitting for the play and exercise of the desiring imagination and the elusiveness and resistance of its object "en vertu de la loi inévitable qui veut qu'on ne puisse imaginer que ce qui est absent" [in virtue of the ineluctable law ordaining that one can only imagine what is absent] (IV, 450–51)—for as Lacan theorized, the very essence of desire is precisely not to be satisfied (1966, 277). We need to ask, then, whether the narrator would indeed *want* to imprison the past in metaphor and risk destroying that charm, for, as Proust had read in Ruskin,

> If the imagination is called to take delight in any object, it will not always be well, if we can help it, to put the *real* object there, before it. The imagination would on the whole rather have it *not* there;—the reality and the substance are rather in the imagination's way: it would think a good deal more of the thing if it could not see it. Hence that strange and sometimes fatal charm, which there is in all things as long as we wait for them, and the moment we have lost them; but which fades while we possess them. (Ruskin V: 181–82; quoted in Macksey 1987, xxxvi)

An indication of residual reluctances and ambivalence is suggested in the notion of possession and "capture" inhabiting a crucial image proclaiming Marcel's intention to write, an image that betrays the uncertainty with which he views the whole project. The triumphant claim is that "style," writing, will capture the past in its "necessary rings" (IV, 468)—certainly a fixed and deadening image, one evoking, as Ellison (9–10) and Doubrovsky (72) point out, the "necessary rings" of chain links and imprisonment figured in the brothel whipping of Charlus "enchaîné sur un lit comme Prométhée sur son rocher" [enchained upon a bed like Prometheus upon his rock] (IV, 394). The chain links recur as an even more fixed, eternal binding in the narrator's description of metaphor as a "rapport unique que l'écrivain doit retrouver pour en enchaîner à jamais dans sa phrase les deux termes différents" [unique connection which the writer must rediscover in order to link forever in his phrase the two different terms] (IV, 468). And an earlier version renders the chain image not only semantically, through the verb "enchaîner," but in an even more vivid depiction of viselike capture of the two terms by the writer, who "les enchaînera *par le lien indestructible d'une alliance de mots*" [will enchain them with the indestructible link of an alliance of words] (IV, 1265; quoted in Roloff 287; my emphasis).

Could this, then, be the insidious price of capturing the past in the "chains" of metaphor, which, as stylistic technique, alone would render "une sorte d'éternité au style," an eternity at the price of imprisonment? Further ambiguities are suggested in an obverse of the chain image, an image of liberation, where the narrator would like to capture past moments in the "necessary rings" of metaphor in order to

free them from time: "pour les soustraire aux contingences du temps."
Following that resolve, however, he comes upon Odette, whose apparent immunity to time has fixed and immobilized her as "une rose
stérilisée" (IV, 528). How will freeing his past from the "contingencies
of time" avoid fixing it in similarly deadening, stifling images? Freedom from time's contingencies through "sterilization" would only
seem a second bondage, following the "chains" of metaphor in a sort
of double-bind: the chaining in metaphor so as to imprison yet further in sterilization. We are led to wonder whether such "freedom
from the contingencies of time" is indeed so desirable a state for
the the narrator's past. The whole apparatus of involuntary memory depends precisely upon those contingencies thrown up whimsi-
cally by time, the chance coincidence of imagination and sensation,
past and present; but the "necessary rings" of metaphor would seem
to deaden the spontaneous coincidence that empowers involuntary
memory. Would the narrator really want to inflict upon his past the
"eternal" fetters and punishment of what he calls freedom, which is
to say capture in metaphor? Or would the effort of his narration precisely be to *distance* and preserve his past from such bondage?

Such curious, ambiguous images in the final pages suggest a need
to look again at the behavior of figuration in Marcel's narration, asking whether it might not act so much to capture the past as to keep
the past from capture, from the "sterilization" that is Odette's fate.
Figuration might ward off such capture by foreclosing the fixedness
of interpretation, allowing experience to remain unconfined, at large.
Metaphoric "chains," rather than binding experience within interpretation, may precisely work to exclude it, to keep interpretation from
domesticating experience, providing thereby traces of a reluctance to
capture the past in writing. This curious use of image in Proust—not
as a mimetic device to render an outside, deeper meaning or reality,
but, rather, precisely to refuse the assignment and fixedness, or fet-
tering, of meaning—is at work not only on the mimetic level, under-
mining the representation of a putative outside world, but on the
textual, or self-representational level as well. Proustian figuration
would then be a sophisticated device that fractures the textual web
and immobilizes textual movement—and this within the representational forms of a mimetic fiction. Instead of understanding figuration
as a failed effort at totalization, we might read it as precisely an attack
on the narrative's confining esthetic and intellectual domination. What
has been read as the failure of totalization might thus instead be understood as the successful resistance to its appropriations.

Discussions of the Proustian image have noticed the mimetic breakdown or explosion it operates. Kamber and Macksey point to a certain

use of "negative metaphor," an anti-mimetic "vertiginous dissolving of appearances" (882) in favor of a deeper capture by the imagination—as in the renowned *Combray* claim that the "obscure coolness" of the narrator's room allows him more fully to apprehend "the total spectacle of summer." It was through this sort of "contradiction in sensorial logic," these critics claim, that "Proust found the distance necessary to embrace his subject" (883). Other analyses, however, cite such mimetic breakdowns to argue instead for the failure of the narrator's totalizing intentions. Genette mentions the anguish of the narrator's effort, as he runs from side to side in the little train to Balbec, to unite in "une vue totale et un tableau continu" [a unified view and continuous tableau] (II, 16) the conflicting scenes on each side of the car, the nocturnal starry sky, and the luminous countryside at dawn. Arguing for an effect of "phantasmagorical over-impression" in which "les profondeurs s'entredévorent" [depths devour themselves] (1972, 52), Genette implies that depth is flattened, negated, disputed by conflicting images.

A similar "fantasmagorie" is cited by Ellison to question the representational function of figure. The disruptiveness of such conflicting images is apparent in the "Soirée Sainte-Euverte" episode, when a footman's tangled hair has the simultaneous appearance "d'un paquet d'algues, d'une nichée de colombes, d'un bandeau de jacinthes et d'une torsade de serpents" [of a bunch of seaweed, a brood of fledgling doves, a bed of hyacinths, and a coil of serpents] (I, 319). Ellison points to the stylistic accumulation of such impossible simultaneity, arguing that "rather than clarifying the description of characters, the similes and metaphors superpose separate, disjunct levels that dispute the same place, the same instant of duration" (16). Suggesting the "challenge" to "interpretive activity" of such accumulation, Ellison implies that the text in such cases no longer functions mimetically to describe a fictive evening at the Marquise de Sainte-Euverte's but is "self-representational" in its insistent reference to its own stylistic technique. Ellison's discussion draws theoretical support from Ricardou's distinction between ornamental metaphor, used to illustrate and thus further the purposes of representation, and "ordinal" metaphor: a metaphor that attacks representation by "dissolving" spatial and temporal categories. "Ordinal" metaphor, rather than serving the purposes of representation, invades the narrative to reroute its direction. Such use of "ordinal" metaphor makes the *Recherche* "une parfaite machine à subvertir la représentation" [a perfect machine to subvert representation], pointing instead to its own mechanisms, or "auto-représentation" (Ricardou 97, quoted in Ellison 4). This claim will be repeated by Lang's argument for the Proustian text as "humorous" and postmodern in its self-referential privileging of "the logic of the signifier . . . over the logic of the signified" (159).

The interpretive challenge posed by such "stylistic accumulation" deserves further scrutiny, however. These critical suggestions that the text ruptures the mimetic illusion to draw attention to its own operations are haunted by a certain "return of the repressed"; representation, understood as the claim to mimetic reflection, is banished only to return in the form of textual *self*-representation. But a text that disputes mimetic representation would necessarily invite suspicion of the way it negotiates representation at any level, including, or perhaps particularly, representation of its own mechanisms. Remembering that "text" from the Latin "textus" suggests the woven, interconnected surface of a web, we might ask whether such very interconnectedness is not disputed by a certain use of image. The connecting work of interpretation itself may well be the "text" that the *Recherche* confounds, the linking and crisscrossing of the same and the different. Interconnectedness engages time, for it is recurrence, repetition; but the Proustian image seems to work to overtake time, to frustrate, to impede, and to throttle it, flattening it to a single timeless screen-image in which all duration is denied. While Ricardou argues for the "ordinal" metaphor's redirecting of textual direction, Proustian figuration functions even more subversively in blocking, immobilizing, and suspending temporality itself, the very trajectory of interpretation.[1]

An investigation of figuration not as the capture and "sterilization" of the narrator's past, but as the rupture and blockage of precisely interpretation's appropriating efforts, might begin by noticing, with Benjamin, that what the narrator calls involuntary memory is "closer to forgetting than what is usually called memory" (202). The world must be forgotten in order to be reconfigured in the images produced by the involuntary memory. But this is not a return or recapture so much as it is the creation of a simulacrum, of a collection of images and figures of the world. It is not a return to the world so much as a turn to the *image* of the world: a turn away, as Flieger puts it, from the daily contiguity of discursive thought, to the figures of "nightliness," of a poetic absent-mindedness or forgetfulness which, rather than memory, "performs the work of figuration" (69). Thus the "moment bienheureux" [privileged moment] in Proust is marked by a lapse of attention, permitting "a somnolence which favors intrusion of dream material" (74). Such dreamlike forgetfulness, while it offers perhaps too mild an account of the power and coercion of involuntary memory and the way it "forces" our nostrils to breathe the air of a different time, does, however, begin to suggest what may be at work in Proustian figuration—a displacement or substitution of experience in favor of image. But this displacement would not be the lapse or mere omission brought about by forgetfulness or dreaminess, but a deliberately strategic rhetorical move whereby figuration, rather than locking in experience, effectively locks out the aggressions of interpretation.

The disruptive power of figuration in the *Recherche* and its more decisive refusal of the "mimetic" world than that suggested by mere forgetfulness is evoked in an early image *of* images.[2] Significantly, the first memory of Combray to be recounted after the waking "images tournoyantes et confuses" [shifting and confused images] is that of the magic lantern and its "surnaturelles apparitions multicolores" [supernatural and multicolored apparitions] (I, 9). The lantern's images, projected on the topography of curtain folds, take on the contours of that topography. "Je distinguais le cheval de Golo," says the narrator, "qui continuait à s'avancer sur les rideaux de la fenêtre, se bombant de leurs plis, descendant dans leurs fentes" [I distinguished Golo's horse advancing across the window curtains, swelling out with their curves and descending into their folds]. But as the passage continues, the reverse seems to happen. Rather than being shaped and rounded by the curtains' folds, the images seem to take into themselves, to "interiorize," the depths of materiality. "Le corps de Golo lui-même . . . s'arrangeait de tout obstacle matériel, de tout objet gênant qu'il rencontrait en le prenant comme ossature et en se le rendant intérieur" [The body of Golo himself . . . accommodated every material obstacle, every bothersome object in his path, by taking it as a skeletal structure and incorporating it]. This interiorized topography is then flattened to the same plane as the projected image: "fût-ce le bouton de la porte sur lequel s'adaptait aussitôt et surnageait invinciblement sa robe rouge ou sa figure pâle" [even the door-handle, over which, adapting immediately, his red cloak or his pale face invincibly floated] (I, 10).

The topography of surface is smoothly converted to a screen for the lantern's images, which, rather than being shaped and given relief by material contour, absorb and flatten *as* image all depth and contour. Depth and thickness are flattened to become surface, screen supporting shimmering image as Golo floats ("surnageait") atop the doorknob. From an initial claim for the shaping and contouring of image by topography—the folds and clefts of curtains and doorknob "emulated" by Golo—the passage concludes with a certain shift in which topography, no longer interiorized, is flattened to prop, screen. The image, having initially been produced and plied, shaped, by the world—as Golo is given skeletal structure by protruding material "obstacles"—seems subsequently to float "invincibly" atop topography, against topography as surface, support, rather than as infrastructure.

The image thus spreads itself out across the world, refusing to accommodate its contours; instead, the image stands against the roughness of depth, opacity, and experience.

The implications of this early image of images are significant, for the "magic lantern" scene has frequently been read as "imaging" forth the narrator's desiring imagination with its appropriations of the world. Arguing that the magic lantern "function" of projection is "the key to the whole system of desire, of possession, of the self's absorption of its prey, endlessly repeated in the Proustian narrative," Riffaterre, for instance, understands projection as leading to absorption by the imagination, a reading indeed suggested by the first part of the Golo passage (1988, 453). But the passage goes on to overturn this model of imaginative absorption, suggesting by the end that the projections of the imagination somehow hold off the world, distancing rather than absorbing it, turning against experience rather than incorporating it.

Further in *Combray*, the "clochers de Martinville" passage again suggests a use of image not to absorb, "comprehend," or somehow interiorize experience, but to refuse it. Admiring the movements of the three Martinville and Vieuxvicq steeples from Dr. Percepied's carriage, Marcel produces a written page of sporadic images.[3] Emphasized in his description is the irregularity of the steeples' intermittent motionlessness and jolts. Initially, he writes, only the two Martinville steeples are visible; then, belatedly, the "clocher retardataire" [dilatory steeple] of Vieuxvicq joins them "par une volte hardie" [with a bold leap]. The steeples hold their positions in resistance to the carriage's speed ("Nous allions vite et pourtant les trois clochers étaient posés sur la plaine, immobiles" [We were traveling fast, and yet the three steeples were perched on the plain, motionless]); the Vieuxvicq steeple then moves away while the Martinville steeples inexplicably remain. The length of time it has taken to approach them makes the young hero think of the time still needed to reach them when "tout d'un coup, la voiture ayant tourné, elle nous déposa à leurs pieds" [all of a sudden, the carriage turned a corner and deposited us at their feet]. The steeples have precipitously flung themselves in the carriage's path ("ils s'étaient jetés si rudement au-devant d'elle, qu'on n'eut que le temps d'arrêter pour ne pas se heurter au porche") [they had flung themselves so abruptly in our path that we had just time to stop before bumping into the porch] (I, 179). The carriage moves on, writes Marcel, the village disappears, but the steeples remain on the horizon. One disappears, the others remain "un instant encore" and they all vanish, only to reappear yet again. The precipitous speed of the carriage ("nous nous éloignions au galop") [we drew away at a gallop] continues to be opposed by the steeples, who "timidly" seek their places in halting, "awkward, stumbling movements" of hesitant collisions and alignments until they finally become "une seule forme noire" [a single dusky shape] and disappear.

In Marcel's description, the steady trajectory of the carriage is thus opposed by the erratic, irregular, belated or precipitous movements of the steeples, their occasional motionlessness as unexpected as their abrupt, premature leaps: a refusal of the metonymic spatial slippage of observation rendered by the young writing hero as a succession of fragmented, disjointed images. The first comparison likens the steeples to "trois oiseaux posés sur la plaine, immobiles" [three birds perched on the plain, motionless]; they next become "trois pivots d'or" [three golden pivots], and then "trois fleurs peintes sur le ciel au-des- sus de la ligne basse des champs" [three flowers painted upon the sky above the low line of the fields]; finally, the steeples are "trois jeunes filles d'une légende, abandonnées dans une solitude où tombait déjà l'obscurité" [three maidens in a legend, abandoned to a solitude in which night was already falling] (I, 179). Each image thus negates and replaces the preceding in a fractured, disjointed succession whose rup- ture of all progression has escaped critical attention.[4] Interestingly, there is no continuity here, no approach-and-retreat progression or development; rather, a series of disjointed, unrelated images arrests and fixes the steeples in immobilized "stills" that fracture the narra- tor's moving perspective from the carriage. The effect of the images is thus to fix the spectacle: "immobiles," "pivots," "trois fleurs *peintes*," "trois jeunes filles d'une *légende*." Reference to the shifting, evolving world of experience is patently refused here; nor can it be said that the text is self-referential, since the "web" of textuality is sundered anew with each conflicting, unrelated image. Incoherent, flagrantly unlikely images of fixedness and immobility are here imposed—"pro- jected"—upon a moving, evolving world. Both referential and textual time—that is, progression—are cancelled by images that patently re- fuse temporal development. Within the very material of writing, sig- nifiers as chain—as progression—are denied in favor of image.

In the young hero's page on the "clochers de Martinville," a text is advertised as text, showcased as his first attempt at writing. Through figuration, however, Marcel's text actually fractures the experience it purports to describe. For, curiously, what originally seems to provoke Marcel's "plaisir spécial" is not the fractured effect evoked by his ac- count; instead, an altogether different experience, a fluid, continuous movement, is subtly implied. It is the observation of "le *déplacement* de leurs lignes" that makes him feel that "quelque chose était derrière ce *mouvement*" [something lay behind that movement]; and he indicates significantly, "J'avais envie de garder en réserve dans ma tête ces lignes *remuantes* au soleil" [I wanted to store away in my mind these lines stirring in the sunlight] (I, 178). Why should the rendering of a fluid, moving impression in fixed "stills" then produce the young writer's pleasure? Why would the formulation into words, the fixing and immobilizing of an impression of fluidity and movement, so increase the narrator's joy?

The answer may lie in the preceding page, where a distance is maintained between image and experience when the narrator refers to his habit of turning aside from an impression, of protecting it somehow from the aggressions of his attention. He calls the impression "cette chose inconnue" [this unknown thing] protected precisely by a screen or covering, a "clothing," of images—"protégée par le revêtement d'images sous lesquelles je la trouverais vivante" [protected by the clothing of images beneath which I would find it still alive] (I, 178). This protective distance shields the impression, continues the narrator, "comme les poissons que les jours où on m'avait laissé aller à la pêche, je rapportais dans mon panier couverts par une couche d'herbe qui préservait leur fraîcheur" [like the fish which, on days when I had been allowed to go out fishing, I used to carry back in my basket, covered by a layer of grass keeping them cool and fresh] (I, 178). While the narrator offers his recourse to this "revêtement d'images" as a failure of will, a reluctance to penetrate the truth contained in the impression—"la réalité pressentie que je n'ai pas eu assez de volonté pour arriver à découvrir" [the reality I once sensed, but never had the strength of will to bring to light] (I, 177)—we have now learned to read his stated claims with more suspicion. In this surprising passage, figuration–rather than being produced and shaped by experience in order to convey it—acts as a "covering" to preserve the cool, fresh "unknown" of an impression. Rather than the "setting before the eyes" Aristotle claimed for metaphor, its sudden revelation of truth, figuration seems here to work to hide, distance, and protect the world it claims to represent. Virtually antimimetic images thus seem to distance the world by forestalling the progressive temporality of experience, and of interpretation; a "revêtement d'images" would seem to act as a protective screen against interpretation's aggressions.

The sundered textuality implied by the "clochers de Martinville" page—a ruptured signifying chain in favor of a succession of powerfully hallucinatory images—is suggested in Jameson's discussion of the peculiarly "schizophrenic" postmodern condition. Jameson points to the "monstrously" material and glowing, nearly hallucinatory schizophrenic experience of the world, and, drawing on Lacan's understanding of schizophrenia as essentially a language disorder, suggests that the schizophrenic condition is the breakdown of "the relation-ship between signifiers." This breakdown of language, of linkage and threading, then produces the breakdown of time and of the ability to negotiate one's way through past, present, and future—a collapse in ability to order a temporal itinerary, a direction. "It is because lan-guage has a past and a future," claims Jameson, "because the sentence moves in time, that we can have what seems to us a concrete or lived experience of time" (1983, 119). With the dimension of past and fu-ture collapsed, the schizophrenic is stranded in a world of monstrous, perpetual presents, each "overwhelmingly vivid and 'material,'" "glow-ing with hallucinatory energy." In this analysis of schizophrenia, the world becomes an immense, monstrous screen supporting a fractured succession of images, each displacing and erasing the preceding, each a universalized present. The image as screen suggests, then, a mo-mentary hegemony; the screen image is the only image, admitting of no other, displacing all past and future. The emergence of the hal-lucinatory, fractured, schizophrenic image seems, in Jameson's dis-cussion, to be produced by the collapse of an ability to order signifiers in time. But this linguistic collapse would seem to be part of a more general deterioration in ordering capacity, in the ability to thread one's way through experience—to devise not only temporal itinerar-ies, but to order one's way among categories and generalizations. This collapse would seem, then, more generally to be a collapse of inter-pretation, with each successive present monstrous and hegemonic, unconfined by the webbing of interpretive context and ordering.

Drawing on this connection linking the emergence of image to the breakdown of interpretation, we notice a similiar configuration in-volving the cancellation of temporal continuity in favor of figuration in further passages in Proust. Here such a configuration seems to oc-cur not only with a succession of disjointed images, but even in the context of *sustained* metaphor, eventually producing an arrest and foreclosure of the evolving temporality of interpretation. Three epi-sodes, the extended comparison of the Opéra to a marine cave in *Le côté de Guermantes*, the "première apparition" of the little band at Bal-bec, and the Charlus/Jupien encounter opening *Sodome et Gomorrhe*, suggest a breakdown of the signifying movement under the emer-gence of image.

The Opéra-marine cave comparison is initiated when a sudden "pas-sage éventuel vers un monde nouveau" [a potential passage into a new world] (II, 338) interrupts the vulgarity, says the narrator, of his every-day life. The passage describes the corridor as "humide et lézardé" [moist and fissured]; the Guermantes and their guests are the white goddesses and bearded tritons of "ces sombres séjours" [these sombre

abodes]. Critics have argued that the comparison is generated not by efforts of representation, but, in a turn away from worldly experience, motivated by the cliché, or sleeping metaphor, of "baignoire" [bathtub] for "loge" [box]. Lang, for instance, suggests not that the scene inspires the metaphor, but that the metaphor produces the scene by creating semantic needs demanding particular images; the text remains enclosed within itself, its references and figuration generated by the signifier "baignoire." Thus the pearls—marine jewels—worn by the Princesse de Guermantes and the bald pates likened to "galets" [pebbles] in the audience are derived from the (marine) needs of the metaphor (Lang 164). Such an argument, however, is based upon perhaps too ready an analogy between "baignoire" and "grotte marine." Genette, in fact, points to the very tenuousness of their connection; in his claim, the profusion of points of resemblance *appears* to create a relationship—"l'illusion d'une continuité, et donc d'une proximité, entre comparant et comparé" [the illusion of a continuity, and thus of a proximity, between the "comparing" and the "compared"]—between the marine cave and the Opéra. Suggesting that the metaphor thus justifies itself through its very proliferation, Genette argues that this, more than any "motivated" connection, serves to bind the marine cave and the Opéra in an apparently "natural" relationship.

But the metaphor's textual mass, rather than binding it to the diegetic Opéra, places the "comparant" in dangerous competition with the "comparé." The very profusion of metaphoric detail produces an excess that eventually overwhelms, immobilizes, and ruptures the "continuité" between "comparant" and "comparé." At one point in this "production," the marine metaphor, suggests Ellison, receives new energy from a literal prop, the Princesse's crown of pearls and white seashells, "mosaïque marine à peine sortie des vagues" [a marine mosaic newly emerged from the waves] (II, 41)]. But this literal intrusion of the marine cave in the Opéra—the seashell crown—also names the instant at which figuration's excesses rupture their confines as description and begin to usurp the world described. Representation invades and disrupts not only the level of story, but of text, as the passage indicates in its closing lines. Temporality *and* textuality as slippage, deferral, and difference are finally halted in the explicit "immobilisation" of

un panorama éphémère que les morts, les scandales, les maladies, les brouilles modifieraient bientôt, mais qui, en ce moment était immobilisé par l'attention, la chaleur, le vertige, la poussière, l'élégance et l'ennui dans [une] espèce d'instant éternel et tragique d'inconsciente attente et de calme engourdissement. (II, 354)

an ephemeral panorama which deaths, scandals, illnesses, quarrels would soon alter, but which was now immobilized by attentiveness, heat, dizziness, dust, elegance, and boredom, in [a] sort of eternal and tragic instant of unconscious expectancy and calm torpor.

The very weight of the extended comparison would seem to have brought the text to immobility, arresting all textual movement and energy; textual slippage is suspended, fixed in a "panorama." From such an immobilized point, any resumption of the narration seems equally arbitrary, unmotivated; we are at a loss as to what to expect next—whether this "panorama" is a device to close the episode, or merely a passing scene. This "suspended" instant suggests a rupture that subverts narrative progression, throttling narrative momentum, which then can only pick itself up and begin again almost at random. The "engourdissement" of this "panorama" is the text's own, run aground by the weight of figuration.

A further demonstration of the interruption and immobilization wrought by figuration upon narrative occurs in the narrator's description of his initial encounter with the "little band" of girls at Balbec. Marcel's appreciation grows as the "vision" resists assimilation by the mind's interpretive "narrative." The fragmented collection of features is an "ensemble merveilleux" precisely because of its resistance to the organizing effort of the intelligence. It is "confus comme une musique" [confused as a piece of music], says the narrator, "où je n'aurais pas su isoler et reconnaître au moment de leur passage les phrases" [in which I would not have been able to isolate and recognize at the moment of their passage the different phrases] (II, 148). The text specifically relates the group's beauty to its very refusal to be domesticated by the "démarcations" his mind will soon impose upon what momentarily remains a resistant "vision," "fluide, collective et mobile" (II, 148).

As if to oppose the appropriative work of interpretation, the text produces a disjointed series of images. The girls are "nobles et calmes . . . statues exposées au soleil sur un rivage de la Grèce" [noble and calm . . . statues exposed to the sunlight on a Grecian shore]; "une lumineuse comète"; their passage along the boardwalk is like that of "une machine qui eût été lâchée et dont il ne fallait pas attendre qu'elle évitait les piétons" [a machine which might have been released and which could not be expected to avoid pedestrians]; their movements are compared to Chopin's most melancholic phrases, where a "marche lente" [slow walk] is embellished with "gracieux détours où le caprice se mêle à la virtuosité" [graceful deviations in which caprice mingles with virtuosity]. The bird image recurs, as if to erase the intervening comparisons; the girls are likened to "un conciliabule d'oiseaux qui s'assemblent au moment de s'envoler" [a conglomeration of birds assembling at the moment they take flight] (II, 150).

Interpretation, however, has set in, and Marcel formulates a hypothesis: the girls must be "les très jeunes maîtresses de coureurs cyclistes" [the very young mistresses of professional cyclists] (II, 151). In conclusive tones, he announces a definitive evaluation: "En tous cas, dans aucune de mes suppositions, ne figuraient celle qu'elles eussent pu être vertueuses" [In any event, in none of my suppositions did the possibility of their being virtuous figure]. Subsequent images seem initially to cooperate with this conclusion of "nonvirtuousness," as when the hero's glance crosses that of "une petite péri, plus séduisante pour moi que celle du paradis persan" [a little Peri, more seductive to me than any from a Persian paradise]. Unaccountably, however, the unlikeliest image of all recurs. Earlier, the girls were likened to "noble" Greek statues, a comparison that refused to coincide with their "dandinement de hanches si dégingandé" [such an unabashed swing of the hips], their "termes d'argot si voyous et criés si fort" [such guttersnipe slang terms, and shouted as such volume]. Impossibly, however, the austere Greek-statue image recurs; they are "divines processionaires" of a "frise attique ou quelque fresque figurant un cortège" [some Attic frieze or a fresco representing a procession] (II, 153). The young hero, however, has long since concluded that the girls cannot possibly be "virtuous," and the direct reversal posed by this metaphoric vision of Greek virgins would seem to disturb and unravel his "intellectual" supposition.

The interpretive, appropriative work of the mind is confounded by a persistently impossible image, and this explosion of the assimilative enterprise, the mind's efforts to "know," allows the narrator to continue to make claims for the little band's "inaccessibility," its "unknownness": "Je n'avais rien vu d'aussi beau, imprégné d'autant d'inconnu, aussi inestimablement précieux, aussi vraisemblablement inaccessible" [I had never seen anything so beautiful, impregnated with so much that was unknown, so inestimably precious, so apparently inaccessible] (II, 155). An initial vision is rendered again and again in a series of unrelated images, culminating as the "vision" slows almost to "immobility." Although it is merely "un extrait de la fuite innombrable de passantes" [an excerpt from the endless flight of passing women] that has excited his imagination and desire, says the narrator, "cette fuite était ici ramenée à un mouvement tellement lent qu'il se rapprochait de l'immobilité" [that flight was here reduced to so slow a movement as to approach immobility] (II, 154). Again, figuration seems not so much to convey the world as explicitly to oppose that world, overturning referentiality; worldly experience is made to serve as screen, prop, support for pure image.

The "immobilization" of narrative progression and interpretation is configured in the closing image of the episode, in curiously precise, elaborate detail. The narrator, "avec une satisfaction de botaniste," draws the sort of esthetic conclusion rendered possible by the recurring and flagrantly improbable Greek-virgin image: "Il n'était pas possible de trouver réunies des espèces plus rares que celles de ces jeunes fleurs" [It was not possible to find gathered together rarer varieties than these young flowers] (II, 156). This comparison of the girls to "jeunes fleurs" is strangely extended in a long dependent clause:

Entre lesquelles tient tout le trajet de l'océan parcouru par quelque steamer, si lent à glisser sur le trait horizontal et bleu qui va d'une tige à l'autre, qu'un papillon parasseux, attardé au fond de la corolle que la coque du navire a depuis longtemps dépassée, peut pour s'envoler en étant sûr d'arriver avant le vaisseau, attendre que rien qu'une seule parcelle azurée sépare encore la proue de celui-ci du premier pétale de la fleur vers laquelle il navigue. (II, 156)

Between whose blooms is suspended the whole tract of ocean crossed by some steamer, so slow in slipping along the blue, horizontal line that stretches from one stem to the next that a lazy butterfly, dawdling in the cup of a flower which the ship's hull has long since passed, can wait, before flying off in time to arrive before it, until nothing but the tiniest speck of blue still separates the prow from the first petal of the flower toward which it navigates.

In this passage, the text images the overtaking of interpretation by figuration, configuring what the text has just enacted: the arresting and overturning of interpretation's linear, time-bound appropriative effort by the whimsy, capriciousness, and unpredictability of the image, whose movements are as erratic as those of the butterfly.[5] Curiously here, the image's status *as* image is advertised in an explicit flattening of dimension: the far-away horizon of the steamer's trajectory pasted to the same plane as the nearness of rose and butterfly, in a direct race between steamer and butterfly to the same petal.[6] Dimensionality, depth, is collapsed in a final arrested image *of* an image. Much later, the same flattened image of an image recurs

Je me rappelais Albertine d'abord devant la plage, presque peinte sur le fond de la mer, n'ayant pas pour moi une existence plus réelle que ces visions de théâtre où on ne sait pas si on a affaire à l'actrice qui est censée apparaître, à une figurante qui la double ou à une simple projection. (II, 656)

I remembered Albertine first of all on the beach, almost painted against the backdrop of sea, having for me no more real an existence than those theatrical tableaux in which one does not know whether one is looking at the actress herself who is supposed to appear, at an understudy taking her part, or at a simple projection.

The image is finally a "simple projection," effacing the world itself of Albertine and the sea, just as the magic lantern's "projections" refused the world in flattening it to mere surface. Similarly, the first chapter of part 2 of *Sodome et Gomorrhe* closes upon just such a flattened plane in which horizon is pasted to the same dimension as foreground; noticing the apple trees in bloom, "les pieds dans la boue et en toilette de bal" [their feet in the mire, and in ball-dresses], Marcel goes on to observe that "l'horizon lointain de la mer fournissait aux pommiers comme un arrière-plan d'estampe japonaise" [the distant horizon of the sea gave the trees the sort of background of a Japanese print] (III, 177).

The image as a disrupting mechanism forcing open the closure of desire's appropriations, arresting and overturning time, is also at work in the first chapter of *Sodome et Gomorrhe* where the homosexual encounter of the Baron de Charlus and Jupien is "imaged" in the fertilization of an orchid by a bee: an extended figure that subtends the encounter in apparent support, but that finally breaches its containment as image to invade and overturn the narrative proper. The episode opens in the irregular mode of postponement, deferral; according to the logic of the narrator's "story," it should have been recounted in *Le côté de Guermantes*, occuring as it does while Marcel watches their courtyard for the Guermantes's return. At the appropriate moment in the "story," however, the narrator merely notes the importance of an episode he chooses to recount later; "Or cette attente sur l'escalier devait avoir pour moi des conséquences si considérables . . . qu'il est préférable d'en retarder le récit de quelques instants" [Now this wait on the staircase was to have for me consequences so considerable . . . that it is preferable to postpone the account of it for a few moments] (II, 861). The episode is thus deferred in the narrative until the narrator is able to give it the "extension" it demands—for, he says, it is "une découverte . . . si importante en elle-même que j'ai jusqu'ici, jusqu'au moment de pouvoir lui donner la place et l'étendue voulues, différé de la rapporter" [a discovery . . . so important in and of itself that I have until now, until the moment I could give it the prominence and development it deserves, postponed giving an account of it] (III, 3). The ambivalence of this deferral, signaled by the narrator's indication of its importance even as he postpones it, is repeated by the main botanical image, which apparently supports the homosexual "conjonction" but in fact contests and over-turns it.

From his post on the stairway, Marcel watches for the Guermantes's return, noticing, with "la contemplation du botaniste," a courtyard orchid awaiting fertilization—and wondering "si l'insecte improbable viendrait, par un hasard providentiel, visiter le pistil offert et délaissé" [whether the unlikely insect would come, by providential fortune, to visit the offered and neglected pistil] (III, 4). Observing Charlus and Jupien in the courtyard, he resolves not to be distracted from "l'arri-vée presque impossible à espérer . . . de l'insecte envoyé de si loin en ambassadeur à la vierge qui depuis si longtemps prolongeait son at-tente" [the arrival, almost beyond the possibility of hope . . . of the insect sent from so far away as ambassador to the virgin whose wait had lengthened into so long a time] (III, 4). Noticing, however, that the baron and Jupien are now face to face in the courtyard, Marcel's attention begins to shift, carrying with it the bee-orchid image now reduced to the supporting status of analogy. Jupien suddenly seems, before the baron, "enraciné comme une plante" [rooted as a plant] and "prenait des poses avec la coquetterie qu'aurait pu avoir l'orchi-dée pour le bourdon providentiellement survenu" [struck poses with the coquetry that the orchid might have adopted upon the provi-dential appearance of the bee] (III, 6). Jupien leaves the courtyard, pursued by Charlus, who follows him at the same instant a real bee enters—having ruptured its metaphoric status to invade not only the courtyard but the "histoire": "Au même instant où M. de Charlus avait passé la porte en sifflant comme un gros bourdon, un autre, un vrai, celui-là, entrait dans la cour" [At the same instant as M. de Charlus passed through the gate humming like a great bumble-bee, another, a real one this time, flew into the courtyard] (III, 8). Intriguingly, the bee enters as the baron exits into the street in pursuit of Jupien, in a chiasmus or criss-crossing of action that inaugurates the opposition brought now into the diegetic space. Jupien and Charlus return, and as the door of Jupien's shop closes upon them, the hero simultane-ously loses sight of the bee, saying "Je ne savais pas s'il était l'insecte qu'il fallait à l'orchidée, mais je ne doutais pas, pour un insecte très rare et une fleur captive, de la possibilité miraculeuse de se con-joindre" [I did not know whether he was the insect needed by the orchid, but I had no longer any doubt, in the case of a very rare in-sect and a captive flower, of the miraculous possibility of their con-junction] (III,9).

Marcel here pursues a meditation inspired by the comparison: the overlapping of "certaines lois de la botanique et ce qu'on appelle par-fois fort mal 'Homosexualité'" [certain botanical laws and what on occasion is quite inappropriately termed "Homosexuality"]. In the case of both botany and homosexuality, he concludes, sexual gratification depends upon "la coincidence de trop de conditions et trop difficiles à rencontrer" [the coincidence of too many conditions, and of conditions too difficult to meet] (III, 28).

Marcel then realizes that, his attention usurped by Charlus and Jupien, he has neglected to notice whether the bee brought the long-awaited pollen, but observes that he has just witnessed a similar sort of "miracle." As a "botaniste moral," the narrator has just observed Jupien "tourner autour de M. de Charlus comme l'orchidée faire des avances au bourdon" [circling round M. de Charlus like the orchid making overtures to the bumble-bee] (III, 32); and the episode closes with a final explicit parallel equating "la conjonction Jupien-Charlus" with the fertilization of the orchid by the bee (III, 33). But the orchid-bee image carries on simultaneous activity of its own, appearing to sustain and support that of the baron and Jupien while, in fact, acquiring such independence as to become an explicitly disruptive episode. The narrator frequently refers to the rivalry that develops between the two "foyers" of activity; observing Jupien and Charlus in the courtyard, he resolves, he says, "de ne plus me déranger de peur de manquer . . . l'arrivée . . . de l'insecte envoyé de si loin" [not to let myself be disturbed for fear of missing . . . the arrival . . . of the insect sent from so far away]. Yet the homosexual encounter so absorbs his attention that he forgets to watch the bee; "Mais je fus distrait de suivre les ébats de l'insecte, car au bout de quelques minutes, sollicitant davantage mon attention, Jupien . . . revint" [But I was distracted from following the frolicking of the insect, for, a few minutes later, engaging my attention more insistantly, Jupien . . . returned] (III, 8). Initially fastened on the hoped-for arrival of a bee, Marcel's attention shifts so definitively to Charlus and Jupien that the episode closes with the remark, "J'étais désolé d'avoir, par attention à la conjonction Jupien-Charlus, manqué peut-être de voir la fécondation de la fleur par le bourdon" [I was distressed to find that, out of attention to the Jupien-Charlus conjunction, I had perhaps missed seeing the fertilization of the blossom by the bumble-bee] (III, 33). Here, critical claims for the "concomitance" of the two encounters (Genette) are overturned by the narrator's mystified, uncertain "perhaps"; the fertilization of the orchid by the bee has perhaps and perhaps not taken place.

The tensions produced between the two "conjunctions," which explicitly vie for the hero's attention and between which he is explicitly obliged to choose, suggest that figuration here no longer supports narrative purposes, but ruptures the narrative surface to grow into a rival narrative of its own—to the point that the episode's closing sentence is, instead, a sentence of non-closure. The "conjunction" of the Baron and Jupien is complete; the general lines of their future are even suggested—"Il rendit la place de Jupien de plus en plus lucrative jusqu'à ce qu'il le prît définitivement comme secrétaire et l'établît dans les conditions que nous verrons plus tard" [He made Jupien's position more and more lucrative, until he finally engaged him as secretary and established him in the situation in which we shall see him later on] (II, 31). But such closure is overturned when the image forces narrative back upon itself, pointing to the unknown, blank spot of what did or did not happen, in the narrator's expression of regret at having missed—"peut-être"—the fertilization of the orchid by the bee. Originally read as one of Ricardou's docile ornamental metaphors, the figure becomes more subversive even than Ricardou's "ordinal" metaphor. It not only "reorders" and reroutes the narrative, but confounds, stalls, and suspends it, pointing insistently to the unknown of a gap eternally enigmatic.

We are thus in a position to take issue with such claims as Genette's "la description, chez Proust, se résorbe en narration . . . est tout sauf une pause du récit" [description, in Proust, is absorbed by narration . . . is anything but a pause in the narrative] (1972, 138). Description as image is precisely a "pause du récit," in fact, an immobilization and overturning of the narrative's energies, invading the narrative to set up a rival narrative of its own. While this is a far more visible maneuver in the "nouveaux romanciers" and particularly the post-1970 "nouveau nouveau roman," the putative absence of such subversive behavior in the *Recherche* is often cited to separate Proust from postmodernist writers. McHale's discussion of Proust's marine cave and orchid pollinization, for instance, suggests that Proust is merely a "precursor" in his use of such subversive, or what Ricardou would call "ordinal," figuration. "Of course," writes McHale, "Proust is careful to 'ground' his hypertrophied metaphorical developments, motivating them at every point to prevent his reader from mistaking the 'minor' world of the metaphor for the 'major' world of the novel" (138). McHale goes on to claim that "postmodernist writers are not always so considerate," while in fact, their use of images to reroute narrative and confuse "ontological" levels (McHale) is far more visible as a deliberate effort. Proust's postmodern use of figuration, however, is coercive in its subtlety, imperceptibly entwined as it is within the very mimetic conventions it overturns.

Such eclipsing of life by image, the displacement of worldly experience by the smooth screen of figuration, is described in the genesis of the "faire cattleya" metaphor—where the term "simulacre" occurs explicitly. Thrown against Odette by a jolt of the carriage, Swann adjusts the orchids in her décolletage, which leads to the initial, long-deferred act of physical possession: an act henceforth referred to as "faire cattleya." Like other Proustian metaphors, this one also has a performative purpose, erasing and negating cumulative time. In linking the possession of Odette to the "larges pétales mauves" of the orchids, a banal act of love-making for the blasé Swann is endowed with sudden newness: an unfamiliar novelty named by the metaphor as "un plaisir qui n'avait pas existé jusque-là . . . un plaisir—ainsi que le nom spécial qu'il lui donna en garda la trace—entièrement particulier et nouveau" [a pleasure until then nonexistent . . . a pleasure—whose trace remained in the special name he gave it—entirely singular and new] (I, 231). Defying temporal wear, the metaphor conserves the excitement of novelty.

Interestingly, the word "simulacre" occurs in an important definition of the expression "faire cattleya." Swann's arrangements and adjustments, after the first evening, become simulacra of themselves, stylized gestures: "L'arrangement (ou le simulacre rituel d'arrangement) des cattleyas" [The arranging (or, rather, the ritualized pretense of arranging) of her cattleyas] (I, 231), just as the term itself "faire cattleya" eventually becomes a simulacrum of love-making, the appearance or ritual miming of physical possession. The text, suggesting that the very idea of "physical possession" is a simulacrum screening the possession of nothing, "L'acte de la possession physique—où d'ailleurs l'on ne possède rien" [The act of physical possession—in which, by the way, one possesses nothing] (I, 230), produces an endless chain of appearances: possessing nothing, screened by the notion of "physical possession," screened itself by the "vocable 'faire cattleya.'" But this chain of simulacra disguises its own evolution, erases its own past, for Swann and Odette use the term "faire cattleya" "sans y penser" [without thinking].

Such an eclipsing of narrative by image, the negation of extension and successive temporality, suggests Baudrillard's discussion of the simulacrum, which effaces the "real." Arresting time, the simulacrum absorbs attention, which forgets the world and fixes obsessively on the suspended present of the smooth screen. Proustian figuration, originally a "signifiant" pointing to the "signifié" of the intradiegetic (Genette) world, here eclipses the "signifié" according to Baudrillard's model: "Le signifiant devient son propre signifié s'il y a confusion circulaire des deux au profit du signifiant, abolition du signifié et tautologie du signifiant" [The signifier becomes its own "signified" if there is a circular confusion of the two in favor of the signifier, an abolition of the signified and thus a tautology of the signifier]

(1969, 188). Baudrillard continues, "Au lieu d'aller au monde par la médiation de l'image, c'est l'image qui fait retour sur elle-même par le détour du monde (c'est le signifiant qui se désigne lui-même derrière l'alibi du signifié)" [Instead of referring to the world by the mediation of the image, it's the image that returns to itself via the detour of the world (it's the signifier that designates itself behind the alibi of the signified)]. Forgetfulness, induced by the power of the image, jettisons the world itself as poor imitation. The world no longer gives rise to an image that reflects it, returning energy to the world itself; rather, the image, as simulacrum, now precedes the world, rendering the world an archaic artefact, a useless, obsolete reference. From an initially reverential, submissive function in which the image merely reflects a deeper reality, it then proceeds to mask and displace that reality, ultimately severing all relation to any other referent: it is "son propre simulacre pur" [its own pure simulacrum].

Such an eclipse of the "real" by its image, or simulacrum, is argued in a specifically Proustian context in Bersani's discussion of the *Recherche*'s "mortuary esthetic." According to Marcel's theory, writing will render his life more real than that life itself. "The myth of art as both a 'translation of life' and as more 'real' or more 'essential' than life could itself be thought of as a simulacrum of a realistic esthetic: in this myth, the imaginary adheres to the real . . . to demonstrate the superiority of the image to the model" (417–18).

The use of simulacra, however, may not be a dismissive move away from life and experience, as Bersani argues, but a protective effort to shield experience from capture. Such glossy, hallucinatory images act as protective shields against the narrator's aggressive, "sterilizing" interpretive efforts.

This creation of simulacra, of glossy, hallucinatory shieldlike appearances that explicitly interrupt and explode the mind's domestication of experience, arresting and cancelling the progressive temporality of interpretation, suggests the baffling power of the sublime. For Kant, the sublime was what could not be absorbed by the mind, which, encountering the sublime, could only fall back upon itself; for Burke, this became a moment of awe and terror as the mind encountered the threat of its own obliteration, its own extinction, in a pleasure-in-pain masochism suggestive of Charlus whipped in his brothel chains. Recently, however, a certain postmodern sublime has taken shape, its glossy surfaces the spectacular object of fascination, but no longer of terror—for the postmodern self lives the experience of the sublime with exhilaration but not pathos, feeling only euphoria at the implication of its dissolution.

In the Proustian text, such euphoria seems suggested in the arresting and suspension of interpretive temporality, the re-creation of a moment of involuntary memory when the mind is powerfully overcome by sensation, without as yet being able to interpret its cause. As the narrator realizes in the madeleine scene, "Certes, ce qui palpite au fond de moi, ce doit être l'*image, le souvenir visuel*, qui, lié à cette saveur, tente de la suivre jusqu'à moi" [Undoubtedly what is thus palpitating in my depths must be the *image, the visual memory* which, linked to that taste, is trying to follow it up to my awareness] (I, 45; my emphasis). Holding off interpretation, this imaged sublime keeps experience from capture, and thus impoverishment, depletion, in Sontag's terms; it fends off the mind's domestication of its object through interpretation. The narrator goes on, "Mais il se débat trop loin, trop confusément; à peine si je perçois le reflet neutre où se confond l'insaisissable tourbillon des couleurs remuées; mais je ne peux distinguer la forme" [But it struggles too far away, too confusedly; I can scarcely perceive the neutral reflection in which the elusive whirlwind of stirred-up colors is dissolved; but I cannot distinguish its form] (I, 46). Marcel's rapture and felicity arise, it would seem, in the gap between experience and interpretation, in the hesitation and suspension of interpretation's time-bound effort.

We now have further reason to agree with critics such as de Man and Ellison that the *Recherche* is essentially allegorical. The power and "étrangeté saisissante" [arresting strangeness] of allegory has long been known to the narrator, who, as a child, was initially mystified by Giotto's curiously uncharitable Charity and distracted, cheek-distended Envy, who has no time for envious thoughts and looks more like a medical illustration for a tumor of the tongue. As the narrator later comes to realize, however, there is something powerfully material and compelling—"effectivement subi ou matériellement manié" [actually felt or materially handled] (I, 81)—concrete, realistic, and precise in these images so different from their purported meaning, so indifferent to the meaning that works through them. But as de Man suggests, we know what the allegory means only because "Giotto, substituting writing for representation, spelled it out on the upper frame of his painting: KARITAS" (77). In this model of the "arresting strangeness" of meaning separated from representation, even in conflict with its own representation, we discover the pattern of Proustian figuration: representation actively contradicting, disrupting, and foreclosing what it purports to describe. The difference is that Giotto's allegories curiously end up coinciding with their meanings; the narrator later comes to appreciate the verisimilitude of Giotto's unlikely Charity once experience reveals to him "le visage sans douceur, le visage antipathique et sublime de la vraie bonté" [the severe, unsympathetic, sublime countenance of true goodness] (I, 81). In Giotto, empirical experience is ultimately consonant, then, with allegorical meaning; in Proust, however, experience is contradicted by the very figures that purport to convey it, thereby blocking the aggressions of interpretation. Such an allegorical mode of figuration would seem appropriate to the narrator's own purposes in recounting his past without imprisoning it. The "setting before the eyes" of Aristotelian metaphor may be precisely what the narrator would not want to do to his past—understanding, with Ruskin, that the imagination "would think a good deal more of the thing if it could not see it."

Such protection and preservation of the past, its screening from capture, would then imply a certain fetishizing of that past. After such prolonged delay and hesitation, how could the narrator not approach the long-awaited material of his "oeuvre" with trepidation? The psychic stakes of recording that past—the act's charge of anxiety and desire—would now be much greater than they were when life was simple, so to speak, for Marcel. Now that he has decided, however, that his past is to be the "matière" of his long-awaited, long-deferred oeuvre, that past becomes charged with obsessive ambivalence, object of both dread and desire. The traces of such ambivalence emerge in the *Recherche*'s work of figuration, where image, rather than conveying and reflecting experience, acts, curiously enough, against it, throttling and suspending interpretation's appropriations. But his past, as the next chapter will show, is not the only object of Marcel's ambivalence; other hesitations and reluctances, other resistances, inhabit his intention to record the past in a work of literature.

Notes

1. Ricardou develops the distinction between ornamental or descriptive metaphor, which serves the purposes of representation, and ordinal metaphor, which "re-orders" narrative direction by overturning the text's "catégories du temps et de l'espace" (93–104).

2. This move—to scrutinize an image *of* images for what it might suggest about the behavior of figuration in the *Recherche*—parallels Paul de Man's effort to trace the *Recherche*'s "allegory of reading" by reviewing a seminal reading scene.

3. The "clochers de Martinville" experience is given twice in the text, first by the older, remembering narrator, and then in the young hero's written piece: the two accounts thus stand in some contrast, as Collier and Whitely have pointed out in suggesting that the older narrator's description functions as a "blank page" in order to set off the child's version, which is laced with metaphor.

4. Among critics whose commentary of this scene does not account for the disjointedness of its figures is Picon, who observes merely that the metaphori-

cal possibilities of the steeples capture the narrator's attention (159). Ricardou points to other metaphors at work in the text, for instance, that the very relationship of the young observer to the steeples is metaphoric (119–20). Understanding metaphor as a linking operation based on a "point commun," Ricardou suggests that the narrator and the Martinville steeples are brought together by a common point, which is ordinal metaphor itself. The Martinville steeples, as "églises," *name* ordinal metaphor: "Més-églises," the shortcut of "point commun" with Tansonville; and the young narrator *writes* ordinal metaphor ("c'était sous la forme de mots qui me faisaient plaisir que cela m'était apparu" [it was within the form of pleasurable words that this came to me] (I, 181)). The "common point" linking the *Recherche* hero with the Martinville steeples is ordinal metaphor, which the steeples "name" and the hero "writes" (119–20). Stambolian observes that the narrator's "habitual consciousness of time and space enters a new world in whose freedom he senses his own liberation (76)—but confidently concludes that "succession and multiplicity in time and space are given identity and unity within a work of art." The young writer's explosive, disjointed images, however, would seem to refuse all "identity and unity."

5. Intriguingly, the Pinter script for the film that eventually became *Swann in Love* apparently called for a shot of a butterfly partly masking in the foreground a far-away steamer. The shot had to be omitted, however, for reasons of expense: "How can one hire a steamboat captain to sail to and fro trying to follow the course of a butterfly on a mountain top twenty miles away?" (J. Theodore Johnson, Jr., ed., vol. 11 (1974): 10–11).

6. I am indebted to Anne-Catherine Smith for the observation that depth is flattened in this image of steamer and butterfly pasted to the same plane.

Chapter 6
Skipping Love Scenes: Marcel's Repression of Literature

Rehearsing the recalcitrant behavior of figuration, the preceding chapter argued that Proustian figure, rather than capturing the past, may precisely work to preserve the past from capture by the aggressions of interpretation. Similarly, other narratorial claims might yield, upon further scrutiny, doubts, hesitations, uncertainties; there might thus be further traces in the text of resistance to overt assertions. We might then turn to the Proustian text's ultimate claim, as extreme as it is renowned: "La vraie vie, la vie enfin découverte et éclaircie . . . c'est la littérature" [True life, life at last laid bare and illuminated . . . is literature] (IV, 474). It marks the abrupt reversal of the narrator's artistic fortunes: the occasion on which, having despaired of becoming a writer, he finds renewed faith in literature and in his own literary talents—and he resolves to write the story of his past. But is this tautological relationship between truth and literature—literature as a repository for the "truth" of a life—as unproblematic an equation as the narrator and many of his readers seem to think in the final pages?

This ecstatic solution implies a belief in being able to move smoothly from narrating to writing, from experience to "truth," from life to the literary work. Lately, however, the "smoothness" of such a move has become more knotted in critical discussions, as if we somehow need more explanation than what the narrator gives us about his next step. Implicit in Macksey's reference to the narrator's "supremely problematic encounters with literature" and the "highly suspect language" (1987, xiv) of his accounts of these encounters is a suspicion perceptible in further symptoms of unease with narratorial claims. The narrator's euphoric resolve, for instance, is undermined by Ellison's suggestion that the literary work is produced out of failure to take possession, whether of Albertine or of meaning (1984, 128), implying a certain disjunction in tone between the final triumphant pages and what would actually be a far more resigned move to writing. This disjunction widens in Bersani's argument for a fundamental divide between narrating and writing, experience and "truth," life and literature; literature and truth may precisely entail the erasure of experience and its replication as a sort of "sanitized" account, a simulacrum, now liberated from the damaging anxiety and desire that disfigure experience itself. But the divide between life and literature is rendered as a veritable rupture in Paul de Man's suggestion that perhaps the narrator doesn't move on to literature after all. His demonstration of how the *Recherche*'s actual practice fails to "coincide" with its explicit esthetic claims suggests that a "metaphor" with high ethical stakes is in fact a metonymy, a relationship of association and habit, allowing de Man to question the narrator's exalted visions of metaphor and literature—and to suggest the mystification of Marcel's constant "plus tard, j'ai compris" [later on, I understood] claim: his deluded belief in a "later on" that would mark "the passage from experience to writing" (78).

There are further reasons to justify such critical preoccupation with the "passage from experience to writing." The embracing of literature may not, in fact, be the successful completion of Marcel's artistic quest and the "happy ending" with which many readers have concluded; for inter- and intratextual elements in the presentation of literature suggest hesitation, reluctance, and ultimately an outright refusal on the part of the narrator. Complicating his esthetic equation is his discovery of the frought, tangled improbability of literature, which, like psychic truth, is a fragile compromise of contradictions.[1] Time, de Man has suggested, is "truth's inability to coincide with itself" (78); as an agent in life and in literature, time produces ragged aporias that refuse to be domesticated by any equation for truth. Exploding the narrator's esthetic tautology is his own final image of time as living stilts, vertiginous heights of past lifting the present self aloft and from which it finally topples (III, 1048)—for what unwrites Marcel's climactic intuition is the disruptive potential of this past, recorded in what Riffaterre calls the "intertextual unconscious."[2] Scrutiny of this inter- and intratextual network suggests that the *Recherche* concludes not with the sudden espousing of literature as the narrator's vocation, but with the confirmation of what has long been suggested: the narrator's continued refusal of literature.

This refusal is implied in the very scene that introduces the young Marcel to literature: the "drame du coucher" evening in which his mother, having initially refused the ritual good-night kiss, calms her distraught son by reading George Sand's *François le Champi* aloud to him. Scholarship on this episode has tended to focus either on the Oedipal implications of the nocturnal bedroom scene played out between mother and son,[3] or on its connection to the child's future writing career by emphasizing the reading act as anticipatory of writing.[4] More rarely have both Oedipal and scriptural scenarios been conjugated, as in Henrot's argument for the sensual, sonorous "littérarité" discovered by the listening child in this densely Oedipal scene. Doubrovsky, however, goes further in accounting for both readings by linking each to the madeleine episode; just as Marcel's mother gives him the madeleine as a substitute for herself, so also does she feed him words as she reads aloud to him. Thus, for Marcel—in Doubrovsky's equation—to write is to read in the place of the mother, usurping her mastery of language: appropriating that language as his own. Doubrovsky accordingly locates the reading scene as the origin of the narrator's own writing (63). In fact, however, this attempt to engage both readings fails to recognize that the first, the Oedipal, would seem to "unwrite" in palimpsest the second, the scriptural. Doubrovsky's focus on ingestion (ingesting the madeleine, ingesting the mother's words) as the act that enables Marcel to become a writer—in the coalescing of Oedipal and scriptural scenarios—refuses to honor their occluded difference: that the word "madeleine" harbors opposing semiotic resonances whose tensions precisely throw the narrator's climactic embracing of writing into question. The madeleine as the instrument that opens the narrator's way to writing by restoring memories of Combray is threatened by its semiotic inscription as an interdiction, a taboo only too explicitly sounded within the Biblical resonance of the name Madeleine: forbidden sexuality. The embracing of literature in the final pages of the novel is thus stamped with a resistant ambivalence: literature as the desired, the idealized (literature as generally understood by Proustian criticism) is also the forbidden, the proscribed. Blocking the invitation to writing proposed by the madeleine pastry is the interdiction of writing, the "pro-scription" posed by Madeleine the sinner. "La place de la Madeleine," contrary to Doubrovsky's claim, is the place of hesitation, immobility: the place of Marcel's failure to become a writer. One "madeleine" scene is unwritten, negated by another, inscribed in an indelible palimpsest, just as one "scriptural" scenario (the reading scene as inaugural of writing) is apparently unwritten by another "Scriptural" verse naming Madeleine as the "immoral one."

If the *François le Champi* reading scene has implications for the would-be writer, it is perhaps not so much for what he ingests, in Doubrovsky's claim, as for what eludes him: the mystery of "littérarité," as Henrot points out (131). At the time of this seminal introduction to literature, the narrator had not yet read any "real" novels and believed dimly that Sand was a "typical" novelist (I, 41); much later, he will recognize that *François le Champi* contained "l'essence du roman" for him, and the novel's depiction of "les progrès d'un amour naissant" [the progress of a nascent love affair] (IV, 462) indeed suggests a primitive, paradigmatic narrative shape. Furthermore, *François le Champi* was chosen for him by the narrator's grandmother with particular care, again suggesting its function as model: selected because his grandmother cannot bring herself to give the child "quelque chose de mal écrit" [something poorly written] (I, 39).

However, for all its initiatory significance, *François le Champi*, the work that introduces the child to literature and presumably to his future vocation, is swathed in hermeneutic mystery (Henrot). Compounding the incomprehensibility of the word "champi" [foundling] in its title and the incoherences inflicted on the text by Marcel's daydreaming inattention is his mother's discreet omission of love scenes.[5] Marcel's official introduction to literature will thus be important not for what it tells the child about literature, but for what it doesn't—what it withholds, producing the impression of strangeness and mystery that seems to excite the curiosity, desire, and fascination he will thereafter associate with literature. Much later he will say it was *François le Champi* that gave him "l'idée que la littérature nous offrait vraiment [un] monde de mystère" [the idea that literature really offered us [a] world of mystery] (IV, 462). The narrator's interest in literature seems thus to be awakened precisely by that part of Sand's text that is silenced or repressed; the reading scene simultaneously represses and raises, or idealizes literature in an "Aufhebung": a negating and yet a conservation through transformation.[6]

François le Champi, however, not only depicts an Oedipal "amour naissant" between mother and adoptive son, but stages a narration in which literature as "Aufhebung," as repression and idealization, is further impressed upon the listening child. In Sand's foreword, an authorial voice ponders the difference between instinct and the intelligence, speaking wistfully of the rural life of peasants as "la vie primitive"—opposed to the sophistication of "notre vie développée et compliquée, que j'appellerai 'la vie factice'" [our own elaborate and complicated life, which I'll call "artificial life"] (206). Can the two be reconciled? wonders the author aloud to a friend, who challenges her to attempt just that: to retell the story of François in such a way as to satisfy the exigencies of both. The tale is to be recounted as if there were a peasant to the left and a Parisian to the right—thus the need to speak naïvely and sensuously, with image and color, for the peasant, and with elegance and sophistication for the citified Parisian

(216).[7] The simple account of the champi, the child found in the "champs," becomes a careful and difficult—even improbable—exercise before it even begins in Sand's text. The narration will unfold painstakingly among the skeptical silences judging each word pronounced, their power suggested in the friend's warning, "Je t'arrêterai où tu broncheras" [I shall stop you where you go wrong] (218), with its explicit threat of an arresting and premature foreclosure of the story: a threat realized when the friend stops the author at her title, objecting that "champi" is not a French word (219).

This role of the skeptical and fastidious judge is repeated in the narrative proper as the act of narration is dramatized by two embedded narrators. Monique, the parish priest's old maidservant, having ceded her role as narrator to the hempworker, then objects to his use of the word "secousse" [shake], saying "vous dites un mot qui ne convient pas. Une 'secousse' ne dit pas un moment, une minute" [You're using a word that isn't right. A "shake" doesn't mean a moment or a minute]. This lexical objection from "la vieille puriste" [the old purist] is disputed and overridden by the hempworker, who replies stoutly, "Je dis donc une secousse, et je n'en démordrai pas" [I say a shake, and I'm not budging] (335). The procedural tensions traced out in the foreword are thus inherited by and enacted in the narrative proper, reminding any listener (whether intra- or extradiegetic) too engaged in the "histoire" that this is also a perilous exercise in "narration."[8]

An earlier moment of interruption, suspension, and deferral has already occurred when Monique claims she no longer remembers the story. This is the point at which the narration is assumed by the hempworker, who says scornfully,

Je sais bien pourquoi vous n'êtes plus mémorieuse au milieu comme vous l'étiez au commencement; c'est que ça commence à mal tourner pour le champi et que ça vous fait peine, parce que vous avez un coeur de poulet comme toutes les dévotes aux histoires d'amour. (279)

I know very well why you suddenly don't remember the tale the way you did at the beginning; it's that things start going badly for the Foundling and that upsets you, for you're as chicken-hearted as all the other silly fools for love stories.

Monique's prim "forgetfulness" and hesitation suggest a possible reluctance in the face of the story's increasingly apparent incestuous eroticism. But this interruption is also marked by a moment of more explicit "littérarité," the conferral of a literary definition and status upon the story. "Ça va donc," says one of the listeners in response to the hempworker's remark, "tourner en histoire d'amour?" [So it's going to turn into a love story?]. The emergence of literature is thus further presented to the listening child as punctuated with blockages, ruptures, that would seem to mark a struggle between the incestuous interdiction and its recuperation and legitimization in narrative form: the difficult elaboration of a compromise between instinct and intelligence, peasant and Parisian, the forbidden and the idealized, the repressed and the permitted.[9] Literature as symptom, as the trace or mapping of the struggle between repression and expression, is introduced to Marcel by his mother's careful editing and repeated recurrently within the edited text itself.

Such simultaneous repression and idealization of literature would then offer an explanation for the narrator's long delay in embracing his vocation as a writer, a delay that might be read as an expression or symptom of the repression of literature, a return of the repressed. For to write, or produce literature, would be to reproduce *François le Champi*—repeating, it seems, the love story of mother and adoptive son, a story of incestuous, forbidden desire. To correct Doubrovsky, then, to write would not be to appropriate the mother's voice, but the mother herself—to realize the Oedipal dream of possession. The long delay during which Marcel hopes to become a writer but incessantly postpones getting down to work might then be understood as a substitute satisfaction—a compromise-formation allowed by the interdiction, permitting Marcel to aspire to be a writer *as long as* he doesn't write. This delay would explain the interminability of narration, the "monstrosity" (Genette) of the narrating voice: a voice unable to move on to writing.

This long resistance to writing is explicitly linked to *François le Champi* in the episode that stages a literal "return of the repressed," the narrator's rediscovery of Sand's novel in the Prince de Guermantes's bookcase during the climactic day that renews his faith in himself as a writer and in literature. His meditation on the position *François le Champi* occupies, figuring as it does the two poles of his life, argues for its psychic resonance as literature; for the book both marks the long detour away from writing, what the narrator calls "le déclin de ma santé et de mon vouloir, mon renoncement chaque jour aggravé à une tâche difficile" [the decline of my health and my will, and my renunciation, each day more definitive, of a difficult task]—and, much later, seems to confirm his sudden embracing of literature, rediscovered, he says, "par le jour le plus beau [de ma vie] et dont s'éclairaient soudain . . . les tâtonnements anciens de ma pensée" [on this most beautiful day of my life, suddenly illuminating for me . . . the old gropings of my thought] (IV, 465). The early repression of literature imposed by the *François le Champi* reading scene, producing the narrator's incessant deferral of writing, would seem to be recuperated, legitimized—"aufgehoben"—by this rediscovery of Sand's novel: the embodiment, says the narrator, of "le but de ma vie et peut-être de l'art" [the purpose of my life and perhaps of art itself]. Has the interdiction then been lifted; has the story of incestuous desire been sufficiently transformed, as art, to permit its appropriation by the narrator? Does this represent the recuperation of repression, its definitive "cure" and transformation or "Aufhebung" as cultural artifact? Freud's study of Jensen's story "Gradiva" proposes just such a model of repression lifted by the very instrument of its cause. Freud remarks on how appropriately Jensen's love-fleeing archaeologist is wrested "from his retreat from love" by "the marble sculpture of a woman" (IX, 49).

That the rediscovery of Sand's *François le Champi* lifts the repression of literature and inaugurates the narrator's writing career is certainly implied in his remark on Sand's "magnetized pen":

Mille riens de Combray . . . sautaient légèrement d'eux-mêmes et venaient à la queue leu leu se suspendre au bec aimanté, en une chaîne interminable et tremblante de souvenirs. (IV, 463) [10]

A thousand subtle details of Combray . . . came lightly and spontaneously leaping, in single file, to suspend themselves from the magnetized nib in an interminable and trembling chain of memories.

Sand's "magnetized pen" thus not only writes François's story, but also "recounts" memories of Combray, ordering them "single file" into an "interminable chain": an explicitly textual image that prefigures the narrator's celebrated remark on metaphor as "les anneaux nécessaires d'un beau style" (IV, 468) [the necessary rings of a beautiful style]. Such a peculiarly ordered and discursive resurrection of Combray would seem to herald the narrator's position on the threshold of his vocation as a writer; memories of Combray, no longer the imaged shapes that take on "form and solidity" provoked by the tea-dipped madeleine, are now, instead, inscribed one after the other in textual alignment, "magnetized" by Sand's pen.

But an indication that things might not be so simple for the narrator is implied in his curious initial reaction of distaste upon identifying *François le Champi* in the prince's bookcase: "Je me sentis désagréablement frappé comme par quelque impression trop en désaccord avec mes pensées actuelles" [I felt myself disagreeably struck, as by an impression too discordant with my present thoughts] (IV,

461). This aversion is soon claimed to be corrected as the narrator apparently realizes how consonant *François le Champi* is with his new belief in literature. He reasons that he initially recoiled from the book because it represented so old a memory that he hadn't immediately been able to place it:

C'était une impression bien ancienne, où mes souvenirs d'enfance et de famille étaient tendrement mêlés et que je n'avais pas reconnue tout de suite. (IV, 462)

It was quite an old impression, in which memories of childhood and family were tenderly intermingled and which I had not immediately recognized.

Could the explanation of his distaste lie not in the age of the memory, but rather in the images of childhood and family "tenderly mingled" with it—memories that include scenarios of repressed incestuous desire? Perhaps the renewed apprehension of *François le Champi* as literature—as art—still can't indemnify *François le Champi* as forbidden desire; and his sense of being "disagreeably struck" by a "discordant impression" suggests the persistence of repressed scenarios identifying incestuous desire with literature.

Another sort of repression may be at work here, however. *François le Champi* is not only a story of incestuous desire, but, we remember, a story of story: a demonstration of the difficult, belabored production of literature. Even more "discordant" for the narrator may be the unwelcome reminder—in the form of the prince's copy of Sand's novel—that literature is the improbable product of selection and omission, their tenuous compromise. Most threatening for Marcel may not be the book's scenarios of interdicted desire, but its fitful production of those scenarios; *François le Champi* may be a far more unpleasant reminder for Marcel the aspiring writer than for Marcel the Oedipal son. Could the drama of interdicted desire be a "screen" tactic—a "leurre" (Barthes, 1970) for Marcel as well as his readers—to obscure the more anguished drama of literature as difficult compromise?

Continued repression of literature is confirmed by the remainder of the scene, an example of Riffaterre's "syntagm," or text generated by the repressed material as compensation and within which the repressed meaning obtains a measure of expression (1987, 375). As the narrator contemplates *François le Champi* in the prince's library, the early gesture of silencing and suppression is repeated. The book is summarily dismissed from the literary canon, excluded as an example of "l'idée fort commune de ce que sont les romans berrichons de George Sand" [the quite pedestrian idea of "one of George Sand's

Berry novels"] (IV, 462): a refusal that would seem safely to segregate *François le Champi* and literature, the repressed and the idealized, defusing the danger of the "Aufhebung." But—in a move that attests to the subliminal threat of Sand's story—the narrator proceeds to a more decisive dismissal. Pursuing his reverie of *François le Champi* as a "tendre mélange" of childhood memories, the narrator realizes that such books have now been enriched by vast "enluminures" [illuminations] of remembered images and asociations, and, as such, are worthy of illustrated editions "que l'amateur n'ouvre jamais pour lire le texte mais pour s'enchanter une fois de plus des couleurs qu'y a ajoutées quelque émule de Foucquet et qui font tout le prix de l'ouvrage" [which the collector never opens to read the text but to be enchanted once more by the colors added to it by some follower of Foucquet and which make the volume such a treasure] (IV, 466). The original gesture of refusal continues with the indication that such "illustrated editions," which *François le Champi* has become for him, are never opened in order to read their texts, but to contemplate the vivid childhood memories now associated with those texts.[11] *François le Champi* will thus remain unread by the narrator, Sand's story eclipsed and silenced by Marcel's own imaged memories. In a final repressive move, the narrator claims that *had* he his old edition of *François le Champi*, not only would he never read it, he would never even look at it. "Je ne le regarderais jamais" [I would never look at it], he says,

j'aurais trop peur d'y insérer peu à peu mes impressions d'aujourd'hui jusqu'à en recouvrir complètement celles d'autrefois, j'aurais trop peur de le voir devenir . . . une chose du présent. (IV, 466)[12]

I should be too afraid of gradually inserting into it my impressions of today, to the point of smothering those of the past; I would be too afraid of seeing it become . . . a thing of the present.

Curiously, then, this prototypical novel representing the "essence" of the form, the work that introduces the child to literature and presumably to his future vocation as a writer, is ultimately refused by the narrator at the very moment he apparently embraces that vocation. The two encounters with *François le Champi* stand at seminal moments of the narrator's life. Marking the movement away from writing that seems to articulate the narrator's story, *François le Champi* reappears at the moment of apparent illumination, the intuition that this same resistance to writing (claims the narrator) will be the very material of his writing. Not only does this final "I would never look at it" repeat an original repression of literature, but, as well, a refusal or silencing—masked by fetishistic reverence—of the narrator's own past in the book that contains the imaged story of Marcel as well as that of François. Literature and his past, which coalesce in *François le Champi*, are refused in the narrator's very claim to embrace them.

What is Marcel really avoiding—literature as interdicted, Oedipal desire or literature as agonistic, contested effort? Some clue might be provided by returning to the *François le Champi* reading scene once again—this time not for its diegetic value as an event in the narrator's past or "histoire," but for what it might tell us as a much-later moment in his "narration." In his still-to-be-written work of literature, how will he recount this scene? In fact, his "narration" of the reading scene repeats the repressive gestures enacted in the scene itself. In speaking of "les progrès d'un amour naissant," the narrator neglects to mention that this "nascent love affair" is incestuous: the tale of the growing erotic bond between the miller's wife and her adoptive son, François. More interesting, however, is the narrator's refusal to name the heroine, whom he obliquely calls "la meunière" [the miller's wife]. Her name, of course, is Madeleine, bespeaking her sinful predecessor of the Gospel according to Luke, the "immoral" woman, the sinner of illicit sexuality: the one who cedes to forbidden desire.[13] Marcel's own "narration" arises, like his mother's, from discreet editing, the careful silences and omissions that shape "literature"; like his mother, the narrator skips the love scenes. Literature indeed seems available to him in this handy demonstration of how he might negotiate the conflicting demands of expression and repression, voice and silence, selection and omission. But in silencing the name "Madeleine," he also silences the little tea-dipped cake that gives birth to his narration in a sudden welling-forth of lost memories of Combray: the initial involuntary memory that seems to open the way to writing. To silence the name "Madeleine" is merely to honor the lesson of *François le Champi* and accept literature as belabored editorial compromise; but to silence the "madeleine" (cake) is to refuse literature altogether.

Could, then, the story of how Marcel becomes a writer really be the story of how he doesn't? He may proclaim that the truth of life is literature as often as he likes in the final pages, but his equation, it seems, must remain constative; Marcel's passage to a performance of that equation is foreclosed by his final refusal of *François le Champi* and literature. As the unquestioned esthetic conclusion of the *Recherche* narrative, the narrator's chosen artistic form, his tautology for "truth," literature is perhaps not available to him as the long-sought answer to his "gropings" after all. Literature as the idealized is doubled by an intertext that recounts a story of literature as the repressed; literature thus stands as an incomplete, failed "Aufhebung": as both idealization and repression, conservation and negation, selection and omission—

suspended terms unable to realize the "Aufhebung"'s promise of transformation. This "compromised" understanding of literature *as* compromise is taught Marcel in the intra- and intertextual lessons of his mother and *François le Champi*. But his refusal of literature at the end of *Le temps retrouvé* and in the silences of the narration itself indicates that Marcel is not only skipping love scenes, but foregoing the story altogether: unable to engage the agonistic process of compromise. Throughout the *Recherche*, literature as interdicted desire masks the real interdiction: literature as performance, as the execution of an improbable act. Literature *as* repression—depicted in *François le Champi*'s careful compromise of permitted and interdicted—produces Marcel's own repression *of* literature, the compromise between wanting to become a writer and being unable to write. Literature is the desired and dreaded object of his ambivalence: a conflict whose energy insidiously ironizes the triumphant esthetic proclamations of the final pages and confers not closure but continued delay, deferral.

Interestingly enough, Marcel's refusal of literature at the end of the *Recherche* leaves us with a far more intriguing notion of literature than the traditional reading provides. Concluding with the embracing of literature flattens and falsifies it somehow, commodifies it; for literature as the esthetic solution, period, precludes any further, more difficult investigation as to what literature might really be. Concluding without literature, however, leaves us with something of the impression Marcel himself must have had that night listening to his mother read *François le Champi*: renewed respect for the strangeness of literature, its elusiveness and mystery, the fascination of its enigma. We are close here to the Russian formalist esthetic of "defamiliarization"—of art, as Shklovsky put it, as "the process of 'singularizing' objects, and the process that consists of obscuring forms, of increasing the difficulty and duration of perception" (83).[14] Such "singularization" of literature is perhaps the "art" of the *Recherche*, which renews literature far more decisively for us by leaving Marcel nowhere near a pen.

Notes

1. Using Freud's *Beyond the Pleasure Principle* as a "template" for the dynamics of narrative, Peter Brooks elaborates an analogy between psychic and narrative function. In each, he suggests, the birth of appetancy or desire releases energies variously exercised and bound as they seek an appropriate resolution.

2. Riffaterre develops the idea of intertextuality as repression by tracing what might more accurately be an "intratextuality" of unconscious phantasms repeated within the Proustian text itself. He points in particular to the

"repressed" desecration of the mother through such surrogates as the grand-mother, the vulgar Marquise de Villeparisis, and the grotesque lavatory-attendant "marquise" presiding over her clients (1987).

3. The scene's portrayal of mother and son is emphasized, for instance, in Joubert's suggestion that the musicality of the mother's reading voice reveals her character (35). Mehlman sees the mother's voice as a "metaphor of presence, sheer immediacy" (26), but doesn't account for the significant absences of all the scenes her voice omits. Rousset argues that the story of *François le Champi* adds thematic support to "l'idylle ardente et pure" of the nocturnal reading scene, without recognizing the subversive energy released by scenarios of incestuous desire. The episode is read in an explicitly Oedipal vein by Reille, who construes it as a "primal union" of mother and son, and by Didier, who observes that the evening symbolizes an "inceste imaginaire" (140) for the narrator.

4. Compagnon's chapter "Proust I: contre la lecture" retraces the various forms of idolatrous reading rejected by Proust in the *Recherche* and preceding texts, suggesting that for the narrator, writing is the ultimate authentic (non-idolatrous) act of reading (1983). Blumenthal discusses *François le Champi* as a "pre-text" for the narrator's own (7), a view anticipated by Doubrovsky in his claim that the "bedtime drama" scene ultimately produces "le Livre" [the Book] (59). Lang points to the digressiveness of the *François le Champi* account, which suggests the disregard of story in favor of text, signifier, and nonreferentiality—attesting the narrator's "progressive discoveries about the truth of art" (160), while Descombes argues that since *François le Champi* is incomprehensible as a novel to the listening child, it is received not as story, but as style ("doux langage") and represents a moment of prudish maternal morality that must be overcome for the narrator to proceed on to "l'art du roman" (125–26) and a more aggressive penetration of life's truths and laws. These genetic interpretations of the source of the narrator's writing, however, ignore the ambiguities and ambivalences that undermine his "progression" toward writing.

5. In *Jean Santeuil*'s version of the "bedtime drama," it is not only the love scenes that are skipped, but reading and literature altogether. There is no mention of Sand's text, and Jean's mother merely remains with the child until he falls asleep (208–9). Literature appears in Proust's drafts at the same time as omitted love scenes, endorsing their association throughout the various phases of textual elaboration; in Cahier 6, the protagonist remarks that, in reading Sand's *La Mare au diable*, "Maman . . . passait tout ce qui avait rapport à l'amour" [Mummy . . . skipped everything to do with love]. The evolution of the *François le Champi* reading scene, originally one episode, with its return in *Le temps retrouvé* is traced by Roloff, Brun, and Henrot.

6. The rich paradoxes of Hegel's seminal concept, the "Aufhebung," echo in the work of Freud—who understands civilization itself as an "Aufhebung" in *Inhibitions, Symptoms and Anxiety*—and Lacan, as Jean Hippolyte suggests in tracing the term's various uses. Derrida rewrites "Aufhebung" in *Marges* as "la relève," suggesting not only a lifting up but a relaying or relieving, an effect of substitution: a play of "différance" or transfer that the "Aufhebung" can never entirely master through its process of raising, conserving, and negating, as Alan Bass particularly points out (20n).

7. Didier reads this impossibility ("Comment s'adresser à la fois au paysan et au Parisien? et quel langage employer alors?" [How might one simultane-

ously address both peasant and Parisian? and what idiom might one use?] (150)) as productive of "un genre marginal," "le roman paysan" [the rustic novel]—which, in Didier's argument, offered Sand the opportunity to develop an "écriture de la femme" [woman's writing].

8. Genette's analysis of narrative as the product ("récit") of an act of recounting ("narration") at work upon events ("histoire")—later suggesting that "histoire" is itself as artful a product of narration as "récit" (1983, 11)—allows for the isolation and scrutiny of any narrative as recounting act: the effort, as we have seen, of my third chapter. This difference will also be important later in this chapter when we return to the *François le Champi* reading scene to note its function in the *Recherche* as "narration," rather than as "histoire."

9. The fitful starts and stops that punctuate the narration of *François le Champi* occurred as well in the production of the text. In one of the two preliminary texts that delay the narration of François's story, Sand indicates that the tumultuous advent of the July monarchy postponed the novel's serialized appearance in the *Journal des Débats*. Sand addresses her explanatory "Notice" to "ceux des lecteurs qui . . . s'intéressent aux procédés de fabrication des oeuvres d'art" [those readers . . . interested in the procedures with which works of art are accomplished]. As an allegory of the "fabrication" of works of art, Sand's text cannot but impress upon the listening Marcel the laboriousness of the production of literature.

10. The source of this "magnetized pen" image would seem to be Plato's *Ion*, where Socrates suggests that Ion's eloquence is a divine power, impelling him like a magnet which not only draws iron rings, but magnetizes them in turn to produce an interlinking magnetic chain (220). Socrates likens this magnetic attraction to the power of the Muse, who inspires poets and, through them, a "chain" of other men.

11. A similar usurpation of text by childhood memories occurs in Proust's preface "Journées de lecture" to his 1906 translation of Ruskin's *Sesame and Lilies*, a piece first published as "Sur la lecture" in *La Renaissance Latine* in 1905. In that early text, praising childhood reading, Proust instead dwells on the images and impressions that accompanied the reading act—an intruding friend, an inconvenient bee or ray of sunlight, the nearby untouched tea, the sinking sun, the dinner interrupting a chapter (1971, 160). Ellison suggests that this relationship between the actual text read and the memory of childhood reading passes from a chance or metonymic association to a necessary or metaphoric bond (90), a movement I have discussed at greater length in Chapter 3. I am concerned here, however, to point to the refusal of text that such "nonreading"—the remembering of sensual impressions rather than the text read—constitutes.

12. The fetishism of such a refusal is apparent, and has been documented in Compagnon's discussion of bibliophilia and idolatry in the *François le Champi* rediscovery scene (1983). Compagnon, however, does not account for the refusal of literature, the repressive gesture, implicit in such a fetishizing of Sand's text.

13. It may be argued that Madeleine's redemption in the Gospel provides a successful example of "Aufhebung," a completed transformation through a literal "raising up": a transfiguration that would also transform and redeem her semiotic resonance of illicit sexuality. Yet the intertext cited by the *Recherche* appears interrupted and blocked at the notion of forbidden sexuality, for *François le Champi* refuses to carry out the transfiguration of Madeleine; the

story ends just short of Madeleine and François's wedding, the moment of official legitimization of their incestuous love ("Là finit l'histoire, dit le chanvreur, car des noces j'en aurais trop long à vous dire" [That's the end of the story, said the hempworker, for it would take me too long to tell you about the wedding] (403)). Madeleine's redemption is thus foreclosed by Sand's text, producing a conspicuous nontransfiguration inherited by the listening Marcel.

14. Lang mentions "defamiliarization" as part of the *Recherche*'s esthetic manifesto; art should force us to new perceptions, according to Proust (Lang 133). But the *Recherche*, I maintain, goes further in obliging us to see art itself—literature—anew.

Chapter 7
Proust, Narrative, and Ambivalence in Contemporary Culture

It seems apt ("appropriate," in an irresistible pun provided by the lexicon of this chapter), having begun with Proust's own critical writing and the "violence and desire" of its appropriations, to conclude by addressing the symmetrical (now at the other end of this discussion as well as this century) "violence and desire" of contemporary pop-cultural appropriations of Proust. For few canonical modernist writers, certainly, have provoked such response in popular culture as Proust, whose proliferating presence in jokes, puns, cartoons, advertisements, magazine articles, and the newspaper columns of Russell Baker has made him something of a media cliché. If he is not yet quite what Baker, the self-proclaimed "man who took Marcel Proust out of the cobwebs in the library stacks and made him a vital presence at the center of American consciousness"[1] asserts, Proust is certainly encountered with intriguing regularity on the surfaces of contemporary culture. His current reader thus approaches the *Recherche* amidst a thick atmosphere of popular myth and cliché, violent and desiring appropriations that refigure the text as a sort of vernacular, popularized simulacrum.

This mass-cultural appropriation of a canonical literary text is the sort of gesture Huyssen may have in mind in his argument for a cultural climate now post-Great Divide, an era in which the segregation of high modernism and mass culture "no longer seems relevant" (26). It also suggests Baudrillard's analysis of "homogenization" in which opacity, resistance, and difference are collapsed, flattened, and scrambled in a "totalité consommatrice" [consuming totality]; he offers the example of the mall "effect," in which the monotony of successive, indistinguishable storefronts abolishes all differences between elegant grocery boutiques and art galleries, between *Playboy* and treatises

on paleontology (1970, 22). For Baudrillard, such collapse of difference is fostered by the fetishizing of the object, whose function then
becomes no longer to serve usefully as instrument, but to be manipulated as sign. The object itself in its density and opacity thus disappears behind the slick surface of its now-fetishized sign value, a
process Baudrillard calls "réduction sémiologique" (1972, 96). Such
reduction levels and abolishes all difference in favor of a circulating
economy of interchangeable signifiers.

Yet neither Huyssen nor Baudrillard seems to account for anything
beyond an indiscriminate leveling of signs. More energy is at work
here, a more acute attention in the vigor with which mass culture
encounters the elitist signs of a text perceived to embody the high
modernist canon. Might we then understand this popularization of
Proust as revolutionary, the bringing down of an elitist text in order
to rewrite and replace it with a "democratized" version? This media
energy has no revolutionary program of its own to propose, however,
nor would today's fractured cultural surfaces any longer seem to provide the cohesiveness necessary to animate a revolutionary agenda. In
Baudrillard's metaphor, this "homogenization" of signs is not revolutionary and convulsive, but viral, insidious. Animating this "viral"
contamination, however, is an ambivalence neither Baudrillard nor
Huyssen accounts for, and whose anxiety and unease announce a
more complicated negotiation with the *Recherche*. Fraught with both
dread and desire, this activity might be read in Hal Foster's terms as a
"recoding" of elitist signs, its ambivalent energy attesting to the persistence of cultural hierarchies.

When a review in *Le Nouvel Observateur* of eleven comic books claims
that the comic strip is as vivid a "signifier" of French culture as "Proust
et le camembert, Jean Renoir et le papier à cigarette Job,"[2] scrutiny
of this cheeky collapse of Proust, camembert, and comic books to the
same resonant, culturally symbolic function is in order. Recalling the
gesture of Barthes's *Mythologies*, we might proceed by moving past
the "Proust" signifier to its immediate "signified," and on to yet another level of meaning at which this original signified is re-engaged
as itself a cultural signifier. At this deeper signifying level, what is the
new cultural *signified*: the cultural "myth" indicated by the signifier
"Proust?" How does "Proust" signify, along with camembert and
comic books, on the jumbled postmodern cultural register?

An attempt to engage this "myth" would notice that to a frenetic
consumer culture, Proust's narrative—indeed, narrative itself as form—
evokes what most resists consumption. In an age that values speed,
brevity, efficacy, performance, and appearance, Proust "signifies"
slowness, length, labor, contemplation, resistance, transcendance.

Contemporaneity values the ever-more-rapid accessing, processing, and transmission of information—hence the acronym, the thirty-second TV spot, the "filename" spelled as one word, the "bite patrol" of presidential-candidate speechwriters with their credo, "Make it short, keep it bite-sized." Reading Proust at the other end of the twentieth century is to trace the encounter of the acronym and the adjective; the "filename" and the sentence; the "sound bite," or condensation, and narrative, or extension. Proust is the scandalous imperative not only to read, but to reread: to move backward in time rather than ever more frantically on. And contemporary culture has no time for time, as suggested by Russell Baker's bathroom parody of a man overwhelmed with memories provoked by the scent of his shaving cream; pounding on the door, someone angrily demands, "Are you going to be there all day?"[3] We seem to be back in 1913, when one of three editors to refuse Proust's novel explained that he couldn't understand how anyone needed thirty pages to describe tossing and turning in bed before falling asleep.[4]

Since then, Proustian length has become a favorite target in an information culture measuring time in microseconds. Russell Baker's column "Don't Invite Proust" reviews the writers one might contemplate receiving at the White House; Proust does not qualify, as he would thereupon pronounce one sentence lasting seven hours and forty-five minutes.[5] Infamous here is the Monty Python "All-England Summarizing Proust Competition" in which contestants have fifteen seconds to summarize the *Recherche*. One opens with the only word distinguishable in his hasty and incomprehensible effort, "time," and the competition goes instead to the most buxom contestant.[6] Proust's lengthiness is even advertised as a cure for stress incurred by "Type A" temperaments. Two cardiologists "repeatedly" advise their Type A patients to read Proust's novel "because the author needs several chapters to describe an event that most Type A subjects would have handled in a sentence or two."[7]

Proustian length becomes synonymous with boredom and effort in this "vernacular." "This great length," claims Baker, "is due not only to the incredible number of strained similes entwined in the novel's seven volumes, but also to the dense layers of tedium packed into every paragraph" (1980, 252). "Do not give up," admonishes another reader, "Proust gets better in the second volume and by the time you reach Charlus, it's whizzo."[8] In similar vein, it is asserted that D. H. Lawrence felt that reading Proust "was trying to till a field with knitting needles."[9]

Unlike the 1913 editors, however, we no longer refuse to publish Proust's thirty pages of insomniac reveries, we reduce them to the thirty-second "sound bite." An energetic article entitled "Huit clés pour lire Proust" [Eight Keys to Reading Proust] urges us to start with the ending, and advises in particular to skip the long sentences. We are admonished not to forget the main theme of a vocation in search of itself: "Ne pas perdre le fil conducteur: l'histoire d'une vocation qui s'ignore" (Leuwers 54). Symptomatic of such zestful "sound-biting" is Proust's inclusion in the *Reader's Digest* page of quotations, culled from seven writers, entitled "Points to ponder."[10] The Proustian "point," from *Le temps retrouvé* (IV, 474) is the sentence "Thanks to art, instead of seeing a single world—our own—we see it multiply until we have before us as many worlds as there are original writers." (In fact, as J. Theodore Johnson notices, the "point" is not exactly Proust's, whose sentence instead suggests there are as many worlds as original *artists* and goes on to mention Rembrandt and Vermeer). Proust himself is reduced to an element in that most postmodern of genres, the list: in *The Book of Lists*, he is fifteenth in a list of twenty insomniacs.[11]

Yet another example of reduction is implied in Genette's discussion of recent publishing patterns. Genette points out that the *Recherche* went from Proust's original hope for a single large volume to a binary division: the whole entitled *Les intermittences du coeur* and composed of two volumes, *Le temps perdu* and *Le temps retrouvé*. The Grasset edition, however, became so swollen as the proofs were being printed that a ternary structure was imposed: *Du côté de chez Swann*, *Le côté de Guermantes*, and *Le temps retrouvé*. Under Gallimard the novel in fifteen volumes, what Beckett called "the abominable *NRF* edition," gave priority to the overarching title, the individual volume titles listed beneath the title of the whole; the Pléiade edition in 1954 and the return to three volumes produced an even greater privileging of the ensemble title, *A la recherche du temps perdu*. Since the sixties, however, the paperback industry has returned to the fragmentation that privileges volume titles, relegating, in the case of the popular Folio collection, the ensemble title to the back cover. Publishing paradigms thus urge the perception—consonant, it is true, with Proust's own understanding of his work—that each volume is an independent piece, each fragment functioning autonomously. Neglected, however, in contemporary publishing practices, is each volume's function as part of a composite whole.

This fracturing and abbreviation of length, however subtly apparent in the *Recherche* paperbacks, announces the mass-cultural appropriation underway. Proust becomes not only a "sound bite," but "bite-sized" in a general reduction and thus "kitschification" of the *Recherche*: a movement implied by Calinescu's suggestion that kitsch

might be understood as a certain "aesthetic inadequacy," which generally involves the miniaturization—the reduction and multiplication—
of the singular work of art: the Greek statue reduced to the "bibelot."
This "aesthetic inadequacy" applies to "objects whose formal qualities
(material, shape, size, etc.) are inappropriate in relation to their cultural content or intention" (1987, 236). Could the notion of a "kitschified" Proustian text—"reduced" in some fashion inappropriate to
its "cultural content or intention"—help explain this pop-cultural
Proust? A recording of hodgepodge music and recitation of Proust
excerpts tempts its reviewer to proclaim it "le disque le plus kitsch de
la saison" [the kitschiest record of the season]; but that temptation
itself prompts the reviewer to ask, in a question we might repeat here,
"Mais où passe exactement la frontière du kitsch?" [But just where
does the borderline of kitsch lie?].[12]

An investigation of the "kitschification" of Proust might begin by
invoking Benjamin, whose analysis of the depreciation or "withering"
of the work of art's "aura" in an age of mechanical reproduction implicitly anticipates the phenomenon of kitsch. Defining this "aura" as
"the unique phenomenon of a distance, however close it may be,"
Benjamin points to the aggressive, countervailing "desire of contemporary masses to bring things 'closer' spatially and humanly." Such
"bringing closer" sets us squarely in the realm of consumption, an
idea further suggested in Benjamin's observation that the mechanical
reproduction and multiplication of works of art—their reduction to
"signifiers" in a consumer economy—is often the way this "bringing
closer" is accomplished. For the masses, writes Benjamin, "bringing
things closer" is "just as ardent as their bent toward overcoming the
uniqueness of every reality by accepting its reproduction" (223–25).

The link of reproduction and consumption to kitsch is made by
Calinescu, who argues that the way kitsch "works" psychologically has
to do with the "convertibility" potential of artistic cultural expressions
"into something fit for immediate 'consumption,' like any ordinary
commodity" (247). Calinescu notes—and here is the transition from
Benjamin—that reproduction alone is not enough to create kitsch,
but that considerations of context and purpose are also important.
Using slides of the Mona Lisa in an art history course would not be
kitschy, for instance, but the Mona Lisa's image reproduced on plates
and tablecloths would be "unmistakable kitsch" (257).

Using Calinescu's emphasis on purpose or intention in locating the
"frontière du kitsch," we realize that a certain "kitschification" of
Proust is at work when he becomes a mere advertising gimmick: certainly a persuasive example of Benjamin's destruction of the singular
work of art's aura by "bringing closer." Reduced to a bite-sized object

of consumption, Proust is manipulated for purposes of marketing in which other irreducibly "unique" matters are commodified. Reading, for instance, that most Proustian of themes, is aggressively advertised in the poster of a young woman reading Proust in the (expensive) Pléiade edition; the caption (predictably) advises, "Soyez jeune, lisez la Pléiade."[13] Similarly, an advertisement with the headline "Let Marcel Proust put you in the driver's seat!" announces the Modern Library's fiftieth anniversary contest, the winner to receive a bright red replica of a 1931 Model A touring car. "Marcel and the rest of us," claims the ad, "feel this prize is singularly appropriate since it represents style and value that never go out of date . . . very much like The Modern Library which, we hasten to remind you, can be bought in beautiful hardbound editions for very little more than paperbound editions."[14] This exploitation of Proust in order to market not so much the act of reading, but its highly commercially defined Pléiade or Modern Library *objects* implies an eclipse or effacement of reading itself, echoed differently in other encounters with Proust. "I don't read my books over and over," confessed Henry Miller, "I read Proust and that was enough."[15] Even Anatole France, pressed into writing a preface for Proust's *Les plaisirs et les jours*, admitted that he himself didn't read Proust, for life was too short and Proust was too long.

Reduction of "aura" through Benjamin's "bringing closer" via Calinescu's "kitschification," or perversion of cultural purpose, continues in further appropriations of Proust for marketing purposes. Dior advertises its cosmetic line "Les Rouges des (sic) Swann" as "poetic, sensitive, emotional lip and nail colors inspired by Marcel Proust." A romantic hairdo is legislated: "la coiffure de l'hiver, douce et anachronique, à bandeaux et à entrelacs de tresses, rappelle celle des héroines de Proust, la duchesse de Guermantes ou la princesse de Sagan" [the winter hairstyle, soft and anachronistic, with wings and braided interweavings, recalls that of Proust's heroines, the Duchesse de Guermantes or the Princesse de Sagan]. A picture features "une coiffure 'temps perdu'" [a 'time lost' hairdo].[16] An extreme example of ambitious marketing exploitation of Proust might be read in the "poltrona di Proust," an Italian-designed upholstered chair inviting one "to be wrapped in thoughts of lost time" and available by special order for $4,600; it is, apparently, "simply the most important chair that's been done in the last twenty years."[17]

Further commercial appropriations of Proust include tours such as "A la recherche de Marcel Proust" planned by a Delaware travel agency,[18] and another by a British agency including three nights at the Grand Hôtel de Cabourg, a visit to Tante Léonie's house, lunch with the Société des Amis de Marcel Proust, and a lecture on César

Franck and Proust.[19] An extreme example of "kitschy" consumption is the trendy marathon reading session held occasionally on campuses; as one participant put it, "You do it for the bonding, and for the souvenir T-shirt"; least of all, it seems, for the *Recherche*'s "aura" as singular work of art. Then there is the older, stuffier, emblem of kitschification and answer to the college reading marathon, the talk-show appearance. "I've often wondered," runs one query,

how Marcel Proust's fragile psyche would have fared if his publisher had persuaded him to make a fool of himself on the Dick Cavett Show: "Precisely *how* autobiographical is your novel, Marcel? And that lovely country place of your family's, is it really in Normandy? Uh, uh, can you call it fiction, if it's so true to life?"[20]

"Kitschification" is also at work in cunning revisionist titles; a baseball umpire's memoir trivializes and rewrites the activity of memory as activity at the plate in *Remembrance of Swings Past*. Cooking columns with titles like "Remembrance of Things Poached"[21] and "Remembrance of Things Pasta"[22] are particularly energetic sites for "bite-sizing" efforts, offering terrifyingly literal examples of reducing and "consuming." Other titles operate the same collapse of cultural difference. Occupying the position given to time in Proust's title is the corporate chicken king in an article called "A la recherche de Frank Perdue." An article on returning to competitive swimming after twenty years is entitled "A la Recherche du Tanks Perdus,"[23] while the fortieth commemoration of D-Day is similarly headlined as "A la recherche du tank perdu."[24] Proust and such culturally different signifiers as baseball, cooking, chicken, swimming, and war are thus cheekily and nonchalantly flattened to the same collage surface. Such glib paste-ups support Baudrillard's claim for the collapse of difference in a pervasive flattening and homogenization of signs, their reduction to a collection of equivalent signifers positioning them for manipulation and exchange.

More intriguing, however, is an even more aggressive "leveling" in which not only signifiers but their signifieds are "homogenized." One example compares Elvis to Proust's madeleine, concluding that

Elvis is for the war babies what the madeleine was for Proust. One nibble lets loose a flood of remembrances of adolescence past—not the most pleasant remembrances, perhaps, but the most vivid ones they have.[25]

This "leveling" comparison of Elvis and the madeleine, each producing a "flood of remembrances," takes the "kitschification" of Proust to a new level. One function of kitsch, argues Calinescu, is to provide

"an illusionary escape from the banality and meaninglessness of contemporary day-to-day life" (251). Kitsch is unabashed, self-indulgent
escapism, "the systematic attempt to fly from daily reality": to escape
in time through memories of a personal past (souvenirs, mementos,
photographs) and to escape spatially through the curios of exotic
lands. Kitsch "'hallucinates,'" writes Calinescu, "—if we are allowed
to use this word transitively—empty spaces with an infinitely variegated assortment of 'beautiful' appearances" (251).

Such flattening, facile collapsing of Proust's madeleine to the escap-
ist "kitsch" of Elvis's songs necessarily raises an uneasy question.
Could the Proustian surge of memories precipitated by the madeleine,
elaborated over several thousand pages, merely be an extreme expression of narcissistic gratification through nostalgia? Does popular
culture now uncover a narcissistic Proust: a map or at least legitimization of kitschy pleasures, encouraging and even sanctifying the *Recherche* as the "easy catharsis" (Calinescu) of kitsch? Such a move
would be to read Proust's narrator as what Calinescu calls a "kitsch-
man," one who wants passively to "fill his spare time with maximum
excitement . . . in exchange for minimum effort" (259)—hence the
pleasure of nostalgia's "easy catharsis." Indeed, Proust's narrator certainly seems dangerously close to "kitsch-man" behavior. "Accablé par
la morne journée et la perspective d'un triste lendemain" [burdened
by the dreary day and the prospect of a depressing morrow] (I, 44)
on the famous afternoon of the "madeleine," he certainly seems to
"fill" the empty spaces of his life "with an infinitely variegated assortment of 'beautiful' appearances" in his claim that all of Combray, like
unfolding Japanese paper shapes, emerges from his cup of tea.

Perhaps even more unsettlingly suggestive of "kitsch-man" behavior, however, is Swann. The "'kitsch-man' tends to experience as
kitsch even non-kitsch works or situations, . . . involuntarily making a
parody of aesthetic response" (Calinescu 1987, 259). What raises the
possibility of kitsch here is the direction of Swann's synthesizing ten-
dencies, which run from his acquaintance to the work of art. "Swann
avait toujours eu ce goût particulier d'aimer à retrouver dans la peinture des maîtres . . . les traits individuels des visages que nous connaissons" [He had always had that particular taste for the pleasure of
identifying in the paintings of the old masters . . . the individual features of men and women we know] (I, 219). Swann, like the kitsch-
man who experiences "as kitsch even non-kitsch works or situations,"
here parodies aesthetic response by viewing great portraits as like-
nesses of those around him. Odette's listless beauty one day strikes
Swann by its resemblance to that of Botticelli's Zipporah; once the
likeness is established, however, he is no longer able to contemplate

the Zipporah other than through Odette, and Botticelli's Zipporah is "kitschified" as a portrait of Odette which Swann places on his bureau. Rather than mediating Swann's esthetic response to Botticelli's Zipporah, Odette herself now becomes the work of art mediated by Botticelli's; the reproduction of Zipporah on his desk now produces in him thoughts of Odette.

Quand il avait regardé longtemps ce Botticelli, il pensait à son Botticelli à lui qu'il trouvait plus beau encore et, approchant de lui la photographie de Zéphora, il croyait serrer Odette contre son coeur. (I, 221–22)

When he had gazed for a long time at this Botticelli, he would think of his very own Botticelli, who seemed even lovelier still, and, drawing toward him the reproduction of Zipporah, he would imagine that he was holding Odette against his heart.

Odette eclipses and becomes the work of art, an object unworthy of the artistic attention Swann lavishes upon her with "l'humilité, la spriritualité et le désintéressement d'un artiste": an esthetic attention, however, itself constantly kitschified by "l'orgeuil, l'égoisme et la sensualité d'un collectionneur" [the pride, the selfishness, and the sensuality of a collector] (I, 221). Esthetic pleasure for Swann thus approaches the facile, egotistical, sensual pleasure of the "kitsch-man," or collector. Swann's penchant for identifying great works of art in the features of those around him doesn't stop at Odette, of course; he likens the pregnant kitchen maid of Combray to Giotto's Charity; the coachman Odette so dislikes, Rémi, to a bust of the Venetian "doge" Lorédan; M. de Palancy to a Ghirlandajo portrait; and the "docteur du Boulbon" to a portrait by Tintoretto (I, 219). Similarly, Swann's artistic appreciation of Vinteuil's sonata later deteriorates into its "kitschification" as the "hymne national" of his love affair with Odette. Narcissistic gratification is complete when, toward the end of the story, Odette's feelings for him now cooled, Swann again hears Vinteuil's sonata. Stricken by "les refrains oubliés du bonheur" [the forgotten strains of happiness], Swann narcissistically identifies "en face de ce bonheur revécu, un malheureux . . . C'était lui-même" [standing before that scene of relived happiness, a wretched figure. . . . It was himself] (I, 341). Esthetic response to Vinteuil's sonata becomes narcissistic, self-indulgent melancholy in Swann.

Proust's narrator, Swann and the contemporary seeker of kitschy pleasures thus run the uneasy risk of convergence. Can we demonstrate that Proust's narrator and Swann are *not* "kitsch-men?" If they aren't, can we keep them from becoming so, appropriated by the kitschy contemporary reader as heros? Indeed, do we readers at the other end of Benjamin's age of mechanical reproduction have the choice *not* to be "kitsch-people," aggressed as we are by the world reinterpreted through kitsch—and therefore *not* to read the behavior of Proust's characters as kitschy? Proust's narrator dangerously pre- scribes readers who, like Swann with Vinteuil's sonata, read into lit- erary works only themselves ("Chaque lecteur est quand il lit le propre lecteur de soi-même") [Every reader is, while reading, the reader of his own self] (IV, 489), reducing esthetic experience to pas- sive, narcissistic gratification. Noting Oscar Wilde's observation that certain sunsets had come to look like paintings by Corot, Calinescu suggests that "nowadays nature has little choice but to imitate mass- produced color reproduction, to be as beautiful as a picture postcard" (229). Perhaps, similarly, Proust's account of reminiscence has "little choice" but to imitate the "easy catharsis" of a kitschy nostalgia trip.

We need to look further at this facile and ubiquitous escapism from the banality of everyday reality. The escapism of kitsch has been linked by Calinescu to "such questions as imitation, forgery, counter- feit, and what we may call the aesthetics of self-deception." Through kitsch, we want to be "'beautifully' lied to" (259), in the way that Swann willingly deceives himself over Odette; reproaching himself for his initial indifference over so Botticellian a creature, Swann readily forgets that Odette is nevertheless not "une femme selon son désir" [the sort of woman he found desirable] (I, 220–21). As op- posed to a forgery, however, "which illegally exploits the elitist taste for rarity," writes Calinescu, "a kitsch object insists on its antielitist availability" (251), betokening a willingness to be lied to, an easy sus- pension of disbelief in the facile pleasure of self-deception. In the general kitschification of Proust, what sort of "lie" are we willingly embracing, what sort of pleasing self-deception? This would seem to be the "lie" of "bringing things closer"—the breaking-down of the distance between ourselves and great art, or the distance between our- selves and Proust's narrative. "True art," in Calinescu's claim, "always contains a finally irreducible element, an element that is constitutive of what we may call 'aesthetic autonomy'" (240). The "aesthetic lie" of Proustian kitsch would seem to be the reducing of this "irreducible element" that sets his work apart from us; it would be the reduction of Proust to *our* terms, the conversion of the "irreducible" to the "bite- sized": the Proustian madeleine's surge of memories now provoked by Russell Baker's shaving cream.

We are now in a position to return to the madeleine, Proust's most clichéd scene, for further exploration of its kitschified reduction in contemporary culture. This is Proust's most "literary-manualized" passage in the state-imposed pedagogy Barthes so despised. Most available consequently to isolation and appropriation, the "madeleine" scene is thus most often made to "represent" the *Recherche* in a synecdochic eclipsing of whole by part. The madeleine has become so representative of the entire *Recherche* that we now need to be reminded sternly that the work isn't only the madeleine scene: "*La Recherche*, ce n'est donc pas seulement la saveur d'une madeleine trempée dans une tasse de thé. . . . Ne jamais oublier que derrière la petite madeleine, il y a, toujours, la condition humaine!" [The *Recherche* isn't only the savor of a madeleine dipped in a cup of tea. . . . Never forget that behind the little madeleine, there is, eternally, the human condition!] (Leuwers 55). Symptomatic of the madeleine's domination of the Proustian cultural "index" is the anxious query from the colleague in another field:

I am trying to find the famous "tea and madeleine cakes" passage in Proust's *Remembrance of Things Past* (where the taste of the cakes dipped in tea brings back the character's past at Combray with his grandmother [sic]). I have been reading *Du côté de chez Swann*—part in which I thought it appeared and yet have still not come upon it in the first 200 or so pages. Do you know where it is located? In *Swann's Way*? If so, in which section: first, second or third? Perhaps you might even be able to tell me the page number in the Gallimard pocket book edition? If not, if you could tell me approximately where it appears (one half, one third, two thirds of the way through?). I would be *extremely* appreciative if you could send me a short note in regard to this.[26]

Elsewhere, pervasive pastiching of the madeleine scene suggests an effort to "bring closer" (Benjamin) Proust's difficult narrative by rewriting it in one's own cheeky vernacular. One theory claims that Proust's madeleine "was in reality a matzo ball, and the past unfolded itself to the Master as he sat over a bowl of chicken soup in Flanbaum's, the famous kosher restaurant in Paris."[27] A cartoon of a middle-aged man at a typewriter in a cosy apartment gives a vibrantly slangy rewrite of the madeleine scene:

Elle me propose du thé, la mémé. Et des gâteaux. Des petites madeleines, pourquoi pas. Alors là, mes mignons, à peine je commence à en becter une, de ces petites madeleines, que—vous marrez pas—c'est la défonce. Ouais, la vraie défonce; une flopée de souvenirs se ramènent. Flash-back, nostalgeo en diable! Ciné-rétro sur l'air de que-reste-t-il de tout cela! Plein dans la gueule pour pas un rond que j'en prenais avec ses petites madeleines, à la mémé![28]

She offers me some tea, the old bag. And some cakes. Some little madeleines, why not. And now, guys, scarcely do I start munching one of these little madeleines, that—don't break up—I'm tripping. Yeah, the total trip; a pile of memories comes back. The total nostalgic flash-back! Old movies, good-old-days-type stuff! Whammo, straight to the jaw for a total freebie with the old bat's little madeleines.

... *Elle me propose du thé, la mémé.*
Et des gâteaux. Des petites madeleines, pourquoi pas ?
Alors là, mes mignons, à peine je commence à en becter une, de ces petites madeleines,
que — vous marrez pas — c'est la défonce. Ouais, la vraie défonce ;
une flopée de souvenirs se ramènent. Flash-back nostalgeo en diable !
Ciné-rétro sur l'air de que-reste-t-il de tout cela !
Plein dans la gueule pour pas un rond que j'en prenais avec ses petites madeleines, à la mémé !...

Drawing by Sempé in *L'Express* (11–17 June 1982). (Copyright © 1982 by Sempé. Reprinted by permission.)

A short story called "Eating it" features a similar madeleine-scene re-write of a great-aunt whose library contains "Proust's inevitable vol-umes," but in fact "Auntie Drew's taste for French literature was mostly confined to pornography." Auntie Drew coaches the narrator Willie in appreciating a madeleine. "See here, Willie, roll the bite around in your mouth before you swallow! Just don't wolf them down like that! *Feel* the individual crumbs! The texture! Try to understand *taste*!" (54). Willie dutifully practices appreciating taste by biting into an old wicker chair. "Concentrating, I consented to another bite. The flavors were, roughly, sixty-odd years of finely granulated dust, a slight hint of my deceased uncle's oily palms, a dash of the original greenwood fiber, and unmistakingly, a definite essence of nut bread" (57–58).[29]

The "bite-sizing" efforts of further cultural aggressions and appro-priations dislocate the madeleine from its context in the memory scene. Here Calinescu's "aesthetic inadequacy" is expressed through miniaturization's flip side, enlargement—as in the cartoon of Proust riding, like Botticelli's Venus, a gigantic madeleine, whose analogy to the striped grooves of a shell is explicit in the *Recherche*.[30] The multi-plication of kitsch—Benjamin's reproducibility as a way of "bringing things closer"—is apparent in such perversions as the claim by two rival Illiers-Combray pâtisseries to be the original maker of the made-leines purchased by Tante Léonie.[31] Since the pastry in Proust's early, more autobiographical drafts of the madeleine scene was in fact a much more mundane "biscotte," leaving us with no indication that Tante Léonie's Sunday morning "madeleine" was anything but fictive, this argument is both naïve and perverse. The multiplication that characterizes "kitsch" is also expressed in a cartoon depicting Proust with not one, but an entire bowlful of madeleines at his elbow.

This proliferation of madeleines of all shapes and sizes is perhaps nowhere so decisively evident as in the availability and "chic" of the madeleine pan, now found in every pretentious cooking-gadget store. Its ubiquity would seem to be directly produced by the snob-value of Proust; if he had written about a croissant, would madeleine pans now be so trendy? But the Proust connection is increasingly obscured, ef-faced, in favor of the empty but mesmerizing power of the "gadget." The object of consumption, writes Baudrillard, is that object whose use value disappears in favor of its value as sign; it is the car that is no longer used as a car, but manipulated in a signifying system as the status-filled Porsche. Baudrillard suggests that with the disappearance of use value, the object of consumption is then characterized by its very uselessness, the "inutilité fonctionelle" with which "tout peut de-venir gadget" [anything can become a gadget] (1970, 169).

Drawing by Phyllis Herfield in *The New York Times* (19 September 1979): "Recipes for the Foods Proust Loved to Eat and Write About." (Copyright © 1979 by The New York Times Company. Reprinted by permission.)

With the gadgety, useless madeleine pan, however, we are now very far removed from the original "cultural intention or purpose" of Proust's madeleine as the gateway to involuntary memory's powerful joy. The rhetoric of synecdochic displacement—the substitution of part for whole, or the madeleine scene for the entirety of the *Recherche*—seems an inadequate model to account for the cultural part-object the madeleine has become. Such obsessive cultural attention to the madeleine scene as a sort of symbol or signifier for the *Recherche* in its entirety suggests a displaced, excessive emphasis on the part rather than the larger meaning it points to: an interest whose object is the madeleine itself, rather than its symbolic function as the corner-stone of "l'édifice immense du souvenir." The gadgety "madeleine" pan would suggest the extreme veneration of an empty signifier, a signifier now disconnected from its original signified.

Such cultural disconnecting of signifier and signified is again anticipated in Proust's own discourse. Just as Proust's characters Marcel and Swann at times uneasily suggest kitschy behavior, Proust's discussion of idolatry in Ruskin suggests the disconnecting of signifier and signified. Ruskin's sensuous but self-reproving love of images led Proust to claim, in the preface to his translation of Ruskin's *The Bible of Amiens*, "tout chez lui était amour et l'iconographie, telle qu'il l'entendait, se serait mieux appelée iconolâtrie" (1971, 118–19) [in him everything was love, and iconography, as he understood it, would better have been called iconolatry (1987, 40). Several pages later, Proust quotes Ruskin's own definition of idolatry against him. Ruskin defined idolatry as "the serving with the best of our hearts and minds some dear and sad fantasy which we have made for ourselves, while we disobey the present call of the Master" (*Complete Works* 20:66; quoted 1987, 50). Idolatry, then, is displaced adulation, worshipping the image itself rather than the meaning it points to; it is, as Proust puts it, "l'importance excessive que Ruskin attache dans ses études d'art à la lettre des oeuvres" (1971, 134) [the excessive importance Ruskin attaches in his art studies to the literalness of the works (1987, 54)]. As examples of this sort of idolatry of the signifier, Proust offers the act of admiring in a tragedian's costume the same cloth that figures in a Moreau painting, or in a friend's "toilette" the dress and hairdo of Balzac's Princesse de Cadignan (1971, 135). The signifier, suggests Proust, should be appreciated for the signified it points to—Diane de Cadignan's intention, and beyond that, Balzac's purpose. Without this dimension, the dress is merely an empty sign.

Mais une fois dépouillée de l'esprit qui est en elle, elle n'est plus qu'un signe dépouillé de sa signification, c'est-à-dire rien; et continuer à l'adorer, jusqu'à

s'extasier de la retrouver dans la vie sur un corps de femme, c'est là proprement de l'idolâtrie. (1971, 136).

But once stripped of the spirit that is in it, it is no more than a sign deprived
of its meaning, that is to say, nothing; and to keep on adoring it so much as
to be enraptured upon encountering it in real life on a woman's body is, properly speaking, idolatry. (1987, 56)

To admire the dress without its "intentionality" is to confuse literal
and figurative elements, as in Ruskin's tendency to endow an abstract
or superficial image with excessive significance. Kasell identifies this
sort of idolatry as the "error of literality" (552), the production of
"idolatrous literalisms" (555); it is literality at the price of figurality.

Pointing out that while he loves hawthorn, he would never collect
paintings of it, Proust warns of the temptation of a cult of the image
itself rather than the affect it produces in us: "Je me garderai toujours
d'un culte exclusif qui s'attacherait en elles (les aubépines) à autre
chose qu'à la joie qu'elles nous donnent" (1971, 137) [I shall always
guard against an exclusive cult that would attach to the hawthorn anything but the joy they give us (1987, 57)]. Such joy would also be the
"signified" of the madeleine, the powerful and mysterious, incomprehensible joy that marks the work of involuntary memory. But obsessive contemporary attention to the kitschified madeleine is idolatrous
in that it ignores the difference between the literal and the figurative,
the difference between the banal little cake and "l'édifice immense du
souvenir" that it occasions: in Proust's phrase, pop-cultural attention
fixes upon "diversités de pure surface" (1971, 117) [superficial diversity (1987, 40)]. In fixing upon the madeleine, contemporary cultural
attention isolates the image, the signifier, in a veneration that can only
be idolatrous.

Yet as Kasell points out, Proust's own discussion of Ruskin's idolatry
similarly indicts Proust himself as an idolater. Proust goes to some
effort to explain that his own pilgrimage to Amiens is not idolatrous,
not at all the sort of idolatrous pilgrimage a visit to Ruskin's birthplace
itself might be. For, Proust claims, Ruskin's thought may most truly
be appreciated through the Amiens cathedral. The problem, however, as Kasell puts it, is that Proust, in following "à la letter" Ruskin's
prescriptions, himself mistakes the literal for the figurative. "His object," Kasell points out, "is the image in the mind of Ruskin, but
Proust's voyage was to the *real* cathedral" (556). Similarly, madeleines
carry a certain intellectual cachet in contemporary consumer culture
as being symbolic of Proust; but, as guilty of "idolatrous literalism" as
Ruskin and Proust themselves, we "commodify" them, venerating
their cultural chic as we buy gadgety madeleine pans and "name-

drop" Proust and his madeleine in glib cocktail-party settings. This puts the contemporary pop-culturalization of Proust in a new light, for it is becoming clear that Proust himself not only describes but enacts many of the mechanisms of idolatry and kitschification that seem now to take his *Recherche* as object. Proust himself, we realize, is in danger of becoming as idolatrous a "kitsch-man" as Swann and Marcel the narrator. In kitschifying Proust, we are perhaps only emulating Proust's "kitschified" treatment of Ruskin.

But would mere "kitschification" suffice to explain the energy at work in such pop-cultural appropriation of Proust? Other references suggest a more hostile intention in their implicit vengeance on the canon, as in the *New Yorker* cartoon of a woman in cowboy boots (inscribing perhaps a belligerently *American* "stance" on a writer perceived as an icon of French intellectual chic) saying to a well-dressed salesman, "I want something to get even for that new translation of Proust he gave me last year."[32] "Getting even" with the canon continues in a poem that imagines Proust communicating on CB radio, thereby "making friends with every trucker from Deauville to Tours" and, thanks to the "sunshine of CB," giving up writing: a cheeky but pointed effacement of the entire *Recherche*.[33] "Getting even" continues in Bruce Chatwin's *The Songlines*, where the act of closing a Proust volume is described with much vengeful relish. Arkady is depicted "nearing the end of the Duchesse de Guermantes' interminable dinner party." "Then," runs Chatwin's description, "with the satisfaction of concluding a Proustian paragraph, he let out an involuntary 'Ah!,' inserted the bookmark, and slapped the Pléiade shut" (56). Michel Flacon's novel swallows up the entire *Recherche* within a single sentence, obliterating the immense mass of remaining text: "Moi, longtemps je me suis couché de bonne heure, parce que j'avais des parents vieux jeu et qu'ils veillaient sur ma santé" [Me, for a long time I used to go to bed early because I had fuddy-duddy parents who fussed over my health].[34] Even Beckett's Molloy, lying in his ditch, says pointedly about the hawthorn beloved by the Proustian narrator, "La blanche aubépine se penchait vers moi, malheureusement je n'aime pas l'odeur de l'aubépine" [The white hawthorn bent towards me; unfortunately, I don't like the scent of hawthorn] (38). The most expressive and succinct vengeance on the canon might be a one-line letter in the *National Lampoon* reading, "Sirs: A la recherche du temps, *p u!*"[35]

Such "getting even" conveys a hostility that takes us beyond the realm of kitsch and begins to suggest the anxiety with which contemporary culture encounters the canon: an anxiety produced by the si-

"*I want something to get even for that new translation of Proust he gave me last year.*"

Drawing by Ed Arno in *The New Yorker* (20 December 1982). (Copyright ©
1982 by The New Yorker Magazine, Inc. Reprinted by permission.)

multaneous dread and desire that cohabit ambivalence. An account
of such ambivalence is offered in what Hal Foster calls subcultural
"recoding," where the "encoded discrimination" of such elitist signs
as Proust is transformed "through a parodic collage" in which the
"false nature of these stereotypes is exposed." This activity is "pro-
vocative . . . a disturbance, a doubt," a resistance that is "plural
and . . . performed." "It reinvests signs and commodities," explains
Foster, "with a symbolic ambivalence that threatens the principle of
equivalence on which our social and economic exchange is based"
(1985, 170–71). Foster's use of ambivalence as that energy that destabilizes equivalence thus offers us a more energetic entry into this pop-
cultural Proust than Huyssen's and Baudrillard's understanding of a
flattened cultural homogenization, or contemporary kitschified appropriations. In Foster's terms, Proust as the elitist literary canon and
its social equivalences of snobbery, status, intellectualism, refinement,
elegance, and so on is reinvested, distorted, and disrupted in a move
that threatens the "social exchange value" of such terms.

A possible objection to Foster's construction of "subculture" might
be that there would no longer seem to be any opposition by which the

"subculture" defines itself against high culture. It has even been suggested that the term "culture" be replaced with "subculture," evoking instead "a world made up of a complex assembly of interests and factions, each struggling to become *the* culture." Thus "culture" as "the megalith of a normative and all-governing historical paradigm" (Simpson 744) would seem to be obsolete. However, the very energy of "subcultural" recoding only seems to confirm the persistence of cultural hierarchies, including a canonized Proust whose very "canonicity" is affirmed by the ambivalent energies of desire and dread his text excites.

Desire is betrayed, intriguingly enough, in one of the very references to the "unconsumability" of Proust. Status, in consumer culture, is consuming what most defies consumption—as we might have been able to guess from the very energy with which Proustian unconsumability is attacked. Hence, ironically, the *Recherche* as unconsumable object is reinscribed with elitism, as George Will's discussion "Status: A Commodity Up for Grabs" makes clear. Will cites the appeal to status implicit in the advertisements for Dewar's scotch. "You know the kind," writes Will: "'I'm Judy Jones, 28. I am your basic sky-diving, Everest-climbing, Mozart-adoring, Proust-memorizing Boston astrophysicist, and I drink Dewars.'"[36] Status, itself the ultimate commodity, consists in commodifying the uncommodifiable; not merely reading Proust but memorizing him—a more decisive appropriation— as the glamorous Judy, consumer of the unconsumable, suggests. Will goes on ironically to assert that such ads are supposed to "sell whisky to middle-aged businessmen in Duluth . . . who want to think they are like that paragon, Judy Jones." However, concludes Will, in pointedly anti-Proust tenor, "Duluth businessmen have more sense."

But in the structure of ambivalence, dread subtends desire as a parallel energy; can we go so far as to identify dread in this cultural "recoding" of Proust? The obsessiveness of cultural attention to Proust suggests we need to look beyond the self-indulging pleasures of kitsch and idolatry. The very "fetishizing" of Proust betrays a cultural dread, a more acute energy than that of the "easy catharsis" of kitsch, or the veneration of idolatry. We realize, however, that the fetish has always implicitly inhabited the kitsch object, however, as etymology suggests. The Portugese "feitiço" points both to what is artificial, contrived, as in the manufactured kitsch object, and to what absorbs, fascinates, mesmerizes: the fetishized object of fascination (Baudrillard 1972, 99). Another similarity links the kitsch object to the fetish; both are readily available as sources of gratification, whether the "easy catharsis" of kitsch or the sexual pleasure afforded by the fetish. In Freud's claim,

The meaning of the fetish is not known to other people, so the fetish is not withheld from the fetishist; it is easily accessible and he can readily obtain the sexual satisfaction attached to it. What other men have to woo and make exertions for can be had by the fetishist with no trouble at all. (Vol. 21, 154)

But fetishistic desire is animated by an anxiety that distinguishes it from the more passive, easy attention commanded by the kitsch object and the idolatrous detail. The fetish is a defensive move, theorized Freud, created out of fear of castration, fear of losing the self's integrity; the fetish emerges as substitute for the woman's absent member in order to protect the observing subject from the implied threat of his own castration. Just what threat might Proust (perceived by popular culture as the rich, meditative, interiorized, and mythified experience of subjectivity as developed over narrative) pose for the "schizophrenic" (Jameson, Baudrillard) postmodern self in its endless, mediatized, screen-imaged present?

The fetish is not only a defense, but also a denial, as Mannoni shows. The subject would not *appear* to be denying the lack of the woman's phallus, but the fetish exists precisely in place of a denial. What is being denied in the fetishization of the madeleine? Freud further suggests that the fetish-object—a piece of fur, a foot, underclothing—is not chosen by chance, but is often the last item glimpsed before the trauma of discovering the woman's missing phallus (155). The fetish would then suggest an attempt to turn time back; it would be a denial of progressive time, a wistful, nostalgic attempt to deny what time brought, the accession to painful knowledge. This painful knowledge would be that of difference, the knowledge that the other is Other; the fetish would then the subject's means of defusing the threat of his own castration and thereby maintain an illusory state of sexual sameness, neutralizing the danger of Otherness. Fetishizing the madeleine would then suggest a need to avert, to postpone, defer, the Otherness of Proust for the postmodern self: the effort to suppress a threatening knowledge the self secretly knows it cannot escape. As Mannoni puts it, "Il n'y a de fétiche que parce que le fétichiste *sait bien* que les femmes n'ont pas de phallus" [The fetish only exists because the fetishist *knows very well* that women don't have a phallus]. Mannoni describes the divided self thus produced in the fetish formation: "l'enfant à la fois conserve sa croyance en le phallus féminin *et* l'abandonne, maintenant une attitude divisée" [the child simultaneously retains his belief in the feminine phallus *and* renounces it, maintaining a divided attitude] (13).

Beyond the kitschification of the madeleine and of Proust, then—or within them, as the etymological root of "fetish" suggests in its link to the kitsch object—fetishized anxiety might be read in a perverse recipe for "Proust's Chocolate Chip Cookies Madeleine." This, in fact, turns out simply to be the *Joy of Cooking*'s recipe for chocolate chip cookies with one intriguing and suggestive change: minus two minutes of that most Proustian of ingredients, (cooking) time.[37] Fetishization is complete here in the implicit play of familiarity and otherness. Annexed to the chocolate chip cookies, Proust's madeleine loses its threatening difference. Like the fetishized foot, the fur, and the underclothing, the madeleine, here tacked onto a recipe for the most familiar of cookies, seems to assure the anxious cook of sameness, familiarity, identification. One has the comforting feeling that "Proust's Chocolate Chip Cookies Madeleine" pose no threat to any cook having mastered chocolate chip cookies. But the madeleine only registers in the title of the recipe; there is no "organic," so to speak, participation of the fragile buttery-lemon madeleine in the All-American chocolate chip favorite, and the improbable conjunction occurs only in the title. Proust's madeleine is thus pure signifier, uselessly adrift—not even the kitschified, gadgety madeleine pan is put to use here. As pure signifier, however, the madeleine can only point beyond itself, elsewhere, deferring meaning to its signified. Similarly, the fetish object also points to the dreaded otherness, to difference. While the fetish seems to be a denial of difference, in the way that "Proust's Chocolate Chip Cookies Madeleine" seems to deny difference in merging two unlike cookies, the fetish, again, only exists *because* the subject knows very well there is difference (Mannoni). The fetish exists *in place of* a denial, that of otherness; the postmodern self no longer has time for selfhood, for subjectivity, particularly the deeply interiorized subjectivity suggested in Proust. And perhaps this helps to account for the dread experienced by the fetishist, for whom, noticed Freud, "an aversion . . . to the real female genitals is never absent" (154). The fetishized object, the madeleine, substitutes for, yet points obsessively to, the dreaded place of Otherness, Proust's account of a subjectivity now apprehended as threatening to the postmodern self.[38] Such a tangle of desire and resistance, complicity and denial, is apparent in one writer's answer as to why we read Proust.

There is a fascination in such egocentricity. Hypnotized by such monumental gall, the reader is gulled into complicity. Surely there must be a reason for such swollen satisfaction, such a wealth of self-importance? As Zero Mostel once said . . . "If you've got it, baby, flaunt it—flaunt it." Yet those who flaunt it, alas, have not always got it.[39]

Contemporary culture's fetishized madeleine cannot but raise the final version of the same persistent, uneasy question with which we began to suspect in Proust's characters more kitschy "kitsch-men," more idolatrous idolaters, than we; might we also then identify in the Proustian text more "fetishizing" a fetishist than his contemporary readers? We may fetishize the madeleine scene as a way of deferring our knowledge of the Otherness of Proustian (mythified) subjectivity. But within that myth of subjectivity, fetishization is also at work, for the "kitsch" object of indolent, nostalgic pleasure, the past, is more than just that for the Proustian narrator. It is, in fact, the fetish-object of dread and desire, as we saw in the resistances of figuration in Chapter 5. The past, for the Proustian narrator, anticipates the dreaded and desired object that the myth of Proustian subjectivity itself represents for the contemporary consumerist reader.[40]

Returning to the madeleine of "Chocolate Chip Cookies Madeleine" as empty, drifting signifier, we might hope at least that Proust, reduced to pure signifer, would then be preserved from commodification and its ensuing danger, obsolescence. Even as signifier, however, as the emptiest of commodities, Proust is susceptible to the obsolescence of any other "market" failure. The editors of the *Penguin Dictionary of Quotations* "are jettisoning quotes which haven't worn well, lots of Proust, for example": the reduction of Proust to cliché sentences has not been a market success.[41] The Grand Hôtel of Cabourg, having vigorously attempted to cash in on its Proust connection, is a case in point, with its reconstructed "Chambre Proust," its "Salle Marcel Proust" dining room, its "Restaurant Balbec," its "Du côté de chez Swann" bar ("un bar pas comme les autres"), and its madeleines served on silver trays. This, however, has not seemed to "sell," and lately, "économie oblige," the madeleines have disappeared. Proust as commodified signifier only seems to invite the fate of many commodities, subject all to the whim of a fickle market: obsolescence.

Is Proust's narrative as obsolete now in the contemporary consumer economy as the Grand Hôtel's madeleines? What remains of Proust and narrative after such aggressions? We might look to Duchamp's 1919 appropriation of the *Mona Lisa* by framing her smile in a mustache and goatee and cheekily re-entitling the work *LHOOQ* ("Elle a chaud au cul," or, put rather less vulgarly, "She's on the make").[42] Huyssen points out that Duchamp's 1965 invitation to the opening of a retrospective of his work was a *Mona Lisa* now minus mustache and goatee, now entitled *Rasé LHOOQ*. "Through this reconstruction of her identity," mourned one critic, "the 'Mona Lisa' has as a matter of fact completely lost her identity." It would indeed seem impossible to restore canonicity in a full return to Benjamin's "aura-ed" work of art.[43] But Huyssen implies that the canon itself has the last word when he wonders whether the *Mona Lisa*'s "certain smile" is not "ironically directed" at an audience that accepts the tired repetition of provocation as art (147–48). Perhaps every canonical work has that "certain smile" as it contemplates the frenetic energies of subcultural recoding. If the work did not continue to be maintained as canonical (in part, through just such obsessive, ambivalent cultural attention), we would certainly not devote such energy—nor such *time*—to pretending otherwise. The madeleines no longer served by the Grand Hôtel resurface tenfold in jokes, cartoons, advertisements, magazine articles and newspaper columns in untiring attention to the canon and to Proust.

Notes

1. Russell Baker, "Whippersnapper Blues," *The New York Times* 29 June 1986; quoted in J. T. Johnson, ed., vol. 25 (1986): 29.

2. François Cérésa, "B.D.," *Le Nouvel Observateur*; quoted without further reference in J. T. Johnson, ed., vol. 24 (1984): 51.

3. Russell Baker, "Man with Pasty Face Detects the Faint Aroma from Grade-School Days," syndicated column, 28 September 1981; quoted in J. T. Johnson, ed., vol. 23 (1982): 50.

4. Alfred Humblot, editor at Ollendorff, wrote to Proust's friend Louis de Robert, "Je suis peut-être bouché à l'émeri, mais je ne puis comprendre qu'un monsieur puisse employer trente pages à décrire comment il se tourne et retourne dans son lit avant de trouver le sommeil" [I may be impossibly thickheaded, but I cannot understand how a man could take thirty pages to describe how he tosses and turns in his bed before falling asleep] (quoted in Kolb 1984, viii). The same idea is ·expressed equally colloquially in Russell Baker's query, "Would anybody believe 12,000 words about a man who had a hard time going to sleep when he was a boy?" (1980, 253).

5. Russell Baker, "Don't Invite Proust," *New York Times Magazine* 31 August 1975; quoted in J. T. Johnson, ed., vol. 14 (1975): 7.

6. "Monty Python's Flying Circus," 1972; aired Channel 19, Kansas City, 5 January 1976; quoted in J. T. Johnson, ed., vol. 15 (1976): 11–12.

7. Cardiologists Friedman and Rosenmar, quoted in Cary L. Cooper, "The Wages of Hurry Can Be Terminal," *The Guardian* (10 May 1979): 22; quoted in J. T. Johnson, ed., vol. 22 (1980): 29.

8. Charles Elliott, "How to Read Proust," *The Smithsonian* (October 1984): 150–151.

9. Lance Morrow, "We Need More Writers We'd Miss," quoted without reference in J. T. Johnson, ed., vol. 23 (1982): 31.

10. *Reader's Digest* (March 1978): 48; quoted in J. T. Johnson, ed., vol. 21 (1979): 9.

11. Quoted in J. T. Johnson, ed., vol. 22 (1980): 33.

12. Silvie de Nussac, "A la recherche du temps de Proust," *L'Express* (16–22 avril 1973): 19; quoted in J. T. Johnson, ed., vol. 10 (1973): 9.

13. *L'Express*, no. 1132 (19–25 mars 1973): 91; quoted in J. T. Johnson, ed., vol. 9 (1973): 9.

14. *The New York Review of Books* (12 October 1967): 21–24; quoted in J. T. Johnson, ed., vol. 16 (1976): 16.

15. Henry Miller, television interview, 29 November 1977; quoted in J. T. Johnson, ed., vol. 19 (1978): 16.

16. *L'Express* no. 1371 (17–23 octobre 1977): 18; quoted in J. T. Johnson, ed., vol. 18 (1977):20.

17. *TWA Ambassador* (November 1981): 112; quoted in J. T. Johnson, ed., vol. 23 (1982): 54.

18. Quoted in J. T. Johnson, ed., vol. 22 (1980): 22.

19. David Walker Travel, tour of 31 August–4 September 1983; quoted in J. T. Johnson, ed., vol. 24 (1984): 48.

20. Francine du Plessix Gray, "Max Frisch Considered," *The New York Times Book Review* (19 March 1978).

21. *The New Yorker* (24 September 1979); quoted in J. T. Johnson, ed., vol. 22 (1980): 21.

22. Seymour Britchky, *New York Magazine* (2 October 1978): 123; quoted in J. T. Johnson, ed., vol. 21 (1979): 10.

23. Robert F. Jones, *The Best of Sports Illustrated*, quoted without further reference in J. T. Johnson, ed., vol. 10 (1973): 9.

24. *Le canard enchaîné*, 6 June 1984.

25. George F. Will, syndicated column, *Lawrence Daily Journal World*, 27 March 1975.

26. Name withheld, letter to the author, 17 February 1988.

27. S. J. Perelman, "Recapture Your Rapture in One Seedy Session," *The New Yorker* (29 November 1976): 37–39.

28. Sempé, cartoon, *L'Express* (18 juin 1982); quoted in J. T. Johnson, ed., vol. 23 (1982): 25.

29. William Harrison, "Eating It," *Roller Ball Murder* (New York: Warner Books, 1975); quoted in J. T. Johnson vol. 18 (1977): 16–19.

30. Phyllis Herfield, cartoon, *The New York Times* 19 September 1979; quoted in J. T. Johnson, ed., vol. 22 (1980): 21.

31. Sarah Farrell, "A Remembrance of Things Proust," *The New York Times* 26 August 1979; quoted in J. T. Johnson, ed., vol. 22 (1980): 22.

32. Ed Arno, cartoon, *The New Yorker* (20 December 1982): 45; quoted in J. T. Johnson, ed., vol. 24 (1984): 45.

33. Alice Wirth Gray, "A Present for Poor Monsieur Proust," quoted in J. T. Johnson, ed., vol. 22 (1980): 34.

34. Michel Flacon, "Sous l'oeil des barbares," *Le Point* 463, 3 août 1981: 49–50; quoted in J. T. Johnson, ed., vol. 23 (1982): 47.

35. *National Lampoon* (June 1974); quoted in J. T. Johnson, ed., vol. 14 (1975): 8.

36. George Will, "Status: A Commodity Up for Grabs," *Lawrence Journal World*, 18 October 1981: 4A; quoted in J. T. Johnson, ed., vol. 23 (1982): 51.

37. Tom Nugent, "Of Madeleines and Men: Feasting on the Written Word," *The Washington Post*; quoted without date in J. T. Johnson, ed., vol. 23 (1982): 52–53.

38. It is precisely this pervasive myth of Proust's extreme account of excessively developed subjectivity that I try to overturn in Chapter 2.

39. Andrew Sinclair, "Coming Home to Proust," *The Sunday Times*, 20 March 1977: 79.

40. I am indebted to Richard Goodkin for provoking my thinking on the past as fetish-object for the Proustian narrator.

41. Sally Adams, "Play it Again . . . Who?," *The Guardian*, 15 October 1977: 12; quoted in J. T. Johnson, ed., vol. 18 (1977): 13.

42. Calinescu points out that Duchamp's disfiguration of the Mona Lisa was precisely performed on a reproduction, not on the original, suggesting that Duchamp's target was the very notion of reproducing the painting (1987).

43. Compagnon's claim that in this "restoration" to her canonical un-mustachioed self "la Joconde retrouvait sa gloire" [the Mona Lisa recovered her glory] (1990, 135) is thus unpersuasive; there remains, inscribed upon her pristine portrait, the historic though invisible trace of Duchamp's "appropriation."

Works Cited

Albaret, Céleste. *Monsieur Proust*. Paris: Editions Pierre Lafont, 1973.

Anglès, Auguste. *André Gide et le premier groupe de La Nouvelle Revue Française*. Paris: Gallimard, 1978.

Arac, Jonathan. *Critical Genealogies: Historical Situations for Postmodern Literary Studies*. New York: Columbia University Press, 1987.

Assouline, Pierre. *Gaston Gallimard*. Paris: Editions Balland, 1984.

Baker, Russell. *So This Is Depravity*. New York: Congdor and Lattis, 1980.

Bakhtin, Mikhail. *The Dialogic Imagination*. Ed. Michael Holquist. Trans. C. Emerson and M. Holquist. Austin, TX: University of Texas Press, 1981.

Bardèche, Maurice. *Marcel Proust, romancier*. 2 vols. Paris: Les Sept Couleurs, 1971.

Barth, John. "The Literature of Replenishment: Postmodernist Fiction." *The Atlantic Monthly* (January 1980): 65–71.

Barthes, Roland. *Image, Music, Text*. New York: Hill and Wang, 1977.

———. *Mythologies*. Paris: Seuil, 1957.

———. *S/Z*. Paris: Seuil, Collection Points, 1970.

Bass, Alan, trans. *Margins of Philosophy*. By Jacques Derrida. Chicago: University of Chicago Press, 1982.

Baudrillard, Jean. *Pour une critique de l'économie politique du signe*. Paris: Gallimard, 1972.

———. *Simulacres et Simulation*. Paris: Editions Galilée, 1981.

———. *La société de consommation*. Paris: Denoël, 1969.

Beckett, Samuel. *L'innommable*. Paris: Minuit, 1953.

———. *Malone meurt*. Paris: Minuit, 1951.

———. *Molloy*. Paris: Minuit, 1951.

———. *Proust*. London: John Calder, 1931.

Benjamin, Walter. "The Image of Proust." *Illuminations*. Ed. Hannah Arendt. Trans. Harry Zohn. New York: Schocken Books, 1969.

Benveniste, Emile. *Cours de linguistique générale*. Paris: Editions Gallimard, 1966.

Bersani, Leo. "'The Culture of Redemption': Marcel Proust and Melanie Klein." *Critical Inquiry* 12.2 (Winter 1986): 399–421.

Bertens, Hans. "Postmodern Characterization and the Intrusion of Language." Calinescu and Fokkema: 139–59.

Black, Carl. "Albertine as an Allegorical Figure of Time." *Romanic Review* 54.3 (1963): 171–86.

Blanchot, Maurice. "L'Expérience de Proust." *Le livre à venir*. Paris: Gallimard, 1959.

Blondel, Charles. *La psychographie de Marcel Proust*. Paris: Librairie Vrin, 1932.

Blumenthal, Gerda. *Thresholds: A Study of Proust*. Birmingham, AL: Summa Publications, 1984.

Borges, Jorge Luis. "Pierre Menard, Author of the *Quixote*." Trans. James E. Irby. *Labyrinths*. New York: New Directions, 1962.

Bowie, Malcolm. *Freud, Proust and Lacan: Theory as Fiction*. Cambridge: Cambridge University Press, 1987.

Brée, Germaine. *Du temps perdu au temps retrouvé*. Paris: Belles Lettres, 1950.

Brooks, Peter. *Reading for the Plot: Design and Intention in Narrative*. New York: Alfred A. Knopf, 1984.

Brun, Bernard. "L'Edition d'un brouillon et son interprétation: le problème du *Contre Sainte-Beuve*." *Essais de critique génétique*. Ed. Louis Hay. Paris: Flammarion, 1979.

———. "*Le temps retrouvé* dans les avant-textes de *Combray*." *Bulletin des informations proustiennes* 12 (1981): 7–23.

Buisine, Alain. *Proust et ses lettres*. Lille: Presses Universitaires de Lille, 1983.

Butler, Christopher. *After the Wake*. Oxford: Clarendon Press, 1980.

Calinescu, Matei. *Five Faces of Modernity*. Durham, NC: Duke University Press, 1987.

———. "From the One to the Many: Pluralism in Today's Thought." Hassan and Hassan: 263–88.

———. "Ways of Looking at Fiction." *Romanticism, Modernism, Postmodernism*. Ed. Harry Garvin. Lewisburg, PA: Bucknell University Press, 1980: 155–70.

Calinescu, Matei, and Douwe Fokkema, eds. *Exploring Postmodernism*. Amsterdam and Philadelphia: Johns Benjamins Company, 1987.

Calvino, Italo. *The Uses of Literature*. Trans. Patrick Creagh. New York: Harcourt Brace Jovanovitch, Inc., 1986.

Chaitin, Gilbert. "Lacan's Letter." *MLN* 103.5 (1988): 995–1011.

Chatwin, Bruce. *The Songlines*. New York: Viking, 1987.

Clarac, Pierre, ed. *Contre Sainte-Beuve*. By Marcel Proust. Paris: Gallimard, 1971.

Collier, Peter, and J. D. Whitely. "Proust's Blank Page." *The Modern Language Review* 79.3 (1984): 570–78.

Compagnon, Antoine. *Les cinq paradoxes de la modernité*. Paris: Seuil, 1990.

———. *La seconde main: le travail de la citation*. Paris: Seuil, 1979.

———. *La Troisième République des lettres*. Paris: Seuil, 1983.

Davis, Robert Con. "Lacan, Poe and Narrative Repression." *Lacan and Narration*. Ed. Robert Con Davis. Baltimore and London: Johns Hopkins University Press, 1983.

Debray, Régis. *Le Pouvoir intellectuel en France*. Paris: Editions Ramsay, 1979.

De Fallois, Bernard, ed. *Contre Sainte-Beuve*. By Marcel Proust. Paris: Gallimard, 1954.

De Lattre, Alain. *La doctrine de la réalité chez Proust*. 3 vols. Paris: Librairie José Corti, 1978–85.

Deleuze, Gilles. *Proust et les signes*. Paris: Presses Universitaires de France, 1964. 2nd ed. expanded, 1970. 4th ed. expanded, 1976.

De Man, Paul. *Blindness and Insight*. Minneapolis: University of Minnesota Press, 1983.

———. "Reading (Proust)." *Allegories of Reading*. New Haven and London: Yale University Press, 1978.

Derrida, Jacques. "Cogito et histoire de la folie." *L'Ecriture et la différence*. Paris: Editions du Seuil, 1967.

———. *Marges*. Paris: Minuit, 1972.

———. *La voix et le phénomène*. Paris: Presses Universitaires de France, 1967.

Descombes, Vincent. *Proust: philosophie du roman*. Paris: Minuit, 1987.

Didier, Béatrice. "*François le Champi* et les délices de l'inceste." *Ecriture-femme*. Paris: Presses Universitaires Françaises, 1981.

Doubrovsky, Serge. *La Place de la Madeleine*. Paris: Mercure de France, 1974.

Eagleton, Terry. "Ideology and Scholarship." *Historical Studies and Literary Criticism*. Ed. Jerome McGann. Madison, WI: University of Wisconsin Press, 1985: 114–25.

Edelman, Gerald. *Neural Darwinism*. New York: Basic Books, 1987.

Eells, Emily. "Proust à sa manière." *Littérature* 46 (1982): 105–23.

Eliot, T. S. "The Function of Criticism." *Selected Prose of T. S. Eliot*. Ed. Frank Kermode. New York: Harcourt Brace Jovanovitch, 1975.

Ellison, David. *The Reading of Proust*. Baltimore: Johns Hopkins University Press, 1984.

Felman, Shoshana. *Jacques Lacan and The Adventure of Insight*. Cambridge: Harvard University Press, 1987.

———. "Women and Madness: The Critical Phallacy." *Diacritics* 4 (1975): 2–10.

Felski, Rita. *Beyond Feminist Aesthetics*. Cambridge: Harvard University Press, 1989.

Fiedler, Leslie. "The Death and Rebirths of the Novel." Hassan and Hassan: 225–42.

Flieger, Jerry Aline. "Proust, Freud and The Art of Forgetting." *SubStance* 29 (1981): 66–82.

Fokkema, Douwe. *Literary History, Modernism and Postmodernism*. Amsterdam and Philadelphia: Johns Benjamins Publishing Co., 1984.

Fokkema, Douwe, and Elrud Ibsch. *Modernist Conjectures*. New York: St. Martin's Press, 1988.

Foster, Hal, ed. *The Anti-Aesthetic*. Port Townsend, WA: Bay Press, 1983.

———. *Recodings*. Port Townsend, WA: Bay Press, 1985.

Foucault, Michel. *Histoire de la folie à l'âge classique*. Paris: Plon, 1961.

Freud, Sigmund. *Standard Edition of the Complete Works of Sigmund Freud*. Trans. James Strachey. London: Hogarth Press, 1959.

Friedman, Lillian. "Remembrance of Dividends Past." *International Herald Tribune*, 16 December 1983.

Gallop, Jane. *Reading Lacan*. Ithaca, NY: Cornell University Press, 1985.

Gaubert, Serge. "La Conversation et l'écriture." *Europe* 496–97 (aout-septembre 1970): 171–92.

Genette, Gerard. "Discours du récit." *Figures III*. Paris: Seuil, 1972.

———. *Nouveaux discours du récit*. Paris: Seuil, 1983.

———. *Palimpsestes*. Editions du Seuil, 1982.

———. "Proust palimpseste." *Figures I*. Paris: Seuil, 1966.

Gide, André. *Journal*. 2 vols. Paris: Gallimard, 1939.

Graff, Gerald. *Literature Against Itself*. Chicago: University of Chicago Press, 1979.

Hartman, Geoffrey. "The New Wilderness: Critics as Connaisseurs of Chaos." Hassan and Hassan: 87–110.

Hassan, Ihab. *Paracriticisms: Seven Speculations of the Times*. Urbana, IL: University of Illinois Press, 1975.

————. *The Postmodern Turn*. Columbus, OH: Ohio State Press, 1987.

————. *The Right Promethean Fire*. Urbana, IL: University of Illinois Press, 1980.

Hassan, Ihab, and Sally Hassan, eds. *Innovation/Renovation*. Madison, WI: University of Wisconsin Press, 1983.

Henrot, Geneviève. "Marcel Proust et le signe 'Champi.'" *Poétique* 78 (1989): 131–50.

Hilts, Philip J. . "A Brain Unit Seen as Index for Recalling Memories." *The New York Times*, 24 September 1991.

Hippolyte, Jean. "Commentaire parlé sur la Verneinung de Freud." Appendix. *Ecrits*. By Jacques Lacan. Paris: Seuil, 1966.

Hofstadter, Douglas. *Goedel, Escher, Bach: The Eternal Golden Braid*. New York: Basic Books, 1979.

Holland, Norman. "Postmodern Psychoanalysis." Hassan and Hassan: 291–309.

Houston, John Porter. "Temporal Patterns in *A la recherche du temps perdu*." *French Studies* 16 (1962): 33–44.

Humphries, Jefferson. *The Otherness Within*. Baton Rouge and London: Louisiana State University Press, 1983.

Huyssen, Andreas. *After the Great Divide*. Bloomington, IN: Indiana University Press, 1983.

Ibsch, Elrud, and Douwe Fokkema. *Modernist Conjectures*. New York, NY: St. Martin's Press, 1988.

Irigaray, Luce. *Ce sexe qui n'en est pas un*. Paris; Minuit, 1977.

————. *Spéculum de l'autre femme*. Paris: Minuit, 1974.

Jakobson, Roman. "Two Poles of Language and Two Types of Aphasic Disturbance." *Fundamentals of Language*. The Hague: Mouton, 1956.

Jameson, Fredric. "Postmodernism and Consumer Society." Foster 1983: 111–25.

Jardine, Alice. "Gynesis." *Diacritics* 12 (1982): 54–65.

————. *Gynesis*. Ithaca, NY: Cornell University Press, 1985.

Johnson, Barbara E. "Apostrophe, Animation and Abortion." *Diacritics* (Spring 1986): 29–47.

Johnson, J. Theodore, Jr., ed. *Proust Research Association Newsletter* vols. 5–25 (1971–86).

Jones, Ann Rosalind. "Writing the Body: Toward an Understanding of 'L'Ecriture Féminine.'" *Feminist Studies* 7.2 (1981): 247–63.

Joubert, Claude-Henri. *Le Fil d'or*. Paris: Librairie José Corti, 1984.

Kasell, Walter. "Proust the Pilgrim: His Idolatrous Reading of Ruskin." *Revue de littératire comparée* 4 (1975): 547–60.

Kermode, Frank. "What Nathalie Knew." *The New York Review of Books* (25 October 1984).

Kofman, Sarah. "Ça cloche." *Les fins de l'homme*. Ed. Jean-Luc Nancy and Philippe Lacoue-Labarthe. Paris: Galilée, 1981.

Kolb, Philip. "Inadvertent Repetitions of Material in *A la recherche du temps perdu*." *PMLA* 51.1 (1936): 249–62.

————, ed. *Correspondance de Marcel Proust*. Vols. I–XIX. Paris: Plon, 1970–1991.

————, ed. *Lettres retrouvées*. By Marcel Proust. Paris: Plon, 1966.

————, ed. *Marcel Proust et Jacques Rivière: Correspondance 1914–1922*. Paris: Gallimard, 1976.

Lacan, Jacques. *Ecrits*. Paris: Seuil, 1966.

———. *Encore*. Paris: Seuil, 1975.

LaCapra, Dominick. "Intellectual History and Defining the Present as Postmodern." Hassan and Hassan: 47–63.

Laget, Thierry. Introduction. *Quelques progrès dans l'étude du coeur humain. Cahiers Marcel Proust 13*. By Jacques Rivière. Paris: Gallimard, 1985.

Lang, Candace. *Irony/Humor*. Baltimore, MD: Johns Hopkins University Press, 1988.

Lejeune, Philippe. "Ecriture et sexualité." *Europe* février-mars (1971): 113–43.

Leuwers, Daniel. "Huit clés pour lire Proust." *Télérama* 1990 (2 mars 1988): 53–56.

Levin, Harry. "Introduction." *Letters of Marcel Proust*. New York: Random House, 1949.

Levy, Karen. *Jacques Rivière*. Boston: Twayne Publishers, 1982.

Lloyd, Rosemary. "Mirroring Difference, Figuring Frames." *Nineteenth-Century French Studies* 19.3 (1991): 343–53.

Lyotard, Jean-François. *La condition postmoderne: rapport sur le savoir*. Paris: Minuit, 1979.

———. *Le postmoderne expliqué aux enfants*. Paris: Galilée, 1986.

Macksey, Richard. "Introduction." *On Reading Ruskin*. By Marcel Proust. New Haven and London: Yale University Press, 1987.

———. *La lanterne magique*. Geneva: Librairie Droz, 1958.

Macksey, Richard, and Gerald Kamber. "'Negative Metaphor' and Proust's Rhetoric of Absence." *MLN* 85.4 (1970): 858–83.

Mannoni, Octave. *Clefs pour l'imaginaire*. Paris: Seuil, 1969.

March, Harold. *The Two Worlds of Marcel Proust*. Philadelphia, PA: University of Pennsylvania Press, 1948.

Martin, Wallace. "Postmodernism: Ultima Thule or Seim Anew." *Romanticism, Modernism, Postmodernism*. Ed. Garvin. Cranbury, NJ: Associated University Presses, 1980.

Martin-Chauffier, Louis. "Proust et le double 'je' de quatre personnages." *Problèmes du roman. Confluences* 21–24 (1943): 1011–26.

McGinnis, Reginald. "L'inconnaissable Gomorrhe: A propos d'*Albertine disparue*." *Romanic Review* 81.1 (1990): 92–104.

McHale, Brian. *Postmodernist Fiction*. New York and London: Methuen, 1987.

Mehlman, Jeffrey. *A Structural Study of Autobiography*. Ithaca, NY: Cornell University Press, 1974.

Melville, Stephen. "Psychoanalysis and the Place of 'Jouissance.'" *Critical Inquiry* 13.2 (1987): 161–82.

Merrill, Floyd. "Fiction, Fact, Phalanx, Phantasm." *Diacritics* 19.1 (1989): 2–16.

Milly, Jean. "Cris de Paris et désir des glaces." *Proust dans le texte et l'avant-texte*. Paris: Flammarion, 1985.

Moore, Gene. "The Absent Narrator of Proust's *Recherche*." *The French Review* 57.5 (1984): 607–16.

Morino, Lina. *La Nouvelle Revue Française dans l'histoire des lettres*. Paris: Gallimard, 1939.

Muller, Marcel. *Les Voix narratives dans "A la recherche du temps perdu"*. Geneva: Librairie Droz, 1965.

O'Brien, Justin. "Albertine the Ambiguous: Notes on Proust's Transposition of the Sexes." *PMLA* 64.5 (1949): 933–52.

Ozick, Cynthia. "Science and Letters: God's Work—and Ours." *New York Times Book Review* (27 September 1987).

Paulson, William R. *The Noise of Culture: Literary Texts in a World of Information.* Ithaca, NY: Cornell University Press, 1988.

Picon, Gaetan. *Lecture de Proust.* Paris: Mercure de France, 1963.

Plato. *Ion. The Collected Dialogues of Plato.* Ed. E. Hamilton. New York: Bollingen, 1961.

Proust, Marcel. *A la recherche du temps perdu.* Paris: Gallimard, Bibliothèque de la Pléiade, 4 vols. 1987–89.

———. *Le Carnet de 1908.* Ed. Philip Kolb. Paris: Gallimard, 1976.

———. *Contre Sainte-Beuve.* Ed. Bernard de Fallois. Paris: Gallimard, 1954. Rev. ed. Pierre Clarac, 1971.

———. *Correspondance de Marcel Proust.* Ed. Philip Kolb. Vols. I–XIX. Paris: Plon, 1970–91.

———. *Jean Santeuil.* Paris: Gallimard, Bibliothèque de la Pléiade, 1971.

———. *Lettres retrouvées.* Ed. Philip Kolb. Paris: Plon, 1966.

———. *On Reading Ruskin.* Trans. and ed. Jean Autret, William Burford, and Philip J. Wolfe. New Haven and London: Yale University Press, 1987.

———. *Remembrance of Things Past.* Trans. C. K. Scott Moncrieff, Terence Kilmartin, and Andreas Mayor. 3 vols. New York: Random House, 1981.

Proust, Marcel, and Jacques Rivière. *Correspondance 1914–1922.* Ed. Philip Kolb. Paris: Gallimard, 1976.

Raimond, Michel. *Proust romancier.* Paris: Société d'Edition d'Enseignement Supérieur, 1984.

Reille, Jean-François. *Proust: le temps du désir.* Paris: Les Editeurs Français Réunis, 1979.

Ricardou, Jean. "La métaphore d'un bout à l'autre." *Nouveaux problèmes du roman.* Paris: Seuil, 1978.

Richard, Jean-Pierre. "Proust et l'objet alimentaire," *Littérature* 6 (1972): 3–19.

Ricoeur, Paul. *Temps et récit.* 3 vols. Paris: Seuil, 1983–85.

Riffaterre, Michael. "The Intertextual Unconscious." *Critical Inquiry* 13.2 (1987): 211–25.

———. "On Narrative Subtexts: Proust's Magic Lantern." *Style* 22.3 (1988): 440–66.

Rivière, Alain. "Jacques Rivière et Marcel Proust." *Bulletin de la Société des Amis de Marcel Proust et des Amis de Combray* 27 (1977).

Rivière, Jacques. "Baudelaire." *Etudes.* Paris: Gallimard, 1924.

———. *Quelques progrès dans l'étude du coeur humain. Cahiers Marcel Proust* 13 (1985).

———. "Le roman d'aventure." *La nouvelle revue française* (mai–juin 1913).

Robbe-Grillet, Alain. *Le Miroir qui revient.* Paris: Minuit, 1984.

Robert, Pierre-Edmond. "Notice." In Proust, *A la recherche du temps perdu*: IV.

Rogers, B. G. *Proust's Narrative Techniques.* Geneva: Droz, 1965.

Roloff, Volker. "*François le Champi* et le texte retrouvé." *Etudes proustiennes* III (1979): 259–87.

Rosenfield, Israel. "Neural Darwinism." *New York Review of Books* (9 October 1986).

———. *The Invention of Memory.* New York: Basic Books, 1988.

Ross, Kristin. "Albertine, or, The Limits of Representation." *Novel* 19.2 (1986): 135–49.

Rousset, Jean. *Forme et signification*. Paris: Librairie José Corti, 1962.

Ruskin, John. *The Complete Works of John Ruskin*. Ed. Cook and A. Wedderburn, Library Edition, 39 vols. London: George Allen, 1903–12.

Said, Edward. "Opponents, Audiences, Constituencies." *Critical Inquiry* 9.1 (1982): 1–26.

———. *The World, The Text and The Critic*. Cambridge: Harvard, 1983.

Sand, George. *François le Champi*. Paris: Alexandre Cadot, 1850. Paris: Garnier Frères, 1956.

———. *The Country Waif*. Trans. Eirene Collis. Lincoln: University of Nebraska Press, 1977.

Sarraute, Nathalie. *Enfance*. Paris: Gallimard, 1983.

———. *L'ère du soupçon*. Paris: Gallimard, 1956.

———. *Tropismes*. Paris: Editions de Minuit, 1957.

Sartre, Jean-Paul. "A propos de *Le bruit et la fureur*: la temporalité chez Faulkner." *Situations I*. Paris: Gallimard, 1947.

———. *La nausée*. Paris: Editions Gallimard, 1938.

Schlumberger, Jean. *Eveils*. Paris: Gallimard, 1950.

Schor, Naomi, ed. *Flaubert and Postmodernism*. Lincoln and London: University of Nebraska Press, 1984.

Serres, Michel. *Hermès I*. Paris: Editions de Minuit, 1968.

Shklovsky, V. "L'Art comme procédé." *Théorie de la littérature*. Ed. Tzvetan Todorov. Paris: Seuil, 1965.

Silverman, Hugh, ed. *Postmodernism: Philosophy and the Arts*. New York and London: Routledge, 1990.

Simpson, David. "Literary Criticism and The Return to 'History.'" *Critical Inquiry* 14.4 (1988): 721–47.

Smith, Kathleen White. "Forgetting to Remember: Anamnesis and History in J. M. G. Le Clezio's *Désert*." *Studies in Twentieth Century Literature* 10.1 (1985): 99–115.

Snow, C. P. *The Two Cultures: And a Second Look*. 2nd ed. Cambridge: Cambridge University Press, 1964.

Sontag, Susan. "Against Interpretation." *Against Interpretation and Other Essays*. New York: Farrar and Straus, 1966.

Spanos, William. *Repetitions*. Baton Rouge: Louisiana State University Press, 1987.

Stambolian, George. *Marcel Proust and the Creative Encounter*. Chicago, IL: University of Chicago Press, 1972.

Steel, Gareth. *Chronology and Time in "A la recherche du temps perdu."* Geneva: Librairie Droz, 1979.

Suplee, Curt. "Memory Decline Inevitable, But No Reason to Lose Your Marbles." *The Arizona Republic*, 7 October 1990.

Szegedy-Mazak, Mihaly. "Teleology in Postmodern Fiction." Calinescu and Fokkema 1987.

Tadié, Jean-Yves. *Proust*. Paris: Les Dossiers Belfond, 1983.

Todorov, Tzvetan. *Mikhail Bakhtine: le principe dialogique*. Paris: Seuil, 1981.

———. *Poétique de la prose*. Paris: Seuil, 1971.

White, Hayden. *Metahistory: The Historical Imagination in Nineteenth Century Europe*. Baltimore, MD: Johns Hopkins University Press, 1973.

————. *Tropics of Discourse*. Baltimore: Johns Hopkins University Press, 1978.

Wihl, Gary. *Ruskin and the Rhetoric of Infallibility*. New Haven and London: Yale University Press, 1985.

Willis, Sharon. "Mis-translation." *SubStance* 16.1 (1987): 76–83.

Wittig, Monique. "One is not Born a Woman." *Feminist Issues* (Winter 1981).

Index

Agostinelli, Alfred, 100
Albaret, Céleste, 13, 14 n.8
Albertine (in the *Recherche*), 8, 11, 28, 36
    n.4, 38, 41, 43, 52, 54–57, 60–64, 66
    n.5, 84, 86–88, 92, 93 n.4, 97–114,
    115, 138
Algebra: in the *Recherche*, 11, 76–78,
    83–87
Allegory, 135–36. *See also* Giotto
Ambivalence, 12, 39, 129, 136, 140, 148,
    149 n.4, 153, 169, 174. *See also* Fetish;
    Psychoanalysis
Arac, Jonathan, 9, 28
Aristotle, 123, 136
Arno, Ed, viii, 169
Arnold, Matthew, 68
Astro, Alan, 114 n.14
Author: versus narrator, 42, 43, 106; au-
    thorial intention, 115
Authority, 104–7. *See also* Criticism,
    literary
Autobiography, 26, 42–44, 92

Baker, Russell, 12, 152, 154, 161, 174
    nn. 1, 3, 5
Bakhtin, Mikhail, 46
Ball, David, vii
Balzac, Honoré de, 2; in Brooks, 75; in
    Descombes, 3–4; in Proust, 16, 29, 166
Bardèche, Maurice, 113 n.6
Barth, John, 7
Barthes, Roland, 43–44, 145, 153, 161
Bass, Alan, 149 n.6
Baudelaire: in Compagnon, 6; in Proust,
    9, 17–19, 22–28; in Rivière, 35–37
Baudrillard, Jean: on consumption,
    152–53, 158, 164, 169–71; on the ob-

scene, 49–50; on the simulacrum, 11,
    133; on voyeurism, 10, 51
Beckett, Samuel: *Molloy, Malone meurt,
    L'innommable*, 46, 55, 168; *Proust*,
    54–55, 87
Benjamin, Walter, 12, 17, 36 n.1, 119,
    156–57, 162, 164, 173
Benveniste, Emile, 39
Bergotte (in the *Recherche*), 45, 81–82
Bergson, Henri, 3
Bersani, Leo, 38, 44, 45, 51, 64–65, 134,
    139
Bertens, Hans, 66 n.8
Bildungsroman, 40
Birkett, Mary Ellen, vii
Black, Carl, 97
Blanchot, Maurice, 49
Blondel, Charles, 93 n.4
Bloom, Harold, 27–28
Blumenthal, Gerda, 149 n.4
Borges, Jorge Luis ("Pierre Menard, Au-
    thor of the Quixote"), 8, 14 n.7
Botticelli, Sandro: "Zipporah," 159–61;
    "The Birth of Venus," 164
Bowie, Malcolm (*Freud, Proust and La-
    can*), 10, 56–57, 112 n.3
Brée, Germaine, 26, 66 n.7
Brooks, Peter, vii, 74, 91, 148
Brun, Bernard, 26, 149 n.5
Buisine, Alain, 21
Burke, Edmund, 134
Butler, Christopher, 14 n.3
Butor, Michel, 92

Calinescu, Matei, viii, 5, 6, 46, 68, 155–56,
    158–59, 161, 164, 176 n.42
Calvino, Italo, 44–45

Neurology, 10, 67, 69, 70–73, 78–79.
  See also Edelman, Gerald
New Novelists, 2, 92
Noise, 22, 68. *See also* Serres, Michel
Nostalgia, 1, 159, 171, 173
Nouvelle Revue Française, 30–36

O'Brien, Justin, 113 nn. 5, 10
Odette (in the *Recherche*), 54, 88, 93 n.4,
  117, 133, 159–60
Oedipal, the, 140–45
Ozick, Cynthia, 67, 92

Pastiche, 16–18, 26, 27, 29, 105
Paulson, William, 68, 75
Piaget, Jean, 70, 71
Picon, Gaeton, 45, 65 n. 2, 136 n.4
Pinter, Harold, 137 n.5
Plato, 150 n.10
Plon (publishing house), 33
Poe, Edgar Allan ("The Purloined Let-
  ter") 15
Postmodern, 1–9, 11–14 n.5, 38, 49–50,
  66 n.4, 68–69, 134, 153, 155, 171. *See
  also* Baudrillard, Jean; Lyotard, Jean-
  François
Proust, Marcel: *Albertine disparue* (*La fugitive*), 97–99, 101, 103; *A l'ombre des
  jeunes filles en fleurs*, 126–29; *Combray*,
  44–45, 47, 51–52, 118, 120–23, 139–
  43, 147; *Contre Sainte-Beuve*, 26, 29, 35;
  Du côté de chez Swann, 29, 31, 33, 42,
  100, 132–33, 155, 162; *Jean Santeuil*,
  26, 65 n.2, 149 n.5; "Journées de lecture" ("Sur la lecture"), 149 n.11; *La
  prisonnière*, 56, 57, 77–78, 93 n.2, 100,
  103–12; *Le côté de Guermantes*, 100,
  124–26, 155; *Les plaisirs et les jours*, 33,
  157; *Le temps retrouvé*, 47–48, 155; *Sodome et Gomorrhe*, 41, 52–53, 76–78,
  100, 129–32
Psychoanalysis, 12, 15, 71, 88, 89. *See also*
  Ambivalence; Brooks, Peter; Felman,
  Shoshana; Fetish; Freud, Sigmund;
  Klein, Melanie; Lacan, Jacques

Raimond, Michel, 47
Reading, 7–8, 139–51
Recategorization, 67, 69–74, 76, 80–83,
  85, 89, 91, 93 nn.2–4
Reille, Jean-François, 149 n.3

Rembrandt, 155
Renoir, Jean, 153
Representation, 11, 13, 95–97, 105–14,
  115–19, 125, 135, 136 n.1, 162
Ricardou, Jean, 2, 11, 118, 119, 132,
  136 n.1, 137 n.4
Richard, Jean-Pierre, 105, 108, 110
Ricoeur, Paul, 65 n.3, 75, 91
Riffaterre, Michael, 105, 108, 111, 121,
  139, 145, 148 n.2
Rivière, Alain, 32
Rivière, Jacques, 10, 17, 20, 21, 22–23,
  25, 30–32, 35–36, 37 n.15, 58, 93
Robbe-Grillet, Alain, 92
Rogers, B. G., 56
Roloff, Volker, 116, 149 n.5
Rosenfield, Israel, 70, 72–73
Ross, Kristin, 112 n.2
Rousset, Jean, 40, 149 n.3
Ruskin, John, 116, 166–68

Said, Edward, 9, 16, 22, 28, 33, 37 n.14
Sainte-Beuve, Charles, 16, 17–18, 24, 26
Saint-Simon, Louis de, 16
Sand, George (*François le Champi*),
  139–51
Sarraute, Nathalie, 2, 10, 92
Sartre, Jean-Paul, 2, 11, 14 n.3
Schizophrenia, 11, 123–24, 171
Schlumberger, Jean, 34, 35
Schor, Naomi, 13
Science, 67–68. *See also* Interdisciplinar-
  ity; Neurology
Sempé, viii, 162–63
Serres, Michel, 9, 22, 68
Sexuality, 86; bisexuality, 113 n.9; for-
  bidden, 140–41, 143, 145, 147–48,
  150 n.13; sexual difference, 11, 84,
  95–97, 99–100, 103–4, 107–14.
  See also Feminine, the; Oedipal;
  Homosexuality
Shklovsky, Victor, 148
Silverman, Hugh, 1, 13 n.1
Simulacrum, 11, 12, 132–34, 152
Smith, Anne-Catherine, 137 n. 6
Snow, C. P., 68, 92
Sontag, Susan, 135
Spanos, William, 1, 13 n.1
Spectacle, 51–54, 65
Stambolian, George, 137 n.4
Steel, Gareth, 75

This book was set in Baskerville and Eras typefaces. Baskerville was designed by John Baskerville at his private press in Birmingham, England, in the eighteenth century. The first typeface to depart from oldstyle typeface design, Baskerville has more variation between thick and thin strokes. In an effort to insure that the thick and thin strokes of his typeface reproduced well on paper, John Baskerville developed the first wove paper, the surface of which was much smoother than the laid paper of the time. The development of wove paper was partly responsible for the introduction of typefaces classified as modern, which have even more contrast between thick and thin strokes.

Eras was designed in 1969 by Studio Hollenstein in Paris for the Wagner Typefoundry. A contemporary script-like version of a sans-serif typeface, the letters of Eras have a monotone stroke and are slightly inclined.

Printed on acid-free paper.